Get Control of Your Cash

GET CONTROL OF YOUR CASH

Douglas Garbutt

WILDWOOD HOUSE

First published in hardback 1985 by
Gower Publishing Company Limited as *How to Budget and Control Cash*

This paperback edition published 1988 by
Wildwood House Limited
Gower House,
Croft Road,
Aldershot,
Hampshire GU11 3HR,
England.

© Douglas Garbutt 1985, 1988

All rights reserved. No part of this publication may be reproduced, stored in a retrieval system, or transmitted in any form or by any means, electronic, mechanical, photocopying, recording, or otherwise without the prior permission of Wildwood House Limited.

British Library Cataloguing in Publication Data
Garbutt, Douglas
 [How to budget and control cash]. Get
 control of your cash
 1. Great Britain. Business firms.
 Financial management. Cash flows
 I. [How to budget and control cash]
 II. Title
 658.1'5244

ISBN 0 7045 0603 3

Printed and bound in Great Britain by
Biddles Ltd, Guildford and King's Lynn

Contents

Introduction		vii
1	Cash in business	1
2	Preparing a cash budget	20
3	Trade credit	37
4	Budgeting for expenses	56
5	Budgeting for stocks	82
6	Budgeting for long-term needs	94
7	Credit management	112
8	Cash control of projects	132
9	Cash control of standard operations	156
10	Cash control of jobbing and multiple projects	170
11	Cash control in product management	186
12	The use of computers in cash planning	195
13	The impact of taxes on cash management	209
Conclusion		222
Index		223

Introduction

Positive management of cash flow is essential to business success and survival: that is the message of this book.
To quote Berthold Brecht:

> Ah, how very sorely they're mistaken
> Who think that money doesn't count
> Fruitfulness turns to famine
> When the kindly stream runs out.

Generating a stream of cash is what business is about. But cash must be put to work. Assets must be purchased, wages paid, materials bought. Cash in hand is the key decision point for the manager who pays out today in the hope of receiving back, with profit, tomorrow. Cash flows constantly through the hands of management, unlike other assets which tie up funds and are available for use, but if not used, may be wasted. In itself, cash in hand does not earn; it earns only when it has gone out to use. Once committed to use, the business must hope that the business capacity thus created will result in a return of cash, although it may be weeks, months, or years before that return is seen.

Do you think that so long as your business is profitable the cash can be left to look after itself? If you do, you need to read this book. Many businesses have sold to customers because they offered profitable business but have been shocked to discover that the result was a shortage of cash, leading to a crisis which ended in collapse or take-over at a knock-down price. If, at the end of the day, you cannot find the cash to pay suppliers or your salaries bill, your business will fail, no matter how profitable it may be.

Accountants use a system of accrual accounting in which expenses and cost are matched against the revenue arising in a period of account, irrespective of whether the revenues have been collected or the cost and expenses paid in that period. In the long run, that may not matter, but in the short run, there can be dramatic differences between the profit and the cash positions.

Let us take a simple example of Robert Daimon, a businessman who runs a business making Dongles, which he sells for £10 each. For the moment, assume he has all the assets he needs and the workforce and administrative and sales set-up to keep the business going.

Let us assume Robert's accountant produces the following profit forecast for 1985:

Robert Daimon PLC
Forecast income statement for 1985

	£
Sales	100,000
Cost of sales	80,000
Gross profit	20,000
Fixed overheads	10,000
Net profit	10,000

If we further assume that Robert has capital of £50,000 tied up in the business, we may think that this forecast is acceptable, since it promises 10 per cent profit margin on sales and 20 per cent return on capital. Admittedly, we are ignoring tax, but we want a simple example.

From a management viewpoint, however, the statement is not very useful. For one reason, the sales may not be received in cash in the period, customers normally take time to pay and, on average, two months or more of sales may be outstanding at the end of the year. Admittedly, a going concern will have money outstanding at the beginning of the year which will be collected during it. But if Robert Daimon is just starting up, he may only collect ten-twelfths of his sales in cash, that is, about £84,000. Another reason is that the figure of £90,000 cost charged against sales is no guide as to how much cash he will need to pay out for costs in 1985. Let us assume the breakdown of costs is as follows:

	Cost of 10,000	Unit cost
	£	£
Materials	40,000	4
Labour	30,000	3
Variable overhead	10,000	1
Fixed overhead	10,000	1
Total	90,000	9

The cash needs for 1985 depend not on the number to be sold, but the number to be produced. If Robert is just setting up the production of Dongles, he is likely to produce more of them than he sells, so that he can build up a stock to meet demand as it arises. If he produces 11,000 in 1985, the costs of production will then be:

	Cost of 11,000
	£
Materials	44,000
Labour	33,000
Variable overhead	11,000
Fixed overhead	10,000
Total	98,000
Unit cost £8.91	

Notice that the unit cost has gone down to £8.91 because the fixed costs are shared over 11,000 units instead of 10,000. The other costs increase proportionately.

However, the costs are not a sure guide to cash needs, either. The amount paid for materials will depend on the attitude of suppliers. Sometimes they will extend generous credit terms. For instance, if Robert obtains the same credit as he gives to his customers, two months, he would only have to pay ten-twelfths of £44,000, i.e. £37,000. In effect, he borrows £7,000 from suppliers. Equally, on the selling side, when he grants credit, he can be regarded as lending. His customers owe him £100,000 − £84,000 = £16,000! Somewhere he has to find funds to cover the difference of £9,000.

There are other possibilities. Suppliers sometimes demand payment in advance from new businesses, for obvious reasons. Robert plans to produce 1,000 units in January 1986, but he may find the supplier demanding payment in advance. The result is that his bill for materials in 1985 will be £44,000 + £4,000 = £48,000.

For most of the year, labour payments are closely in line with costs, because employees are paid fairly promptly, weekly or monthly. Labour affects cash flows badly, however, in vacations when the basic payroll cost continues and bonuses or holiday pay may be paid out. If production ceases, it may be some time before payments for supplies show the effect, but the effect of falling, or no sales, may be more immediate.

Overheads cover a variety of payments. Examples are light, heating, insurances, rates and rents. These may be paid in advance or arrear. The variable overheads can be expected to increase as production or sales activity rises. Hopefully, they fall as activity falls. It may be some time before the effects of changes are seen on cash payments. Fixed overheads do not change with activity, but this does not mean they do not go up from time to time.

When fixed costs do go up, the effect is often a serious jump in cash payments. An extreme example of this is depreciation, which is often included in fixed overheads and more rarely in variable overheads. Depreciation is not a cash flow at all. The cash to buy assets like plant and equipment has to be provided up-front, when the asset is first acquired. One argument for charging depreciation as a cost is that it helps your business retain funds for replacement. But this is no guarantee that the funds will be in cash when the time to buy a new asset arrives. Only positive cash management can make sure of that.

For Robert Daimon, his overhead cash requirements could well be something like this:

		£
Variable overhead costs 11,000 @ £1		11,000
	£	
Fixed overhead costs	10,000	
Less depreciation	4,000	6,000
		17,000
Plus prepayments	8,000	
Less arrears	6,000	2,000
Cash required for operations		19,000
Add replacement of plant		5,000
Total deficit of cash		24,000

Putting these various factors together correctly is important for all businesses and senior managers need to be as much alert to the cash consequences of their actions as they do to profit and cost consequences. The cash position cannot be trusted to look after itself. It is not impossible that Robert Daimon's cash position would be affected like this in 1985:

		£
Cash received from sales		84,000
	£	
Cash required: for materials	48,000	
for labour	33,000	
for overheads and plant	24,000	105,000
Cash deficit		21,000

This requirement of £21,000 in extra cash is needed, remember, to support a successful and profitable business!

There are many other factors affecting cash flow which are dealt with in this book. For instance, cash flows are affected by taxes, but the effect is very different in the case of corporation tax compared to VAT. Corporation tax on profits may be payable at 50 per cent, but the profit for tax purposes often differs from the profit reported for commercial purposes. Moreover, the tax is assessed and payable in arrears, so the corporation tax payable by Robert Daimon PLC in 1985 may be that from profits made in 1983. If 1983 was a good year in which the company made taxable profits of £20,000, the corporation tax at 50 per cent could be £10,000 – as much as the *profits* for 1985! This sort of fact is what leads many popular entertainers into the bankruptcy courts. VAT is payable quarterly and at 15 per cent on your sales revenues, this can be an uncomfortably large amount.

Take another example. Robert Daimon PLC is allowing £4,000 per year for depreciation on assets. That could mean the assets cost £40,000 when they were bought. At the end of their ten-year life, what will the company do? They may replace the asset with a new facility which is better in many respects than the old, so the new machine may cost more. Also, we live in inflationary times. Even if the new machine is much the same as the old it may still cost a lot more because the value of money has gone down. The better machine will also be correspondingly higher in price. Either way, the business must put up more cash. Prudent cash management will ensure the cash is there when needed.

You may be thinking that this is all very well, but these days it is fairly easy to borrow cash. So why worry?

It is a fair point. It is easy to borrow. But there are snags. The first is that borrowing has to be paid back. That is not so easy and it reinforces the need for careful management of cash.

The second is that lenders do look carefully at proposals for borrowing to see if they are realistic. The business person who has forecast the cash needs in detail will always carry conviction. If Robert Daimon approaches a bank with the prediction that his business needs £21,000 in cash for 1985, based on his profit forecast and his cash budget, he is likely to meet a sympathetic reaction from the bank. 'To be on the safe side, old chap' they will murmur, 'Why don't we make that up to £25,000? No point in spoiling the ship for a ha'porth of tar...'

By contrast, the businessman who waits until his hour of need to approach the bank may find a less than sympathetic reaction. Here we have a person who has got into deep water and comes dashing red-faced into the bank needing money to pay his wages this week. Can we really trust his figures? Is the firm really profitable? Why did this need suddenly crop up now? Have we heard all the story? If we give him £10,000 this week, he says he will be all right. But will he? What if he asks for another cash injection next month? Where is he taking us?

The actual facts of the situation may be exactly the same in both cases, but the point is that they *look* very different to the lender. In one case, we have a well managed company which anticipates its cash needs.

Maybe they don't always get their sums right, but they try. In the other case, we have a disorganised pleader for support who only appears when there's crisis: an incompetent cash manager. Why should we take the risk?

Another point about easy borrowing is the cost. At the time of writing a reasonably sound borrower can expect to pay about 12 per cent minimum on borrowed money and can easily find himself paying 20 per cent or more. Borrowing £20,000, then, may involve Robert Daimon in interest charges of £2,400 minimum and possibly more in 1985. The net cost of the borrowing is less, because the interest is allowable as a taxable expense. If corporation tax is at 50 per cent, the net cost is halved to £1,200 or more. But that is still a considerable cost and too serious to be ignored. Whilst the first objective of cash management techniques is to ensure that your business always has sufficient cash available for its needs, the second objective is to try to do so at minimum cost.

Without stressing too much the value of planning, it has to be said that the businessperson who sees the need for cash coming and arranges borrowing well in advance will not only get the money more easily; he or she will stand a good chance of getting it at lower cost. The borrower in emergency not only risks refusal: he or she also risks having to pay a much higher cost. Providers of money should not be treated like the fire brigade: they are not set up to deal with emergencies. And if they do finally turn out, the bigger the crisis, the bigger the cost!

A final point about borrowing is that it can rarely be relied upon for all your needs. Most businesses must be financed mainly by their owners. In 1982, British industry raised something like £30,000 millions in new funds but of this, only £7,500,000 or 25 per cent was raised by borrowing from banks, mortgages and loans. The banks actually provided most of this money – £6,307 million. Shareholders provided £22,500 million – a lot more!

You may think that these points are all very well for the unenterprising: in your case, if you need more cash you can always expand the business, sell more and find the funds that way.

Again, this is a dangerous fallacy. The effect of expanding your business depends upon its asset structure and the conditions under which you trade. Expansion can often mean you need more cash, not less.

Take the forecast for Robert Daimon PLC in 1985. Let us assume the business expands sales by 10 per cent. His profit will increase so long as his costs do not rise excessively. He may even improve his rate of profit if he can hold costs down. But what about the cash position? The table opposite shows what the results might be: the net profit increases by 20 per cent from £10,000 to £12,000 because of the fixed overheads not being affected by the increase in sales. So much to the good!

Robert Daimon PLC
Forecast Income Statement for 1985

	Original	After 10% increase
	£	£
Sales	100,000	110,000
Cost of sales	80,000	88,000
Gross profit	20,000	22,000
Fixed overheads	10,000	10,000
Net profit	10,000	12,000

The effect on cash requirements has to be calculated. Even if the increase does not change the terms of trade, the results are not obvious:

		Original		After 10% increase
		£		£
Cash from sales (10/12)		84,000		92,000
Cash required:	£		£	
for materials	48,000		52,800	
for labour	33,000		36,300	
for overheads	19,000		20,300	
for plant	5,000	105,000	5,000	114,400
Cash deficit		21,000		22,400

Given the assumptions, the effect is that the deficit actually increases. So far from solving the problem, increasing sales actually make it worse! We are not arguing that you should never increase sales. What the figures show is that effective financial management must be based on forecasts and budgets of cash needs. Whether you decide to increase sales or not is a matter for management judgement. Cash forecasting is necessary to show what will be the effect of a business plan on the resource needs. In particular, the demand for resources will show itself in the cash forecast. Why cash? Because it is the key decision point in putting resources to work to support your business plan.

These examples should give you the flavour of this book. It is a practical handbook intended for the engineeer, production manager, sales manager, product manager, site manager, entrepreneur and business owner. These are the people who make plans for businesses and, if the plans work, generate its profits.

The book concentrates on the cash implications of management plans and achievements. Cash planning and control is a relatively neglected aspect of management planning. As we have implied, most accounting systems concentrate on profits. But profits are the return to shareholders or other owners. Profits are an important measure of success: they must be maintained at a satisfactory level. But profits do not give insight into the effectiveness of the management of financial resources.

Apart from accounting systems, some businesses operate on the basis of budgets. Again, budgets are an important tool for planning, managing and controlling the resources of a business. In the large organisation the budgets reflect the organisational structure: each department, section and unit will have its own budget to which the manager works. The cash budget brings together the financial implications of all other budgets. For managers working within this kind of organisation, this book will clarify many of the problems which beset the financial planners. It is hoped it will create a more sympathetic awareness of these problems. 'Why can't the cash be found? Surely this organisation is big enough to find the money to ...'

Smaller businesses do not need the full panoply of budgets. Even if this is true, the message of this book is that they should nevertheless use cash forecasts and plans.

The book is not intended for accountants and finance specialists, but the author is aware of some who could benefit from reading it. The trouble with accounting training is that it stresses profit above all else. Budgeting and management accounting are comparatively neglected. Cash budgeting and management are regarded as an optional extra, but as we hope to show in this book, this is a seriously mistaken emphasis. For practical business management, cash management should be given pride of place as the key financial technique.

Everyone manages cash, from the housewife who keeps a lot of little tins in the larder to the treasurer of a multinational company who lends and borrows millions overnight, or the pension fund manager who has to invest millions every day. An effective manager must be alert to the cash aspect of the job. Anyone who controls people, material and services or makes decisions affecting resources has an impact on the cash position of the organisation. Admittedly, not all managerial jobs are equally sensitive in the cash aspect. Managers involved in selling, distribution and production have an immediate impact on the short-term cash position of their firms. The manager of a research and development department has little short-term impact, although his or her activities are expected to be very important in the long run.

This book is directed to the intelligent person in business who realises, perhaps uneasily, that cash is important. Such a person can learn how to budget and how to forecast cash needs. If you work in a small firm you may wish to set up and operate a system of cash forecasting yourself.

Introduction

This book shows the techniques which can be used. If you are a manager in a large organisation with a highly developed system of financial control, the technical aspects of the budgeting will be in the hands of a professional staff under a controller and treasurer. In that environment a knowledge of the techniques of cash control will be useful because it will help you understand the demands the experts make upon you.

Chapters 1 to 7 explain the basics of cash budgeting and control. Then in the next four chapters we look at particular types of business activity and the problems of cash control specific to each of them. You will probably want to read only the one that relates to the kind of business you are in. Finally, in the last two chapters we return to more general issues — using computers, and dealing with taxation.

1
Cash in business

Obviously, cash is important to business, but does it matter all that much? After all, cash is just one form of asset and most businesses keep some in hand. But they also make use of many other kinds of asset. Surely the important things are the plant, equipment, stocks, land, buildings, computers and so on which actually work for the business, making, distributing and selling its products? In itself, cash earns nothing and, in inflationary times, even loses value.

There's a great deal of sense in these arguments, as can be seen from the total assets of a group of large UK companies for 1982 (Table 1.1).

As you see, although these large companies held £10,300,000,000 in cash between them at the end of their financial year, large as that amount is, it was only 5 per cent of their total investment in assets. Even if short-term investments are considered to be equivalent to cash, that would still only put liquid assets to 13 per cent of the total.

Nevertheless, an ICMA research project reported in 1983 that forecasting cash flow was given the highest priority by a sample of 76 British companies. There must be sound reasons for this.

The cash flow cycle

In a business, cash flows in a cycle in which cash is used to buy assets, the assets are used to make profits, and, finally, the original capital plus

Table 1.1
Aggregated balance sheet of a group of large UK companies 1982

Current assets	£ million		%	Current liabilities	£ million		%
Cash	10,300		5	Tax due	6,500		3
Investments	17,600		8	Dividends and interest due	2,300		1
Debtors and prepayments	44,200		21	Creditors and accruals	49,500		24
Stocks and work-in-progress	50,500		25	Bank loans	27,200		13
		122,600	59			85,500	41
Fixed assets				Long-term debentures, mortgages, loans	15,700		7
Investments and intangibles	3,600			Shareholders' interests and deferred tax	107,200		52
Tangibles	82,200						
		85,800	41			122,900	59
		208,400	100			208,400	100

2

the profits is returned in the form of cash.

The short-term and the long-term cycles are rather different and both are reflected in the balance sheet.

The short-term cash cycle

The short-term cash cycle provides for the circulation of working capital. The simplest cycle is where a business buys goods, and sells them immediately for cash. If John Doe buys a microcomputer for £100 and sells it immediately for £150, he has a good deal. If the cycle can be repeated, he has a business going.

The effect of this cycle is that cash of £100 is turned into stock (inventory) costing £100, which is turned into cash, £150. If continued, the next cycle would allow John Doe to buy £150 of stock (inventory) and if profitability is maintained, turn it into £225 cash, as in Figure 1.1.

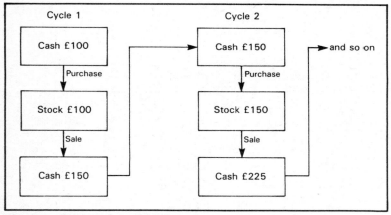

Fig. 1.1 Short-term cash cycle

This cash cycle applies to all businesses, however complex. If John Doe gives credit to his customers, a new stage is introduced: the sales first result in debtors (accounts receivable) which are only turned into cash after a time delay. The cycle is extended as in Figure 1.2.

This succession of cycles is all right but if John Doe's customers are, like most people, impatient for service, they may not be willing to wait around until John receives his cash from the previous customer. If the firm has no cash with which to buy stock, it may lose its next sale.

John Doe overcomes this problem by taking credit from the suppliers. He still has to pay the supplier, but after a time delay. The advantage is that he can expand his business on borrowed money. The two cycles can be combined, so that John Doe can use his £100 cash plus £150 credit to buy £250 stock, which he then sells for £375, as in Figure 1.3.

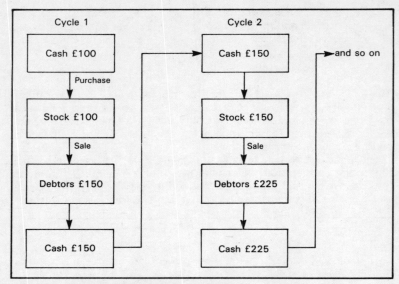

Fig. 1.2 Extended short-term cash cycle

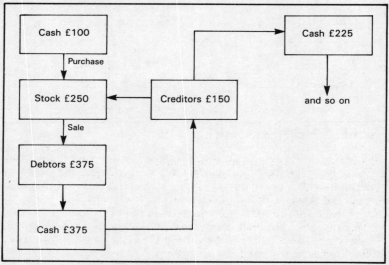

Fig. 1.3 Combining the cycles

Once the £375 cash is received from the debtors, £150 is used to pay the creditors and John Doe is left with £225 cash in hand.

As business becomes more complex, so does the cycle of cash. Let us look at a manufacturing company. In this case, finished goods are manufactured from bought-in raw materials and components, a labour force is paid as is the expense of various services used in production and stocks of both raw materials and finished products are held. The cycle will be as in Figure 1.4.

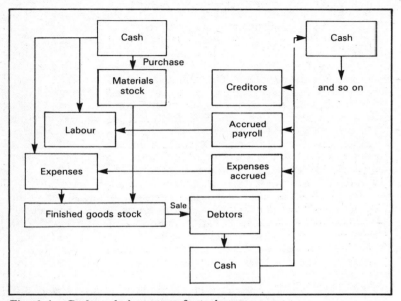

Fig. 1.4 Cash cycle in a manufacturing company

Each form which resources take: materials, labour, expenses, finished goods, debtors and cash is like a reservoir or sump which absorbs a proportion of the funds circulating in the system.

Refer back to the balance sheet in Table 1.1 and you can see the effects of this cycle of working capital in action.

As well as the cash, these large British companies held 21 per cent of assets in the form of debtors and prepayments. Another 25 per cent are held as stocks and work-in-progress. Thus about 60 per cent of all funds in the firms are tied up in current assets.

This figure is an overall average, of course, and some firms such as retailers may have as much as 80 per cent of their assets in current form. Heavy industry will tend to have a lower proportion in this form although the amounts are still substantial. For instance, the oil industry firms included in the group of large UK companies from whom the data in Table 1.1 were collected, had 42 per cent of their assets in current form, significantly less than the average, but still a high proportion.

If you look on the other side of the balance sheet, you can see that

24 per cent of the funds in use was obtained from creditors and accruals for expenses. Adding in borrowing from banks and other items, we see that current liabilities provided 41 per cent of the total assets employed.

To return to our question, how important is cash? One point is that cash is the asset of maximum *choice*. Once a business invests in stock or work-in-progress or allows customers time to pay, resources are tied up. There will be a time delay before they return for re-use. The number of alternatives open to the manager are few; perhaps an asset only has one use.

Another point is that cash is the point where demand for and supply of resources meet. Once a business is ticking along, buying and/or making goods and services, selling and delivering to customers, taking credit from suppliers and giving credit to customers, there will be a constant supply of cash coming available and a constant demand that it be re-invested. We have seen that cash supply and demand are the results of a complex process. Because of this, cash availability can be extremely erratic. Unless strong cash management procedures are established you may find your business staggering from surplus to deficit in quick succession, particularly in the short-term.

You establish routines for making stocks ahead of actual demand because you don't want to lose a sale when a customer appears. But suppose there is a change on the market or a new form of competition and sales do not materialise? What then? For a while, the flow of cash from debtors will continue, and the firm will carry on investing in resources to make stocks. Then, the effect of the drop in sales will work through the system and the flow of cash from debtors will stop. By this time the firm may be vastly overstocked and short of cash to meet essentials like payroll. Desperate measures may be needed simply to survive. If these do not succeed, the firm could be sold off at a knock-down price to a buyer who, with a little money to spare, can sit back and watch the money roll in as sales revive.

The long-term cash cycle

The long-term cash cycle is less volatile. It arises from the provision of long-term capital to the business, partly from owners' contributions and partly from long-term lenders. The cash raised goes partly to the purchase of long-term assets, but it is also used to provide or replenish the supply of working capital. A return must be given to the long-term funds, in the form of dividends to shareholders or interest to long-term lenders.

This cycle is shown as in Figure 1.5.

Other factors which affect the long-term cycle are the need to replenish or increase fixed assets, the need to repay capital sums borrowed and the need to pay tax.

The key factor in the long-term cycle is the sheer size of the amounts involved. If you look at the balance sheet in Table 1.1 again, you will

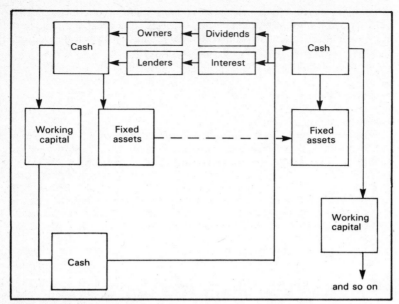

Fig. 1.5 Long-term cash cycle

see on the right hand side that 52 per cent of the funds provided to the large companies concerned came from shareholders: no less than £107,200,000,000. Long-term borrowing was not so important; it only accounted for 7 per cent of the funds. However, if you examine the items under current liabilities, you will see that short-term loans, mainly from the banks, accounted for a further 13 per cent of the funds. So, in total, these large firms were directly borrowing 20 per cent of their funds. Indirectly, they were obtaining a much higher proportion. If you consider trade credit to be a form of borrowing – it is certainly an indirect way of obtaining funds – then the non-owners of these businesses were providing 48 per cent of the funds, compared to 52 per cent from shareholders.

The valuation of assets

A balance sheet such as the aggregate one shown in Table 1.1 drawn up on conventional accounting principles can be highly misleading. For one thing, all the assets have a money value attached to them and naturally, one tends to assume that the figures are comparable. In Table 1.1 the firms have tangible fixed assets of £82,200 million, and working capital of £122,600 million, of which cash is £10,300 million. It is a mistake to imagine that the total asset value £208,400 million could ever be available in cash. Certainly, the £10,300 cash is, but not the fixed assets. They could produce more or less, depending on circumstances.

Historical versus current cost

There has been a great deal of controversy about how to give more reliable accounting figures to businessmen and investors. In the UK, in the early 1980s large businesses have been required to publish two sets of figures. The first set is based on established accounting principles and conventions, historical cost (HCA) and the second set on current cost (CCA) principles.

Since the ruling approach is HCA, we shall consider valuation principles on that basis here but, where appropriate, give some published CCA data to illustrate some of the problems.

Cash

Cash is money which a business actually has. Usually, we don't have to think too deeply about what is meant by cash – it's obvious. But cash can take many forms: currency, bank balances, deposits in building societies, short-term investments and so on. Some forms, such as currency, are immediately available; others involve a time delay. We can draw on cash in the bank by paying by cheque; to draw on a building society we will have to go to their office and draw out the cash and then pay. Normally, this doesn't matter, but suppose you want to buy some bankrupt stock. You could pay by cheque, but there would be no use producing your building society book and trying to pay with that. Cash may also be subject to conditions such as the need to support cheques with a bank card, or to get them signed by two directors. However, we can say that the £10,300 million shown in the balance sheet in Table 1.1 does represent reasonably available funds at the value stated. This figure would be the same if CCA were used.

Debtors and prepayments

The account shown for debtors under HCA, £44,200 million in Table 1.1, is based on the prices at which goods have been invoiced to customers. The valuation reflects what the customers are expected to pay, and that means it is subject to two conditions: that the customer accepts the debt; and that the customer has the cash to pay the debt when due. So that amount is less certain than the cash.

The debtors figure in a balance sheet will also be reduced by an allowance for the possibility of bad debts and for discounts. In other words, the £44,200 million shown should be received, eventually, in cash, but there will be a time delay and, perhaps, not everyone will pay, so the amount could be less.

Stocks and work-in-progress

In conventional accounting, stocks are valued at recorded historical cost with the proviso that if the market value of the stock, at the time of the balance sheet, is known to be lower than cost, then that value will be used. A retailer who paid £500 for a dining room suite for sale will show a valuation of £500 in his trading stocks for that item. Of course, there is no cash there, at least, not until the stock has been sold, and the £500 is no guide to the amount of cash which the suite might produce. If sold in normal trading, it might bring in £900. If sold as bankruptcy stock, it might bring in little or nothing.

Before stocks can be turned into cash, it is necessary to find a buyer. Then the business will have to collect the cash. Although impressive, the statement in the balance sheet that stocks of £50,500 million are held by a number of large companies in the UK must be interpreted with caution. On the whole, it is a fair indication of the amount of money which the companies have put into stocks. It is not a good indication of the cash they will get out! In the normal course of business, the stocks should be sold for much more than cost. In other circumstances, the cash value could be very low.

Assets

Current assets

The variability of the items included in current assets, apart from cash, can be seen by comparing the figures for historical cost and current cost (CCA) published in the *Stock Exchange Handbook* for 1982/83, as shown in Table 1.2.

Table 1.2

Current assets of selected companies for end 1981/early 1982

	HCA	CCA	CCA/HCA % difference
	£'000	£'000	
George Wimpey PLC	501,592	318,000	−37
De la Rue Company PLC	170,984	79,700	−55
Debenhams PLC	118,361	40,800	−65
Talbot Motor Co. Ltd.	168,893	171,880	+2

Not all companies show a dramatic difference and, as can be seen from Talbot CCA can result in higher figures. The point is that the figures do not represent a hard cash valuation.

Fixed assets

Investments in fixed assets may take up a large part of the capital of a firm since land, buildings, plant and equipment may have to be purchased to give the firm the extractive, manufacturing, distributing or selling capacity to put it in business.

Fixed assets are usually valued at cost less depreciation where the assets tend to lose value in use, such as plant and machinery, or computers. Land is not depreciated and, indeed, some companies have their land and property revalued periodically. Marks and Spencer Ltd revalue their land and buildings periodically and in 1982 the profit on revaluation was £64 million, compared with a trading profit of £225 million.

Fixed assets consist of relatively few items which have a high initial cost and a long life. The cash required for them is invested in a large sum at the start of their life, for example, an oil refinery may cost £100 million to build and have a twenty-year life.

Depreciation will be shown as an annual cost in the accounts, say, at £5 million per year, and the balance sheet will show the investment for twenty years, with the value declining from £100 million in year 1 to £5 million in year 20. The balance sheet valuation put on fixed assets is rarely a good guide to their current cash value. This can be seen in the figures published at the end of 1981/beginning of 1982 under HCA and CCA shown in Table 1.3.

Table 1.3

Fixed assets of selected companies for end 1981/early 1982

	HCA	CCA	CCA/HCA % difference
	£'000	£'000	
Taylor Woodrow PLC	63,871	67,648	+ 6
Delta Group PLC	129,220	152,030	+18
Cadbury-Schweppes PLC	328,800	382,000	+16

As may be expected, the difference is not so great as for current assets and it is more usual for CCA to give a higher value, but the variation is still considerable.

Liabilities

Liabilities are money claims on the business. The liabilities are divided into current and long-term in much the same way as the assets.

Current liabilities

Current liabilities arise from short-term factors, such as creditors (the accounts payable to suppliers) and a short-term borrowing such as bank loans and overdrafts.

Current liabilities arise when the business acquires assets and does not pay for them immediately, for instance, when trading stocks are obtained on one month's credit, or cash is borrowed in the short term.

Long-term liabilities

Long-term liabilities arise when funds are borrowed for long periods, typically, for 5–20 years and often in the form of a debenture or a mortgage. In the case of both current and long-term liabilities, the amount shown in the balance sheet is the amount borrowed (and, therefore, repayable) but in the case of long-term liabilities, interest will also be payable, usually on an annual basis. This interest is not normally shown on a balance sheet because it is paid as it becomes due. So future interest does not show because it is not yet due and past interest only shows as a liability if it has not been paid on time.

Liabilities shown on the balance sheet are, therefore, reliable cash figures but they only show the capital amounts which will have to be paid to various creditors. However, it must be remembered that companies which borrow in different currencies may suffer, or gain from, changes in exchange rates, as can be seen in Table 1.4.

Three of the companies show exactly the same figures but Wimpey and

Table 1.4

Long-term liabilities of selected companies for end 1981/early 1982

	HCA	CCA	CCA/HCA % difference
	£'000	£'000	
Talbot Motor Co Ltd	99,549	99,549	—
Taylor Woodrow	37,135	37,135	—
George Wimpey PLC	102,992	70,800	−31
Delta Group PLC	66,950	66,950	—
Cadbury-Schweppes PLC	113,800	33,700	−70

Cadbury-Schweppes show a considerable drop because of the rising value of the pound.

Shareholders' capital

The capital of the owners of a business, whether a sole proprietor, a partnership or a company, appear on the same side of the balance sheet as the liabilities but the figure value shown has a very different meaning. First, we should note that it is calculated as the sum of the capital contributed, plus any retained profits and minus losses, drawings or dividends. It is what the owners have put into the business. Sole traders and partners can add to or draw from their capital and profits as they please, shareholders may receive dividends but not, usually, repayments of capital. If the business gets into a bankruptcy or liquidation position, the owners rank last in order of preference for a return of their money. The owners carry the basic risk of enterprise. If it is successful, they take the profits. If it fails, they carry the losses and will only receive repayments if, and to the extent that, the liabilities have been paid in full. In sum, whilst the liabilities shown on a balance are generally the cash sums claimable at the time of the balance sheet, the capital is not. Owners' capital is a residual claim.

The implications of the uncertain cash value of assets combined with the high certainty of liabilities can be dramatic for the owners of a business. In the UK in 1982, nearly 6,000 businesses were insolvent. Take a balance sheet based on the average for wholesalers and distributors in 1977 (Table 1.5).

Table 1.5

Wholesalers' and distributors' average balance sheet at end 1977, £'000

Current assets			Current liabilities		
Cash	900				
Debtors	4,400		Creditors	4,600	
Stocks	3,500		Short-term loans	1,900	
		8,800			6,500
Fixed assets		2,200	Long-term loans		1,000
			Shareholders' capital		3,500
		11,000			11,000

Of the total capital, £3,500,000 (32 per cent) was contributed by shareholders. Of the assets, £900,000 (9 per cent) is in the form of cash. Given the priority claims of the various creditors, the amount payable to shareholders could be very variable, depending on the cash actually realised from assets, as can be seen in Table 1.6.

Table 1.6

Assets realised	Creditors take	Shareholders take
100% of valuation = £11,000,000	£7,500,000 (100%)	£3,500,000 (100%)
50% of valuation = £ 5,500,000	£5,500,000 (73%)	Nil (0%)
75% of valuation = £ 8,250,000	£7,500,000 (100%)	£ 750,000 (21%)

A final point about the balance sheet is that it is a *static* statement, which states the position of the business at a particular moment in time, and so it is often out of date by the time it is considered. The starting point for controlling the cash position of a firm must always be an up-to-date statement.

Ratio analysis

Despite criticisms of balance sheet valuations it is useful to look at the ratio between items and groups of items on the balance sheet as part of your cash control system.

Working capital

The working capital is the difference between the current assets and liabilities, i.e.

Current assets – current liabilities = WORKING CAPITAL

For the average wholesaler and distributor:

$$£8,800,000 - £6,500,00 = £2,300,000$$

£2,300,000 is the amount of capital in current use in the firm which would still be left if all the current debts were paid off. If the amount is positive, it means that the company could keep on trading even if the suppliers and the bank withdrew their support and demanded their money back. That is good.

Suppose you had a firm, Trueblood PLC, with current assets of £800,000 and current liabilities of £1,000,000. In this case, the working capital would be £200,000 negative and Trueblood would be overtrading.

Another way of looking at the working capital position is to consider the ratio of the current assets to the current liabilities, i.e.

$$\frac{\text{Current assets}}{\text{Current liabilities}} = \text{CURRENT RATIO}$$

For the average wholesaler and distributor:

$$\frac{£8,800,000}{£6,500,000} = 1.34 \text{ to } 1$$

Whether that ratio is satisfatory must depend on the circumstances and the type of industry; there is no one unique ratio which should apply across the board, although 2:1 is a sensible 'norm'.

Quick assets

Before you can turn stocks into cash you have to sell them. First find your customer!

The debtors, or accounts receivable, are different. You have already made the sale and you are simply waiting for payment. Debtors, cash and short-term investments, then, can be regarded as 'quick' assets. We can obtain the figure for quick assets by deducting the value of stocks from the current assets:

$$\text{Current assets} - \text{stocks} = \text{quick assets}$$

For the average wholesaler and distributor:

$$£8,800,000 - £3,500,000 = £5,300,000$$

You can calculate the ratio of quick assets to current liabilities:

$$\frac{\text{Quick assets}}{\text{Current liabilities}} = \text{QUICK ASSET RATIO}$$

For the average wholesaler and distributor:

$$\frac{£5,300,000}{£6,500,000} = .82 \text{ to } 1$$

If you have a quick asset ratio of 1, it means you can meet all your current liabilities from cash or sales already made.

The acid test

Following this logic further, the acid test compares the cash holdings to the current liabilities. This cash ratio is a measure of the extent to which your business could settle current liabilities at the balance sheet date, i.e.

$$\frac{\text{Cash}}{\text{Current liabilities}} = \text{CASH RATIO (ACID TEST)}$$

For the average wholesaler and distributor:

$$\frac{£\ 900,000}{£6,500,000} = .14\ 1$$

Cash in business

It is often suggested that the cash ratio, the acid test, should be .5:1 but the balance sheet of our average wholesaler and distributor shows that cash holdings are well below that figure. This is not necessarily a bad thing. On the one hand, the management has to make sure that it has enough cash at all times to meet claims. On the other, since cash earns nothing, the float should be kept within reasonable bounds, so that the capital of the firm is used most profitably. In this connection, cash capacity is more relevant than cash float.

Cash capacity

Cash capacity is the maximum cash which is available to a firm at any one time.

It is a mistake to consider this purely on the cash figure shown in the balance sheet. Take a simple example of two firms (Table 1.7).

Table 1.7

	Firm A	Firm B
	£	£
Cash	70,000	—
Debtors	120,000	120,000
Stock	260,000	330,000
Current assets	450,000	450,000
Reserve borrowing power	80,000	200,000

The cash capacity is the total cash available to the firm. This includes the cash actually in hand, bank balances, realisable investments and cash equivalent items on the balance sheet. To this must be added cash which the firm has the capacity to borrow. In other words:

Cash reserves plus additional borrowing power = cash capacity
For firm A   £70,000   +   £80,000   =   £150,000
For firm B   Nil   +   £200,000 =   £200,000

This shows that firm B, which has no cash in hand, nevertheless has a better cash capacity than firm A.

The cash capacity of a firm depends on the structure of the business and the policies it adopts (that is, the way it is managed). The major factors determining the cash capacity are:

1 The asset structure. This is the actual composition of the assets held, including cash stocks. To some extent this is determined by the kind of business. For instance, a manufacturing company will probably have a large amount of capital tied up in fixed assets, distributors hold large stocks, suppliers of industrial sub-assemblies probably have substantial accounts receivable, construction companies have a lot of money tied up in work-in-progress.

2   *The financing structure.* This is the actual composition of the sources of finance. We have already seen that current short-term borrowing should be related to the current asset structure, through the working capital ratios. Long-term capital may be provided by owners or by long-term lenders. Here, it is common to calculate the debt:equity ratio. For this purpose, all borrowing, long- and short-term, is included in the debt which is then compared to the total assets. In the case of the data for the companies in Table 1.1, the shareholders provided £107,200 million, that is 52 per cent of the total funds.

Looking at the average financing structure for UK industry in Table 1.1, long-term lenders provided £15,700 million and current liabilities £85,500 million, thus the debt ratio was:

$$\frac{\text{Total debt}}{\text{Total assets}} = \text{DEBT RATIO}$$

For a group of large UK companies:

$$\frac{£101,200}{£208,400} = 48 \text{ per cent}$$

It is often suggested that firms can borrow up to about 50 per cent of their capital requirements. If the debt ratio goes higher, it may be harder to borrow and more expensive, because lenders think the firm is a riskier proposition.

Table 1.8

Euraka PLC balance sheet at 31 December 1984

Current assets	£'000		£'000
Cash	300	Current liabilities	500
Debtors and stocks	2,700	Long-term liabilities	1,000
Fixed assets	2,000	Shareholders' capital	3,500
	5,000		5,000

What is the cash capacity of Euraka PLC (Table 1.8) if comparable firms in the industry can normally borrow up to 40 per cent of their funds? The total borrowing power can be calculated as:

$$\text{Total owners' equity} \times \frac{\% \text{ debt}}{\% \text{ equity}} = \text{TOTAL BORROWING POWER}$$

For Euraka PLC:

$$£3,500,000 \times \frac{40}{60} = £2,333,000$$

From this we can calculate:

Total borrowing power minus actual borrowing = ADDITIONAL BORROWING POWER.

For Euraka PLC:

$$£2,333,333 - £1,500,000 = £833,333$$

The cash capacity of Euraka PLC is thus:

	£
Cash in balance sheet	300,000
Plus additional borrowing power	833,333
Cash capacity	1,133,333

3 *The economic environment.* The general state of the economy, and changes which occur in it, will often affect the cash capacity of the individual firm. If the economy is booming, sales may increase, prices will be firm and profits will benefit. Equity rises and, with it, borrowing power. In the long run, the cash effects will be beneficial, but in the short run, there may be increased demands for cash which have to be met by borrowing or new capital injections.

If the economy is in a bad way, the individual firm may feel the effects in falling sales and a softening of prices. On the other hand, deliveries and prices of supplies may improve so that it may still be possible to keep up profitability. Cash in hand may increase as business activity falls and the firm may need to consider new investments in new products, to find new markets or to increase competitive advertising and discounting. Some businesses perform against the tide, others succumb to the pressures.

4 *The financial environment.* The financial environment is not always in step with the economic environment. An important influence here is the attitudes of the government in power, and, as a consequence, the policies of the financial institutions, both nationally and internationally. In bad times, one government may offer tax benefits and cash grants to encourage business, and they may endeavour to keep interest rates down to encourage recovery: another government might react quite differently. Similarly, the availability of cash from the financial institutions such as the banks, and the interest charged may change rapidly. In the last 30 years the world has seen considerable variations in financial conditions and at the time of writing, in the UK, there are ample supplies of cash at high interest rates, a pound weak against the US dollar, but strong against other currencies.

An important influence is the general expectation about future inflation, since some assets give protection but cash in hand loses value.

Motives for holding cash

Cash is an asset which is valuable because it can be turned into other assets on which profits can be earned. In itself, however, it does not earn. Why, then, should a business hold any cash at all? Cash constantly flows into a business as deals are completed and customers pay their bills. Isn't it good sense to turn that cash back into working assets or to invest it into fixed assets which will create more earning power? In general, these are sound arguments and one aspect of effective cash management is making sure that cash is not left idle, but there are three substantial reasons for holding a stock, or float, of cash. These are:

1 To support business transactions. Sufficient cash should be available at all times to provide for the purchase of stocks, payment of expenses, wages, salaries, and to meet the demands of creditors, interest, dividends, etc. This cash maintains the preferred asset and financial structure.

2 To provide for speculative transactions. Not every firm has this need but many do. This cash is held for the opportunities which arise in an unforeseen way, for instance, to buy bankrupt stock or to take advantage of special offers on supplies, to take over other firms or to enter new markets.

The ability to find cash on the spot may mean a firm can take advantage of many opportunities for profitable dealing. An example in 1984 arose when Thorn Electrical proposed a merger with British Aerospace. The GEC Co., which had considerable reserves of cash, entered a rival bid for British Aerospace.

3 Precautionary cash. Having provided for known transactions and for the possibilities of speculative opportunities, the cash manager may still wish to hold an element of cash on hand 'just in case'. Precautionary cash provides insurance against the fact that our knowledge of the future is always uncertain. As we have seen, there is a complex cycle through which cash flows through the firm before it is converted from asset to asset and back to cash again. One slip-up in the cash chain, a disaster in production, or a failure of a big customer on the sales side and the firm could find itself, despite all its best endeavours, short of cash.

A float of precautionary cash provides against this sort of thing. Some or all of these reasons may explain the large amounts of cash held at The General Electric Company which at 31 March 1983 was sitting on £1.3 billion net cash, 30 per cent of the total assets. The Company has held more than 20 per cent of assets in cash since 1977.

The direct cost of cash

Cash will have an explicit interest cost if it is borrowed from the bank, on hire purchase, or by issuing a long-term debenture.

The indirect cost of cash

Cash also has indirect costs as follows. The first is the cost of cash provided by shareholders. Although interest is not charged on invested funds or on earnings retained, there is an indirect cost since shareholders do expect a return in the form of earnings and dividends. It is a mistake to think that funds provided by owners do not cost anything. Indeed, if risk is to be compensated for, the cost of shareholders' funds should generally be higher than the cost of borrowed money.

The second indirect cost of cash is the opportunity cost, which may take various forms. For instance, in Table 1.7, firm A has stocks of £260,000 compared to £330,000 held by B. Either firm could suffer an opportunity cost as a result of its policies on stock-holding. Firm A may lose sales because it does not have a sufficient range of items in stock. Firm B may lose sales because it has already committed itself to certain types of stock.

Timing

A final reiteration of the basic point about managing cash: timing is of the essence. Cash management tries to ensure that enough cash is available where it is wanted, when it is wanted. The supreme art is to get it just right, not too much and, never, but *never,* too little.

2

Preparing a cash budget

To prepare a cash budget, you need three pieces of information: cash at start; expected receipts during the period; and expected payments during the period.

Cash at start

All reasonably available forms of cash should be taken into account, so long as the amount is significant. Trivial amounts should be ignored. To a small business, trivial amounts might include the £100 float in a cash register. The British Treasury has a daily cash flow model which only deals in amounts over £10 million so, to them, anything less than £10m is trivial. It all depends on the scale of spending.

Expected receipts

The main receipts in business are from sales in cash or from credit sales. Credit sales materialise in the form of payments by debtors. Selling activities largely dominate receipts from the working capital cycle.
    There may also be receipts of a long-term, capital nature such as from the sale of assets, or from new capital raising, but these are not routine.

Expected payments

Payments, also, tend to be dominated, on the current, or working capital side, by two items: payments for supplies (and materials) and payments for labour, i.e. wages and salaries. Businesses vary considerably, of course, but it is generally the case that materials and labour costs account for 70–80 per cent of budgeted expenses. For this reason, these items must attract a great deal of attention if an accurate budget is to be prepared.

The other expenses may also require detailed attention although it is sometimes possible to arrive at a fairly accurate global estimate for them, once the budgeting exercise has been gone through a few times. There can be nasty surprises in these items, however, for instance when annual payments like insurance fall due. Tax demands can be difficult, too, if unanticipated.

There may be long-term payments, or items arising from the long-term capital, such as dividends, interest payments, purchase of new fixed assets or the repayments of loans, but, again, these are unusual.

Short- and long-term needs

On both the receipts and the payments side, the job of estimating tends to centre on current needs, i.e. the working capital, for the very reason that it is the working capital which constantly comes and goes on a daily basis. Also, these needs arise out of the routine, normal operations of the business, so that there is a momentum generated by operations which is closely reflected in the cash flows. Long-term needs arise in more specific contexts and, indeed, are often the reason for having cash planning in the first place. Some of these needs may be predictable, such as the need to find cash to repay a loan. Others may be dependent on cash availability, for example the investment of large blocks of capital into new buildings or equipment. There should be an air of leisured calm about long-term cash planning in contrast to the pressure under which short-term cash is controlled. But, of course, that isn't always so. If long-term planning is done badly, then the large amounts of money involved can contribute heavily to a short-term cash crisis. In that case, the situation is a far cry from leisured calm!

Float – the closing cash

From the three pieces of information, opening cash, plus expected receipts, minus expected payments, the cash budget shows the resultant: the closing cash or cash float. Since the amount is a budget, or a forecast, based on various assumptions, it will be possible to consider, in advance, whether the float is sufficient to meet your needs. If it does, all is well and you can then consider whether, in fact, the float is too high. In that case, you will make plans for putting the surplus to profitable use when it materialises. If the float is too small to meet your needs, then action must be taken to ensure that, in the event, an adequate amount will be available. Later chapters discuss the actions which can be taken.

The float or closing cash is also a starting point, first, for the next period's cash budget. What is left at the end of January becomes the amount we start with at the beginning of February and so on. Second, the float is also used for managerial action to deal with a possible unsatisfactory position or to exploit a favourable one. The purpose of the forecast is to give you time, well in advance, to plan for a more satisfactory outcome *before* you get into the future situation, when it may be too late to act.

Basic data – the data sheet

As a first step in cash budgeting, you should draw up a data sheet. At first, this requires quite a bit of effort but eventually it will become second nature and make cash budgeting far less of a chore. One reason the job is difficult is that it forces you to think about your business in a new way but that is also a benefit of cash planning. It gives you a better understanding of how your business ticks.

There is no one standard form of data sheet. Throughout this book you will be using data sheets for various situations which will provide models but it is likely that, once the use is understood, you will design your own forms for your own circumstances. A simple form of data sheet is shown in Table 2.1.

Like all good business forms, the data sheet has a title showing what it is. There is then provision for you to record the date it was prepared and the fact that you prepared it.

It is then useful to record details of the period for which the budget is prepared, e.g. January to March 1983 and the budget basis, i.e. daily, weekly, monthly, quarterly or annually.

The data sheet then has three sections in which you enter data:

1 Opening cash balances
2 Receipts
3 Payments

The information in each section is recorded under four columns:

(a) *Items*. You list each item to be budgeted for in the appropriate section.
(b) *Cash amount*. You enter the net cash amount involved minus any discounts or allowances in this column. The amount should not generally be an average (except for minor items). If the budget covers three months and £300 is paid in one particular month, then show it for that month.

Table 2.1
Data sheet for cash budget

XYZ PLC
Budget for period: 3 months January to March 1983
Budget basis: Monthly

Prepared by: D. Garbutt
Date: 30th December 1982

Items		Amount	Timing	Conditions and flexibility
Section 1	Opening float			
	Cash in hand	400		
	Cash at bank	600		
Section 2	Receipts			
	Cash sales	5,000	per month	
	Credit sales: December	10,000	Cash after	An extra discount for
	January	12,000	one month's delay	early payment might
	February	8,000		persuade 20% (by value)
	March	15,000		to pay earlier
(Debtors at end of March		15,000)		
Section 3	Payments			
	Salaries and wages	5,840	per month	50% of sales
	To suppliers for materials: January	8,500	Payable within	
	February	6,500	10 days	
	March	10,000		Could be delayed one
				month for loss of 2%
				cash discount
	Other expenses	700	per month	Overheads £800 p.m.
				less depreciation £100
				£700

(c) *The timing of each item listed.* Here you state the exact date or estimated timing of each receipt or payment. Periodic receipts or payments can be stated as such, e.g. monthly salaries. If a single payment of £3,000 is to be made, indicate when it will be paid, e.g. 15 February 1983.

(d) *Conditions and flexibility.* Sometimes, receipts can be brought forward or payments postponed without too much trouble. In other cases, this may not be so. For instance, delaying the payment of creditors for supplies beyond ten days may involve the loss of discounts. Record any information of this kind in this column.

The data sheet as a record

Data sheets should be clearly labelled to show when they were prepared, for what period and by whom. The data sheet is the starting point for preparing the cash budget and should be filed with the budget. Data sheets can save a lot of effort when the next round of budgeting comes along.

Collecting the data for well established items will become a simple routine and attention can be concentrated on changes and new items. If a lot of data are used, prepare each section on a separate sheet.

Working papers

When the cash budget requires supporting calculations, you should keep working papers. These are sheets on which all your calculations are carried out. They are always useful in recording the mental process by which figures shown in the cash budget are arrived at from the basic data on the data sheet. There is no set format for working papers but it is advisable:

(a) To record the data sheet and budget to which they refer.
(b) To organise them in numbered sections. A reference can then be put on the data sheet and the cash budget.

Keeping working papers is surprisingly useful in reminding you exactly how you arrived at a particular figure in your budget. These things are soon forgotten. We illustrate the use of working papers in the next chapter.

Two approaches to cash budgeting

There are two ways in which cash budgeting can be done: short- and long-term.

Short-term cash budgeting (receipts and payments method)

To draw up a short-term cash budget you need the detailed receipts and payments for each budget period. You add receipts and subtract payments from the opening cash. The result is the float or closing cash, which you then use to start the next period. This method is the most practical in day-to-day cash planning. Also, it opens the door to a full understanding of cash budgeting and control problems in business. This method is known in the UK as the *receipts and payments method* and in the USA as the *collection and disbursement method*.

You can use the receipts and payments method for periods of up to one year. For most businesses the method is used on a daily, monthly or quarterly basis and not for periods of more than 90 days. This is because detailed circumstances may not be predictable beyond such a period. Unless a computer is used, the calculations can also be burdensome.

Long-term cash budgeting

A long-term cash budget may be produced from accounting statements which give the income statement (profit and loss account) and balance sheets. You can use this method for periods if you have the accounting statements available. This method has a lot to commend it, but the results are not so dependable except in the hands of a fully skilled accountant and even then, preferably the accountant who prepared the original accounting data. Because it takes the 'broad brush' approach, a great deal of relevant information may be omitted from this kind of long-term forecast. This approach is known as the *adjusted net income method*. If you have sufficient accountancy knowledge, you can use this method at all times.

Example of cash budgeting

Short-term budget – receipts and payments method. The data sheet for XYZ PLC is shown in Table 2.1. The data are for a budget to cover the first three months of 1983, to be made up on a monthly basis.

Section 1

The opening cash amounts of £1,000, of which £600 is in the bank and £400 cash in hand.

Section 2

The receipts consist of cash sales of £5,000 each month and receipts from debtors. Sales on credit are a variable, so the expected value of sales for each month is listed. Also, since the cash is received after a delay of one month, the amount of sales in December is recorded. Thus, the total receipts for each month from sales will be as in Table 2.2.

Table 2.2
XYZ PLC Cash receipts

	From cash sales £	From credit sales £	Total £
January	5,000	10,000	15,000
February	5,000	12,000	17,000
March	5,000	8,000	13,000

In the final column it is noted that it might be possible to hasten up receipts from debtors if additional discount were given, but only 20 per cent of the debtors would pay earlier. The majority would still take a month to pay.

Section 3

Materials, salaries and wage payments account for the bulk of expenses. Salaries and wages amount to £5,840 per month and there is no flexibility on these. Materials cost 50 per cent of sales in the month and are payable within ten days. However payment for materials could be delayed for one month at the cost of a loss in discount of 2 per cent.

The payments have been calculated, as in Table 2.3.

Table 2.3
XYZ PLC Material cost payments

	Sales £	Material cost at 50% of sales £
January	17,000	8,500
February	13,000	6,500
March	20,000	10,000

The sales for each month consist of the cash sales, £5,000 each month, plus the credit sales for that month.

It is also noted on the form that at the end of March £15,000 will be due from debtors, since the last month's sales on credit will not yet have been collected.

In addition to the materials and salaries and wages, other expenses of £700 per month are due to be paid in cash. Overheads are £800 per month, of which £100 has, correctly, been deducted because it represents a depreciation charge.

Depreciation you should eliminate from costs because it is simply an accounting entry. From a cash point of view, you can ignore it; depreciation is not a cash flow. The flow occurred in the past, when the asset was purchased.

Average costs. An average figure may be accurate for the year as a whole but it could be highly misleading in any particular month. Normally, you should not use averages but for small amounts an average may do. In the example, other expenses are not a major item: £2,100 over the three months. In comparison, materials will cost more, £25,000, and salaries and wages, £17,520. However, you should always be cautious in planning cash. There could be circumstances when £2,100 could be the straw which breaks the camel's back.

Table 2.4

Cash budget

XYZ PLC   Prepared by: D. Garbutt
                               Date: 30th December 1982
Budget for period: January to March 1983
Budget basis: Monthly

Items	January £	February £	March £
Section 1			
Cash float at start of month	1,000	960	4,920
Section 2 Receipts			
Cash sales	5,000	5,000	5,000
From debtors (accounts receivable)	10,000	12,000	8,000
Total cash available	16,000	17,960	17,920
Section 3 Payments			
Salaries and wages	5,840	5,840	5,840
To suppliers of materials	8,500	6,500	10,000
Other cash expenstes	700	700	700
Total cash needs	15,040	13,040	16,540
Section 4			
Cash float at end of month	960	4,920	1,380

Receipts and payments cash budget

Having collected the data, you can prepare the cash budget shown in Table 2.4. Again, the cash budget is a form which will be retained for future use. It should state the date of preparation and the name of the person preparing it. In the first column you should list the items, using the same sections as the data sheet. Then, set up a further series of columns one for each period to be budgeted for. In Table 2.4 there is a column for each of the months from January to March.

Now compile the budget for each month from the data sheet. The January budget is shown in Table 2.5.

Table 2.5

XYZ PLC   January budget

	£
Opening float	1,000
Add receipts: cash sales	5,000
from debtors	10,000
Total cash available	£16,000
Deduct payments: salaries and wages	5,840
to suppliers	8,500
other expenses	700
Total cash needs	£15,040
Closing float	£ 960

The cash at the start of January is £1,000. To this you add the receipts from cash sales, £5,000 and from debtors (December sales) £10,000. You total these to show that, during January, £16,000 cash will be available.

Section 3 lists the payments, for salaries and wages, £5,840 per month, for materials, £8,500 in January, and £700 for other expenses. As you see £15,040 will be needed in cash in January. For the final calculation, deduct payments from the total cash available. In the example the cash float is £960 at the end of January. You will see that the cash float has gone down slightly from £1,000 to £960, but that is not a disastrous decline. On the other hand, considering that the firm has had £16,000 in cash through its hands, a float of about £1,000 is not generous. It does not leave much margin for error. Well, February will be better. The budget is shown in Table 2.6.

February starts with a float of £960, to which you add £5,000 from cash sales and £12,000 from debtors to give a total cash available of £17,960. You then deduct the payments of £13,040 (which are low because the cost of materials in February is low) and you are left with a float at the end of £4,920. This represents a big turn-around, as it is more than five times the amount of cash you started the month with.

Now, for March – the budget is shown in Table 2.7. March starts with a healthy float of £4,920, to which you add receipts from sales and debtors of £13,00, to give total cash available of £17,920. This is almost

Table 2.6
XYZ PLC February budget

	£
Opening float	960
Add receipts: cash sales	5,000
from debtors	12,000
Total cash available	£17,960
Deduct payments: salaries and wages	5,840
to suppliers	6,500
other expenses	700
Total cash needs	£13,040
Closing float	£ 4,920

Table 2.7
XYZ PLC March budget

	£
Opening float	4,920
Add receipts: cash sales	5,000
from debtors	8,000
Total cash available	£17,920
Deduct payments: salaries and wages	5,840
to suppliers	10,000
other expenses	700
Total cash needs	£16,540
Closing float	£ 1,380

the same as the previous month's £17,960. From the available cash, you deduct payments of £16,540, and the closing float of cash will be £1,380 at the end. This is another big turn-around, but it is in the wrong direction – down! The reason is obvious: receipts from debtors were low in March because sales in February were low, whilst payments for materials were high because March sales were high.

Looking at the data sheet, you might be forgiven for thinking that it shows a nice, stable business, doing quite nicely, thank you. Looking at the cash budget, it looks more like a roller coaster!

Cash flow from operations

You can estimate the cash flow from operations from an inccme statement (or profit and loss account).

The income statement. Consider, for a moment, the income statement, how it is drawn up and what the figures in it mean. The income statement for XYZ PLC for the period January to March 1983 is shown in Table 2.8.

Table 2.8

XYZ PLC   Income statement for period
1 January – 31 March 1983

	£	£
Sales: January	17,000	
February	13,000	
March	20,000	50,000
Less cost of goods sold		25,000
Gross profit		25,000
Expenses		
Salaries and wages	17,520	
Other expenses	2,400	
(including depreciation £300)		19,920
Net profit		5,080

Gross profit

The first part of the income statement is used to calculate the gross profit. This is the difference between the sales for the period and the relevant cost of sales. The sales for each month are the cash sales plus the sales on credit, whether paid for or not. The income statement is based on the assumption that, eventually, all the sales will be paid for by customers. The cost of sales is, similarly, the cost of the stock disposed of in the sales to customers. Again, whether the stock has been paid for or not is irrelevant for this purpose. Thus:

$$\text{Sales} - \text{cost of goods sold} = \text{gross profit}$$

for XYZ PLC

$$£50,000 - £25,000 = £25,000$$

Gross profit is a useful indicator of whether selling prices have been set at the right level. Most businesses have a clear idea of the gross profit, or margin, which they need to operate on to cover their expenses and make a reasonable net profit.

Net Profit

The net profit is gross profit minus the expenses for the period.

Again, whether the expenses have actually been paid in cash is not relevant. Any expense which was incurred in earning the revenue of the period will be 'matched' against that revenue. You have already seen that depreciation is a cost which arises from the use of assets. It will be one of the expenses in the income statement. Others will be salaries, wages, insurance, rates and so on. Thus:

$$\text{Gross profit} - \text{expenses} = \text{net profit}$$

for XYZ PLC

$$£25{,}000 - £19{,}920 = £5{,}080$$

The cost of salaries and wages is £5,840 per month, i.e. £5,840 × 3 = £17,520 for the three months. The other expenses are £800 per month, i.e. £800 × 3 = £2,400 for the three months. Notice that the other expenses include depreciation of fixed assets of £100 per month, i.e. £100 × 3 = £300 for the three months. Since the expenses for the three months total £19,920, the net profit is £5,080.

The net income, or net profit, of a business shows how much the owners' interest in the business has increased in a period. If there is a loss, this shows the amount by which the owners' interest has declined. From a management point of view, if prices are right, gross profit will be good. If expenses are under control, a satisfactory net profit will result.

The profitability of a business can be looked at in terms of the margin on sales:

$$\frac{\text{Net profit}}{\text{Sales}} = \text{margin on sales}$$

For XYZ PLC

$$\frac{£\ 5{,}080}{£50{,}000} = 10.16\%$$

This is not the whole story of profitability; for that we would have to look at how the profit compared to the capital employed in the business in earning the profit, and that is outside the scope of this book. However, profit is *not* a cash figure and even if profits are satisfactory, there is still a quite separate problem of budgeting for and controlling cash flows. You must plan for both a satisfactory profit and a satisfactory cash position.

You can forecast the cash generated from your business operations by adjusting each item in the income statement. For this, use a form with four columns, as shown in Table 2.9.

In the first column, list each item in the same order as it appears in the income statement, starting with sales revenue. In the second column, enter the amount as shown in the income statement.

Your next step is to enter in column 3 the adjustments which you know need to be made to change the income statement figure to a cash figure.

Table 2.9

XYZ PLC Cash flow from operations

Period: 1 January to 31 March 1986 Prepared by:
 Date:

Item	Income statement amount £	Adjustments	Cash flow £
Sales	50,000	−15,000 not received from March +10,000 received from December −5,000	45,000
Cost of goods sold	25,000		(25,000)
Gross profit	25,000		
Salaries and wages	17,520	No adjustment	(17,520)
Other expenses	2,400	−£300 depreciation	(2,100)
	19,920		
Net profit	5,080	Net cash flow from operations	380
		Add cash float at start	1,000
		Cash float at end	1,380

32

Preparing a cash budget   33

You must reduce sales by any credit sales which will remain uncollected at the end of the period. Equally, you must increase sales by the amount of any uncollected sales (debtors) at the beginning of the period. In the example £15,000 for March sales will not have been collected by the end of that month. On the other hand, £10,000 will be collected in January from December sales. As a result, the cash generated by sales is £45,000.

Now enter in column 4 the results of your adjustments. In the example, sales in the income statement were £50,000 but you have deducted £15,000 and added £10,000. The net result is the cash flow from collections (of debtors) £45,000.

Now, continue down through each item of revenue and expense in the income statement, making a note of each adjustment required and entering the cash figure in the final column.

In the example, you enter £25,000 cost of goods sold as the income statement amount and since you have no information to the contrary, you make no adjustment and the cash outflow in column 4 is £25,000.

Similarly, no adjustment to salaries and wages is made in Table 2.9 but other expenses are reduced by £300 because they include £300 of 'non-cash debits' for depreciation.

When you have entered the adjusted figures for each item in column 4 you can find the resulting figure and that will be your net cash flow from operations for the period. In the example it is £380.

As a final step, you can add the cash float at the start and you will then have the cash float at the end of the period. In the example, you see that this is, again, £1,380.

Sources and uses of funds statements

A statement of sources and uses of funds is included with most company annual reports. Unfortunately, there is no standard form of presentation. The statement can be related to working capital or cash but statements can usually be converted to the cash form. Table 2.10 shows the GEC statement for the year ended 31st March 1983. The statement shows that GEC generated £846.9 million from operations and a further £212.3 million from other sources such as the sale of assets, the sale of investments, increases in trade creditors and payments on account on uncompleted contracts. The company paid £208.2 million for new fixed assets, £213.7 million for taxes and an increase in debtors and inventories took up £177.1 million. Reducing loan capital, repaying capital and loans to associated companies accounted for another £107.6 million, so that a total of £780.6 million was put to these uses. You can see that, large as these payments were, the cash held by the company in various forms increased by £278.6 million in the year.

Reference to the GEC balance sheet shows that investments and cash rose from £1074.8 in 1982 to £1349.8 in 1983, an increase of £275 million. This is £3.6 million less than the £278.6 million in the statement of sources and uses of funds! Large as that amount of money may seem

Table 2.10

The General Electricity Company
Statement of sources and application of funds for year ended
31 March 1983

		£ million
Profit on ordinary activities before taxation		670.4
Adjustments not involving the movement of funds		
Depreciation	139.9	
Exchange valuation adjustments	40.2	
Increase in provisions	13.4	
Undistributed profit of associated companies and changes in minority interests	17.0Dr.	
		176.5
Funds generated from operations		846.9
Funds from other sources		
Sales of fixed assets	27.0	
Sales less purchases of fixed asset investments	7.4	
Increase in trade and other creditors	73.0	
Increase in payments on account of contracts	104.9	
		212.3
		1,059.2
Application		
Purchase of fixed assets	208.2	
Reduction in loan capital	23.3	
Taxes paid in the year	213.7	
Dividends paid in the year	74.0	
Capital repayment	82.2	
Increase in loans to associated companies	2.1	
Increase in debtors	133.8	
Increase in inventory	43.3	
		780.6
Increase in bank deposits, short-term investments and net balances with bankers		278.6

to be, £3.6 million is less than 1½ per cent of £275 million and is probably due to the complications of GEC's organisational structure. For planning purposes, it is not important. A sources and uses of funds statement which reconciles opening and closing cash for XYZ PLC is shown in Table 2.11. As it is only a simple example, the figures *do* agree with XYZ's balance sheet and income statement.

The key features of this method are, first, that you add back the non-

Table 2.11

XYZ PLC Sources and uses of funds for period
1 January to 31 March 1983

	£		£
Cash float at start			1,000
Add cash flow from operations:			
Net profit	5,080		
Plus depreciation	300		
Funds from operations		5,380	
Add non-operational sources of cash:		Nil	5,380
Total funds available			6,380
Deduct non-operational uses of cash:			
Debtors at start 10,000			
Debtors at end 15,000			
Increase of debtors			5,000
Cash float at end of period			1,380

cash expenses in the income statement to the net profit to give a figure: funds from operations:

$$\text{Net profit} + \text{non-cash debits} = \text{funds from operations}$$
$$(\text{e.g. depreciation})$$

For XYZ PLC:

$$£5,080 + £300 = £5,380$$

You will notice that this is *not* the same as net cash flow from operations. If there are other sources of cash these are listed. Examples could be the sale of assets, the proceeds of a loan, or capital stock issues. Both figures are then added to the opening cash to give the total funds available:

$$\text{Cash float at start} + \text{Funds from operations} + \text{Funds from other sources} = \text{Total funds available}$$

For XYZ PLC:

$$£1,000 + £5,380 + 0 = £6,380$$

The adjustment for the credit given on sales (or, if applicable, taken on materials and other expenses) is made in terms of the change in the related asset. Thus, the adjustment to the sales figure is accomplished by calculating the increase (or decrease) in debtors, and this is shown as a source or use of funds. In the case of XYZ PLC, debtors increased by £5,000. This is a use of funds. Other uses of funds might be the purchase of fixed assets, the repayment of loans, or an increase in inventories (stocks). Thus:

Total funds available − uses of funds = cash float at end of period

For XYZ PLC:

£6,380 − £5,000 = £1,380

This presentation shows the total funds available and how these have been used. In the example, £6,380 was available to XYZ PLC in the period and they chose to allow the amount owing from debtors to rise by £5,000. You may argue that this was not so much due to conscious choice as to the fact that March sales rose to £15,000 but it is clear that the rise is due to the policy of allowing debtors one month's credit. The statement of sources and uses of funds brings out the policies of the firm on how it uses cash and where it gets cash from.

As an example of how this form of analysis may be applied in practice, take British Caledonian Airways in June 1984. The latest accounts of B. Cal. to October 1983 showed that the airline had cash of £69 million but of that, £67 million was held overseas and subject to exchange controls. Sir Adam Thomson, the chairman, however, assured Kenneth Fleet that by June 1984, only £7.5 million of that £67 million was still unpatriated to the UK.

B. Cal. then had capital commitments of £217 million for the purchase of Airbus aircraft, and Fleet asked Sir Adam how the company could hope to finance these purchases, especially as B. Cal. had a debt equity ratio of 2.9:1. Sir Adam answered that the debt equity ratio was within the limits set by the banks. Two of the aircraft were already delivered and one more would be received in 1985. The first of the remaining seven would be due for delivery in Spring 1988. B. Cal. would arrange finance for each aircraft when the delivery dates were fixed and no problems were anticipated with the major lenders. If B. Cal. acquired some British Airways routes, they would then hope to reduce their debt equity ratio, even though they expected to need additional assets costing £250 million. Sir Adam was confident B. Cal. would pay a dividend to shareholders in 1984 and also make an allocation to the staff profit sharing scheme.

What emerges from this conversation is the clear and heavy dependence of B. Cal. on borrowed money. Much of this came from the banks but a major lender and shareholder was investors in industry.

3
Trade credit

Trade credit is an important influence on working capital. This kind of credit arises from the separation in time between the delivery of goods or the performance of services and the payment for them.

Trade credit is not usually subject to a formal contract, but it is an important influence on business financing. We have already seen in Table 1.1 that the aggregated balance sheets of a group of large UK companies in 1982 had 21 per cent of total assets in debtors and prepayments. Creditors and accruals accounted for 24 per cent of the funds provided.

These proportions seem to be typical for large firms. A report from ICFC showed that quoted UK companies had 24 per cent of their assets in debtors in 1977 and nearly 26 per cent of their funds were provided by creditors. Small firms were even more strongly influenced by trade credit, with 32 per cent of their total funds in trade debtors and 29 per cent of the total provided by trade creditors.

From the figures it is clear that trade credit, the terms under which you trade as a buyer and as a seller, will have a decisive influence on your cash forecasting and planning.

Trade credit and selling

Essentially, as a seller, you give trade credit to attract and keep customers. Trade credit is a marketing device. As a seller you are willing to wait for cash from sales if this means you get a sale which might otherwise be lost. As a buyer you will prefer a supplier, other things being equal, who gives you time to pay because this is as good as a discount.

Your cash planning should start with a careful analysis of receipts from sales. Receipts may be immediate, from cash sales, or delayed, from debtors. In both cases the net price paid is what is relevant for cash budgeting purposes. This is not always easy to establish.

Net trade price (trade discounts)

The prices of products are usually set according to the volume of business. For instance, a builders' merchant may quote for painted chipboard as shown in Table 3.1.

Table 3.1

Bloggs Builders' Merchants

	Net price	Trade discount on retail
	£	
Retail	5.00 per m^2	—
Trade less than 30m^2	4.40 per m^2	12%
Up to 99m^2	3.60 per m^2	28%
Over 100m^2	2.50 per m^2	50%

The goods are invoiced to trade customers at retail prices less trade discount or the net price may be used. If Pinkham Construction buys 80m^2 of chipboard, the invoice will be as in Table 3.2.

Table 3.2

Bloggs Builders' Merchants

	£
80m^2 at £5/m^2	400
less trade discount 28%	112
Net trade	288

Both the buyer and the seller should use the net price of £288 for cash budgeting. For the seller, the best way to forecast is to prepare a breakdown of sales at each price level. For example, if Bloggs Builders' Merchants expect to sell 8,760 sheets of chipboard, the breakdown would be as in Table 3.3.

Table 3.3

Bloggs Builders' Merchants – budgeted sales of painted chipboard, January

	Sheets no.	Price	Sales value
		£	£
Retail	600	5.00	3,000
Under 30m^2	1,000	4.40	4,400
Under 99m^2	2,000	3.60	7.200
100m^2 and above	6,160	2.50	15,400
	9,760		£30,000

The trouble with this method is that it can mean a lot of work!

Average selling price

A reasonably accurate result can be obtained by using an average selling price. If Bloggs used an average price of £3, then the calculation would still be quite accurate:

$$\text{Quantity} \times \text{average price} = \text{sales value}$$

For Bloggs Merchants in January:

$$9,760 \times £3 = £28,280$$

Weighted average price

A better average price can be worked out by taking the percentage to be sold at each price and adding the resultants. This is called a weighted average price because it does reflect the volume at each price. In our example, the calculations would be as in Table 3.4.

Table 3.4

Bloggs Builders' Merchants

Price	×	Proportion	=	Weighted average price
£				
5.00		.06		.3
4.40		.10		.44
3.60		.21		.76
2.50		.63		1.58
		1.00		3.08

This gives:

9,760 × £3.08 = £30,060

which is much closer to the £30,000 produced from the detailed breakdown. You can use an average or weighted average price if sales at each price are reasonably constant. You should then recalculate it from time to time, as a check.

Annual/volume discounts

A more difficult problem arises when customers are offered a volume discount, determined annually. For most of the period, goods or services are supplied at an agreed price and then the annual volume discount is allowed on the final payment or refunded by the seller to the buyer. The rule here is that you should budget for receipts and payments as they actually occur.

If you supply heating oil at 50p per litre you will budget to receive £5,000 from a customer who takes 10,000 litres. At the end of the year, if the customer is entitled to a quantity discount of £600, that would be deducted from any amount then due.

If receipts are seasonal, as in the case of heating oil, and if the volume discount falls due in a month of low demand, then you might even have to make a cash refund. This would be shown as a payment. The cash budget should be based on realistic forecasts of the discounts for which each customer is likely to qualify.

Cash discounts and terms of trade

The terms of trade are the agreed financial conditions under which sales and purchases are made. In the financial sense, the terms of trade are the understanding between buyer and seller on the price payable and the time when goods or services are to be paid for. The terms may also provide for the allowance of a cash discount if payment is made within a stipulated time limit. The cash discount is an additional allowance off the amount payable for prompt settlement.

As well as appearing in any formal contract of sales, the terms of trade are usually stated on the invoice for the goods or services, for example, as in Table 3.5.

This shows that the net amount on the invoice £700 is expected to be paid within 30 days but if paid in 10 days, a 2 per cent discount will be allowed. If the buyer pays on or before 25th January, he can send a cheque for £686.

Notice that the customer who does not take advantage of the cash discount is expected to pay within a further 20 days, i.e. 30 days from the invoice date. The seller is paying £14 for the privilege of having the use of £686 for 20 days.

Table 3.5

Cash and Curry

	Invoice	Date 15.1.1985
Terms	30 days net/10 days 2%	

To
Customer A. Adamson
43, Eden Road,
Evesham

		£
	To goods at retail	875.00
	less 20% trade discount	175.00
	Net	£700.00

Is it worthwhile? You can answer that question by working out the discount as an annual rate of interest:

$$\frac{\text{Amount of discount}}{\text{Net amount received from customers}} \times \frac{\text{no. of days in year}}{\text{no. of days credit saved}} = \text{annual cost of discount offered}$$

You can reckon on 360 days to the year.

For Cash and Curry this is:

$$\frac{£14}{£686} \times \frac{360}{20} = 38\%$$

This is a high rate of interest.

Cash discount should not be offered if the capital can be obtained more cheaply elsewhere.

Of course, the big variable here is the number of days which may be saved by offering cash discount. Customers are unlikely to wait until the very last moment if they hope to claim cash discount so, on average, the seller may guess that customers claiming cash discount will actually pay in five days.

Also, it is unlikely that customers not claiming cash discount will all pay on the dot at the end of 30 days: the average might be nearer 40 days. In this case, the number of days credit saved by Cash and Curry would be 35, not 20.

The cost of the cash discount will fall for Cash and Curry:

$$\frac{£14}{£686} \times \frac{360}{35} = 21\%$$

The cost of getting the capital back early is lower. At a rate of interest of 21 per cent, the cash discount might well be worthwhile to the seller.

Another benefit of cash discount could be that the risk of bad debts is eliminated.

Trade terms offered and taken

You must distinguish between the terms of trade offered and the terms actually taken. It is the actual terms which customers take which are relevant to cash budgeting.

Deciding to offer credit terms is a managerial decision. Large firms employ credit managers who play a big part in fixing terms of trade and in monitoring them to see that the actual terms conform to planned expectations, or are more favourable. However, some divergence is almost always found.

Percentage debtors to sales

There are a number of ways in which actual trade credit taken can be assessed. One way is to examine the amount of the debtors in relation to the sales on credit, i.e.

$$\frac{\text{Debtors}}{\text{Sales on credit}} \times 100 = \text{percentage debtors to sales}$$

Thus, if Crypto Ltd achieved £3,000,000 sales and at the end of the year had debtors outstanding of £250,000, their percentage debtors to sales would be:

$$\frac{£\ 300,000}{£3,000,000} \times 100 = 10\%$$

Collection period

By itself, the percentage is not very informative, but you can look at it in terms of the year: 10 per cent of the year is:

$$360 \text{ days} \times \frac{10}{100} = 36 \text{ days collection period}$$

So, if Crypto Ltd has terms of trade *30 days* net, the actual collection period is six days longer, on average.

This figure shows that the debtors take 36 days before they pay. The actual collection period is better for forecasting receipts from sales than working on the terms offered. In practice, it is rare for the rate of collection to be the same as the credit allowed. If no reliable data on debtors and sales are available (for instance, if one is looking at a new business), it is safer to assume that the actual rate of collection will be slower than the rate allowed for. So, if customers are allowed 30 days' credit, the cash forecast may well be based on the conservative assumption that cash will, on average, be received after, say, 45 days. Of course, every effort will be made to collect in 30 days and that is what is expected of the customers, but the keynote of cash forecasting is realism!

Ageing schedule

Another way of looking at the status of debtors and the likelihood of receiving payment from them is the ageing schedule. In this method, each amount outstanding is listed, by customer and by age in terms of how many days it has been outstanding. For cash forecasting purposes, only the total figures are required and they are then expressed in percentages. The debtors of Crypto Ltd might yield the summary in Table 3.6.

Table 3.6

Crypto Ltd debtors ageing schedule

Age of debt in days	Amount £	Percentage
0 – 20 days	120,000	40
21 – 30 days	90,000	30
31 – 45 days	30,000	10
46 – 60 days	30,000	10
Over 60 days	30,000	10
	£300,000	100

This shows that the position of Crypto Ltd on collection is not as sastisfactory as might have been thought. When we looked at the average days collection period, it was 36, which was not very much longer than the stated payment within 30 days. But the average conceals the fact that 40 per cent of the debtors are paying within 20 days and another 30 per cent are paying in more than 30 days. Of these, 10 per cent have been outstanding for more than 60 days – always a bad sign.

The main purpose of the ageing schedule is to guide the credit manager on where to press for payment. You will obviously exercise the greatest pressure for payment of the oldest debts, and you will look at the ageing schedule in minute detail.

For cash planning, that is not necessary. Only the total summary figures are needed. They can be very useful. To illustrate, let us assume that Crypto Ltd expect to sell £200,000 of goods in January, £180,000 in February and £220,000 in March. If you prepared a cash budget on the basis of the offered credit terms, the expected receipts from debtors will be:

January	February	March	Total
£	£	£	£
300,000	200,000	180,000	680,000

The debtors at the end of March will be the amount owing from March sales, £220,000.

Now, this budget could be highly misleading, as can be seen if you use the actual age schedule and assume that it will be typical of the following months, too. The cash budget now shows a very different picture (Table 3.7). According to this cash budget, a total of £606,000 will be received over the three months, not £680,000, as calculated in the earlier budget. That is £74,000 less!

Table 3.7

Cash budget

	January £	February £	March £	Total £
Cash receipts from debtors:				
70% in 30 days	210,000	140,000	126,000	
20% in 60 days		60,000	40,000	
10% in 90 days			30,000	
Receipts from debtors	210,000	200,000	196,000	606,000

Of course, the corresponding figure for debtors at the end of March is higher at £294,000. This is a very different picture from our first cash budget, based on the assumption that the stated terms of trade would actually apply! Again, the message is clear – be realistic in your cash forecasting.

Bad debts

The preparation of an ageing schedule of debtors draws attention to the fact that some debts may be outstanding for an excessively long period. We have already suggested that you will direct your efforts as credit manager towards collecting such debts. From a cash planning point of view, it raises the question whether, to be realistic, we can rely on actually collecting cash once a debt has gone beyond a certain time limit.

No general rules can be laid down because debt collection involves many individual factors. In certain types of business where you are dealing with a large number of small customers, it is an unfortunate fact of life that it is safer to plan on the basis of a certain proportion of debtors turning bad.

Take an example. Suppose Perkins Peat PLC sells peat packs for £1.00

each and that sales for the six months September 1985 to March 1986 are expected to be 10,000 peat packs per month. All sales are on credit terms net in 30 days with 2 per cent cash discount for settlement in 10 days. From past experience, as managing director you expect the pattern of credit and cash discount taken to be as in Table 3.8.

Table 3.8

Perkins Peat PLC

Settled within 10 days	10%
Settled within 11 – 30 days	50%
Settled within 31 – 60 days	30%
Settled within 61 – 90 days	8%
Bad debts	2%

On this basis, your collections for each month will be as in Table 3.9.

Table 3.9

Perkins Peat PLC

			£
Month 1	Cash discounted collections	(10% – 2%)	800
Month 1	Settled within 11 – 30 days	50%	5,000
Month 2	Settled within 31 – 60 days	30%	3,000
Month 3	Settled within 61 – 90 days	8%	800
	Total monthly cash receipts		£9,600

The receipts are reduced by £200 cash discounts conceded in the first month and by another £200 in the third month because of bad debts. Looking at the receipts from the September sales, within the cash budget, these will appear as in Table 3.10.

Table 3.10

Perkins Peat PLC

	September £	October £	November £	December £
September sales	800	5,000	3,000	800

Types of market

In practice, many businesses sell into more than one market. The terms of trade and the credit may differ between these markets. So, too, may the prices charged for goods and services.

We have already looked at an example of such a firm, Bloggs Builders' Merchants, when we looked at trade discounts and the calculation of net prices.

Suppose Bloggs Builders' Merchants find that customers for painted chipboard pay on the terms shown in Table 3.11.

Table 3.11

Bloggs Builders' Merchants – terms of trade

Retail	Cash terms
Building trade	During 3rd month after sale
Local authority	During 2nd month after sale
DIY Ltd	Cash terms, 5% discount

The differences in these terms make it necessary to deal with each type of market separately in budgeting for the cash receipts.

For forecasting Bloggs should prepare a predicted breakdown of sales by market, on the lines shown in Table 3.12.

Table 3.12

Bloggs Builders' Merchants – sales market proportions and volume

	% of sales	Volume £
Retail trade	10	3,000
Building trade	40	12,000
Local authority	30	9,000
DIY Ltd	20	6,000
		£30,000

From these two pieces of data you can prepare a reasonable budget for the cash. Bloggs may expect to receive cash from the £30,000 January sales as shown in Table 3.13.

The receipts from DIY Ltd are reduced by the cash discount. What is interesting about the pattern is the complete gap in cash receipts in February and the fact that Bloggs will have to wait until April for 40 per cent of the money from January sales. Since Bloggs are paying expenses in the meantime, the firm may have to find additional working capital.

Table 3.13

Bloggs Builders' Merchants

	January £	February £	March £	April £
Cash from January sales:				
Retail	3,000			
DIY Ltd	5,700			
Local authority			9,000	
Building trade				12,000
	8,700	–	9,000	12,000

Payments to creditors

Payments to creditors in respect of purchases are the other side of the coin to the collection of receipts from debtors, but life often appears different from the other side of the track.

Net trade terms

The first point to be made is that the cost of goods sold will be based on the net prices actually paid for supplies. This may differ between different firms. For instance, early in 1984, the big bakers were selling bread to small shops at 50p less a 30 per cent trade discount, i.e. net 35p.

The price to large chains was 50p less 44 per cent trade discount, i.e. net 28p. Since retail prices are not fixed, the chains may then be able to sell the loaf for 33p!

Each buyer will have very different trading results. If a small retailer sells 100 loaves per day, his gross profit would be £15 per day (100 @ 15p) and a supermarket, selling 1,000 per day, would make a gross profit of £50 (1,000 @ 5p).

The two customers could also have very different cash budgets, if the small shop pays weekly and the chain monthly. Assuming a six-day week, the two cash budgets would show receipts and payments for the four weeks of February 1985 as in Tables 3.14 and 3.15.

These budgets show the large amounts of cash which are available to the supermarket because it is able to postpone payments for its supplies until the end of the month.

Cash discounts

If cash discounts are available on purchased supplies, the decision on whether to take advantage of them will depend on the value of the

Table 3.14
Cash budget – small retailer, February 1985

	Week 1 £	Week 2 £	Week 3 £	Week 4 £
Cash float at start of month	0	90	180	270
Cash sales	300	300	300	300
Total cash available	300	390	480	570
Payments to supplier	210	210	210	210
Cash float at end of month	90	180	270	360

Table 3.15
Cash budget – supermarket, February 1985

	Week 1 £	Week 2 £	Week 3 £	Week 4 £
Cash float at start of month	0	1,980	3,960	5,940
Cash sales	1,980	1,980	1,980	1,980
Total cash available	1,980	3,960	5,940	7,920
Payments to supplier	0	0	0	6,720
Cash float at end of month	1,980	3,960	5,940	1,200

discount compared to the alternative cost or value of the capital involved. The value of the discount is:

$$\frac{\text{Cash discount}}{\text{Net amount payable}} \times \frac{\text{no. of days in year}}{\text{no. of days credit lost}} = \text{annual value of discount taken}$$

This is the same calculation, essentially, as was made by the seller in calculating the cost of the discount but the viewpoint is different. In this case, as a buyer you pay the discounted amount, in order to avoid paying the full amount under normal terms. If you refer to the example used earlier, where a 2 per cent discount was offered for payment in ten days, against payment after 30 days, on a payment of £700, the buyer would obtain £14 discount. In other words, you pay £686 on which you receive £14 for 20 days. The return is:

Trade credit

$$\frac{£\ 14}{£686} \times \frac{360}{20} = 37\%$$

Even in days of high interest rates, that is a good rate of return. On the other hand, the number of days saved is crucial to the calculation. If the seller is rather lax in control of credit, the buyer might be able to delay payment until the end of the second month. In this case, if you pay in 10 days you lose 50 days during which the capital sum could be used, and the rate of interest falls to:

$$\frac{£\ 14}{£686} \times \frac{360}{50} = 15\%$$

At the time of writing, it would be a cheaper source of finance than the bank. If you can use the money profitably, and make more than 15 per cent, you should pay at the end of the second month and lose the cash discount. If you intend to claim cash discount, then reduce the budgeted cash payments for the period in which the payments are actually made. Again, all suppliers may not offer cash discount and the rates may differ between them. Base your forecast on what you expect the actual situation to be, realistically.

Cost of purchases

The basic cost of purchases is the net trade price after deducting trade and quantity discounts but goods are sold in their existing location, so that the costs of freight, insurance, etc. fall on the buyer, unless some other agreement is made. You must include all these other payments associated with purchases in your cash budget.

Creditors' ageing schedule

You should prepare a schedule of creditors showing the time period for which they have been accrued on the same lines as the debtors' ageing schedule. Then, you can schedule payments in order of priority. If this is not done, you will find you are making payments to those suppliers who press hardest. That is wrong. You should plan your payments to your own advantage.

Value added tax, customs duties, etc.

You are liable to pay value added tax on purchases to your supplier, and you charge your customer VAT on sales, thus collecting cash on behalf of the government. This cash must be paid quarterly, but VAT paid on suppliers may be offset against VAT collected on sales. The subject of VAT is exceedingly complex and we do not propose to enter into it here, except to note that payments of VAT to suppliers will be included in cash

Table 3.16

Bloggs Builders' Merchants – data sheet for cash budget

No. 104
Prepared by: J. Entignap
Date: 27th December 1985

Budget period: January to March 1986
Budget basis: Monthly items

		Amount	Timing	Conditions and flexibility
Section 1	Opening float	£		
	Cash in hand	1,600		
	Bank	3,000		
Section 2	Receipts	Quantity m^2		
Sales	January	10,000	30,000	Average price
	February	12,000	36,000	£3 per m^2
	March	11,000	33,000	(Note 1)

Markets	Retail 10%		Cash terms
	Building trade 40%		During 3rd month after sale
	Local authority 30%		During 2nd month after sale
	DIY Ltd 20% (Note 2)		Cash – 5% discount
Debtors at start			
	Building trade	£24,000	
	Local authority (Note 3)	9,000	
Section 3	Payments		
	Cost of board (Note 4)	£1.50 per m²	2% cash discount taken
	Salaries, wages and expenses	per month	Cash

payments and VAT on sales will show as receipts. The payments of VAT to the government will also appear as payments.

Customs duties are payable on some imports and excise duties may be payable on some products. If you pay these taxes, they must be included in payments when the cash is actually paid out.

From time to time, there may also be rebate schemes on various products. If the amounts are significant, you must include them in the cash receipts as and when they are expected. Chapter 13 of this book deals with the effects of tax on cash.

An example of cash budgeting

To summarise this chapter, let us look at an example, the cash budget of Bloggs Builders' Merchants for the three months January–March 1985. You have already looked at some of the relevant information, but the complete data are shown in Table 3.16, in the form of a data sheet. Since some of the calculations are a bit complicated, the preparer, John Entignap, did his workings on another sheet, Table 3.17. On this sheet, he sorted out the data so that the cash budget, shown in Table 3.18, was easier to prepare.

The data sheet (Table 3.16)

Notice that in section 2, receipts, John worked on the quantity of sales expected in each month, at the average price. The notes refer to the calculation on his working paper.

The working paper (Table 3.17)

Note 1. Here, John worked out a new average price of £3 per m^2 on the expectation that the price of deliveries over $99m^2$ would be reduced to £2.40 per m^2.

Note 2. Here, John worked out the value of sales in each month at the expected average price and then broke it down between the markets. Against each market, he put in a note 'when?' to indicate when the sales revenues would be collectible. Sales to both retail and DIY Ltd are collectible in January–March, but building trade sales will be collected in March–May and local authority sales in February–April. This reminds John when to 'plug in' the receipts in the cash budget, but also comes in useful in calculating debtors. In a further calculation, he calculated the effect of the 5 per cent discount on receipts from DIY Ltd.

Note 3. The debtors at the end have been calculated because the information may be needed for the next cash budget, April to June, unless actual figures are then available. By working from Note 2, it is

Table 3.17

Bloggs Builders' Merchants – working paper

Date sheet no. 104   Prepared by: J. Entignap
                     Date: 23rd December 1985

Calculations

Note 1 Average price

	Quantity	%	Price, £		
Retail	600	.06	5.00	=	.3
Under 30m^2	1,000	.1	4.40	=	.44
Under 99m^2	2,000	.2	3.60	=	.72
Over 99m^2	6,400	.64	2.40	=	1.54
	10,000				3.0

Note price reduction on larger quantities (was £2.50 per m^2)

Note 2 Sales to markets

	January	February	March	When?
	£	£	£	
Total	30,000	36,000	33,000	
Breakdown				
10% Retail	3,000	3,600	3,300	January – March
40% Building trade	12,000	14,400	13,200	March – May
30% Local authority	9,000	10,800	9,900	February – April
20% DIY Ltd	6,000	7,200	6,600	January – March
DIY Ltd	6,000	7,200	6,600	
	– 300	– 360	– 330	Take 5% discount
	5,700	6,840	6,270	

Note 3 Debtors at end

	April	May	Total
	£	£	£
Retail – none			
DIY Ltd – none			
Building trade	14,400	13,200	
Local authority	9,900		
Total £37,500	24,300	13,200	37,500

Note 4

	January	February	March
	£	£	£
Net cost of board			
Quantity	10,000	12,000	11,000
x £1.50m^2	£15,000	£18,000	£16,500
Less 2% cash discount	300	360	330
Net payment	£14,700	£17,640	£16,170

Note 5 Receipts from customers

	January	February	March	
	£	£	£	
Opening debtors				
Building trade	12,000	12,000	–	Represents 2 months' receivable
Local authority	9,000	–	–	One month's sales
Sales				
Retail	3,000	3,600	3,300	
DIY Ltd	5,700	6,840	6,270	
Local authority	–	9,000	10,800	
Building trade	–	–	12,000	
Total	29,700	31,440	32,370	

easy enough to calculate the amounts receivable in April and May and, thereby, the total.

Note 4. John calculated the cost of the quantities sold at £1.50 per m^2 and, then, the 2 per cent discount which he deducted to get the net amount payable each month.

Note 5. Having prepared the data sheet, and commencing to prepare the cash budget, John decided to keep the detail of the amounts to be received in his working papers, to avoid cluttering up the cash budget. Here, he calculated his receipts. Knowing that the building trade pay in the third month, he expects the £24,000 receivable will be equally split between January and February. All the amount receivable from local authority will come in January.

Table 3.18

Bloggs Builders' Merchants – cash budget

Budget period: January – March 1986 Prepared by: J. Entignap
Budget basis: Monthly   Date: 27th December 1985

	January	February	March
	£	£	£
Section 1			
Cash float at start of month	4,600	3,600	1,400
Section 2 Receipts			
From debtors (Note 5)	29,700	31,440	32,370
Total cash available	34,300	35,040	33,770
Section 3 Payments			
To board suppliers	14,700	17,640	16,170
Salaries, wages and expenses	16,000	16,000	16,000
Total cash needs	30,700	33,640	32,170
Section 4			
Cash float at end of month	3,600	1,400	1,600

The cash budget (Table 3.18)

The cash budget shows that the expected position for January to March is not very satisfactory.

First, the opening cash float will decline from £4,600 at the start of

January to £1,600 at the end of March. Second, the cash float is, in any case, rather slim in comparison to the total cash handled each month, when about £34 or £35,000 comes available. Perhaps the opening situation is all right – the closing position looks very tight.

Obviously, the basic problem is that the cash receipts are less than the cash needs in January and February, and only £200 in excess in March (Table 3.19). Thus, these figures would be the starting point of some hard thinking about how they could be improved.

Table 3.19

Bloggs Builders' Merchants – cash deficits/surplus

	January £	February £	March £
Receipts from debtors	29,700	31,440	32,370
Total cash needs	30,700	33,640	32,170
Cash deficit	1,000	2,200	–
Cash surplus	–	–	200

4

Budgeting for expenses

If the cash budget is to be accurate, it is absolutely essential that it should include all payments for expenses. We have already considered how to budget for the payments to suppliers which are a major expense in many businesses. There is a danger that other expenses may be overlooked or underestimated and that could be fatal. On the other hand, expenses often consist of many small payments and there is a danger of getting bogged down in a mass of detail. This might make you give up the whole budgeting exercise in despair, which again could be fatal! So, this chapter will try to look at expenses in sufficient detail, but not too much. We will tackle the problem in four stages:

1 *Typical expenses.* We will look at some typical expenses just to make clear what kind of items we are talking about.

2 *Drawing up a list of expenses.* We will look at some ways in which you can draw up a list of expenses for use in your cash budgeting.

3 *Estimating the amount of each expense.* There are several ways in which you can produce useful forecasts of the level of expenses.

4 *Establishing the timing of expenses.* The timing of expenses is crucial to your cash forecast. The general approach fits Section 3 of

Budgeting for expenses

the data sheet. If there are likely to be a lot of expenses, the data sheet can be divided, so that one or more separate sheets are used for expenses. A case study at the end of this chapter sums up the whole approach.

Typical expenses

The first point to be made is that different organisations often have their own pet names for expenses. In making a list use the names which are in use in your firm. Don't worry if these aren't used by anyone else. The purpose of the exercise is to produce a useful statement for your own use.

Supplies

The main expense of materials was dealt with in Chapter 3, but many parts of a business use secondary materials which can be a major item. For instance, general administration, design and the computer centre use vast quantities of various grades of paper. Roll on the paperless office! Other supplies may be microfiche, film, processing chemicals, promotional give-aways, floppy disks, printer ribbons and so on.

Freight and carriage

These expenses arise mainly from buying materials components and sub-assemblies and from delivering sales when that service is provided.

Personnel

Wages and salaries are a major expense in most businesses. The amount paid in wages and salaries in the UK for 1983 was just over £145,000 million. For the 21 million in employment, this is an average of just under £7,000 per annum. There is only one self-employed person for every eleven in employment so, again, the great majority of people who work do so as employees.

Gross pay before deduction is an expense to a business. As an employer, you may withhold part of the gross pay in the form of deductions for your employees' personal tax (PAYE), social security (national insurance), trade union dues, contributions to saving clubs and so on.

In 1983, employers were responsible for withholding nearly £21 million from employees for their national insurance contributions and nearly £34 million for income taxes. Together, these two account for 37 per cent of gross pay!

As an employer, you hold these amounts in trust and must hand them on to the agency for which you, as an employer, are collecting them. However, for cash budgeting, withholdings can be ignored unless there are significant timing differences.

What you cannot ignore are additional employee-related payments on top of the gross pay. In 1983 these accounted for over £22 million, that is just over 15 per cent of gross wages and salaries. For British employers, the cost of paying employees was therefore over £167,000 million, not the £145,000 million gross pay. Since employers also pay for schemes of medical insurance, welfare funds, superannuation and other fringe benefits such as luncheon vouchers, it can be seen that personnel expenses are easily underestimated. Make sure that all the items involved are listed.

Fuel and power

Most business activities involve costs for lighting, heating and power. These are paid for in bills for coal, gas, electricity, oil, supplies of wood, oxygen, and so on. List each form of energy used although you can often combine them into one item later.

Services

Most businesses use a number of services such as telephone, postage and cleaning. These are almost sure to appear on your list, but don't forget that there may be others such as special deliveries, information services, computer bureaux, modelling agencies, advertising agencies, office interviewing and reception services, consultancy and so on. These services may be paid for on a fee-charging basis or be provided by a section of your own firm.

Maintenance

Where the business owns assets such as land, building, plant equipment, vehicles and so on, there will be associated expenses arising from their maintenance and security. These costs may be contracted or paid as and when they arise.

Hire/lease/rent

When the business does not own assets, it may then pay rentals, lease payments, hiring fees and so on to obtain the relevant services. The rent of premises may be a major item, as may be the lease payments on equipment, or hiring charges for vehicles.

Travel

Costs involved in train, plane and other transport should be listed if not already covered, together with associated costs such as hotels and subsistence payments. The cost of company cars is often a large item which needs to be separately listed.

Security

Most businesses pay considerable sums for security in all its aspects. These may include guards for its supervision, nightwatchmen, internal and external audit, detective services, anti-bugging devices and so on.

Insurance and pension schemes

Insurance may be an aspect of security in which premiums are paid to provide compensation for losses which might arise from theft, burglary etc. Premiums may be paid to cover possible loss of profits, fires, stock losses and goods in transit such as purchases of materials and supplies.

Insurance may also be used to provide for pension schemes and for the retirement of partners.

It is possible to have several different companies providing different forms of insurance and certain types, such as export credit guarantees, are provided by the government. All should be listed.

Taxes

Major payments may arise from various forms of tax. In the case of VAT and PAYE the business is simply acting as a collector for the government. In other cases, such as local authority rates, the payments are an annual expense to the firm and treated as part of costs. Income and corporation tax may be major items and should be listed. VAT and customs duties are paid on imports and excise duties on certain products such as alcoholic drinks. They may be listed separately or included in the cost of materials and supplies. In some cases, there may be refunds and grants which may be listed under receipts. The treatment of tax in cash budgeting is dealt with fully in Chapter 13.

Licences

Certain types of business such as premises serving alcoholic beverages, or conducting gambling may require a licence, usually renewed annually.

Royalties

A rather different type of licence may be granted to allow the use of an invention; the exploitation of natural resources, such as quarries or mines; the publication of books, videos and tapes. For the business operating under this type of agreement, royalties may be a significant expense.

Advertising and selling

Most businesses selling to the public advertise in the press, on TV, on radio, through billboards and so on. Firms who sell to industry use more specialised channels to obtain the attention of industrial buyers. Considerable expenses may be involved from the production to the final appearance of the material.

Drawing up a list of expenses

Preparing your own list

One way you can start listing expenses is to identify the main functions of your business and the expenses connected with each, for example:

FUNCTIONS	DIVISIONS
Production	Mines and forests
Warehousing	Manufacture
Distribution	Administration
Marketing	Sales

Now, check through each of the relevant functions and divisions and make sure the expenses have been identified in each. For instance, looking at the functions, you would expect some expenses, such as wages and salaries, to appear in each function but others, such as travel or maintenance of plant and machinery might not.

If you approach the list from more than one angle, you often bring to light a major expense which has been forgotten.

Always take a commonsense approach based on your own understanding of the business for which you are budgeting. Ask yourself what expenses arise in each section or department. Some items appear in all departments but each has some special needs. Even at this stage, you will need a category for 'Miscellaneous' or 'Sundries'. No one expects to keep track of all the bits and pieces like ballpoint pens and paperclips, but try not to put too many items under this heading. If in doubt over an item, list it. Small items can always be eliminated or grouped together at a later stage.

Using an existing list

A great danger in drawing up a list of expenses, especially the first time, is that you miss an item of importance. A useful ploy is to obtain a list that is already in use, for instance, by the accountants or the auditors, by a trade association or by a computer bureau. There are two main forms: the income statement or the accounts code.

The income statement This is the best source because it should list expenses under a few key headings. For the small and medium-sized business, this list should give you sufficient detail for accurate cash budgeting.

The accounts code A more dangerous ploy is to approach the accountants for a list. They are likely to have what they call an accounts code, but the trouble is that it may have too much detail for ordinary managerial cash budgeting. This is the point at which many attempts to produce a cash budget fail. In fact, it is often why the accountants have not produced cash budgets in the past. Resist the suggestion that another accountant should be appointed as a cash budgets officer: it may well still not be successful! A problem in working from an accounts code is that it contains items which are not cash flows, such as depreciation, allowances for bad debts, interdepartmental transfers, provisions and reserves of various kinds. If you are not careful, you can become bogged down.

The scope for argument over whether 'head offices charges' or something similar should be included in your cash flow statement as a payment is endless. If this kind of situation arises, tactical retreat is advised. In large firms, it is often possible to get hold of a blank copy of the accounts code without any figures, simply listing the headings, which is all you want. Computer-based accounting packages will also have an accounts code as part of the software. Again, this will include a section for expenses, and you should have no difficulty in obtaining a printout of the blank code.

New businesses are likely to experience the greatest difficulty in preparing a list of expenses but even here it is possible to get advice from accountants who have clients in the same line of business or from a trade association. Some trades have 'uniform accounting' systems which incorporate a standard list of expenses. These, at least, give the main categories to work on.

As an experienced manager you should know your business well enough to be able to draw up a full list of expenses for each of its parts, but you may still find it a salutary exercise. The completed list is often far longer than you would have guessed when you started.

Estimating the amount of each expense

You can take several approaches to estimating the amount of each expense. Four basic approaches are:

General budget factors
Fixed/variable factors
Expense-type factors
Special circumstances

You can use each of these as alternatives or in combination.

General budget factors

The approach here is to adjust the previous budget figures, overall, for instance, a 10 per cent increase across the board or a 5 per cent decrease.

Whilst rough and ready it is easy to apply and can be very accurate. Bear in mind that any adjustment factor should not just be an allowance for inflation. It should also reflect any general change in activity level and efficiency.

For example, if inflation is expected to run at 5 per cent in 1986, but Hilal Hotels expect their room occupancy to go up by 10 per cent, also, then they should adjust for both factors.

This can be done by adjusting for the increase in activity first and then the increase in prices, or by using a general adjustment factor. For example, if Hilal Hotels had revenues in 1985 of £600,000, they could forecast their 1986 revenues as shown in Table 4.1.

Table 4.1

Hilal Hotels

	£
1985 revenues	600,000
Add 10% increase in activity	60,000
	660,000
Add 5% for price increase	33,000
Forecast revenues in 1986	693,000

For the mathematically minded, the adjustment factor can also be obtained by multiplying the two adjustments:

Activity adjustment × price adjustment = general adjustment

For Hilal Hotels:

$$1.10 \times 1.05 = 1.155$$

This gives the forecast £600,000 × 1.155 = £693,000.

Notice that adding the two adjustments does not give the right factor. For Hilal, if the factors are added, the sum is 15 per cent but the correct adjustment is 15.5 per cent. In practice, this might not matter much unless the two adjustments were large. After all, forecasting is not so precise that you can be sure of being absolutely right at any time.

Fixed and variable factors

Fixed expenses. The amount payable for an expense is sometimes fixed in advance. In this case, you must make sure you use the forecast rate for the budget period, not current figures. For instance, rates are set at the start of the local authority year, in April. The amount can be obtained from the rates notice or calculated from the rateable value if the rate level is known. Insurances, too, are set in advance, and the amount is stated in the demand for payment. The rental element in telephone bills is partly payable in advance. The only problem in estimating is that you must guess whether further increases, as yet unannounced, are likely to occur in the budget period. Here the press can be useful in alerting you to the likelihood of increases.

Variable expenses. Where expenses are not fixed in advance, it may still be possible to get a good estimate if you know some factor determines or influences the expense. These factors are measures of some aspect of business activity.

Business activity. Some expenses may vary with sales activity; others with production or distribution activities. Some may depend on servicing and administrative activities. For instance, the cost of freight may average 10 per cent of sales revenues, or warehouse wages may generally amount to 50p per carton. Royalties may be £2 per ton of ore mined. Authors may be paid 15 per cent of the net cash receipts from sales of books, the administrative cost of preparing a sales invoice might be 60p. You can use each of these measures to give an estimate of the relevant expense, as in Table 4.2.

Expense-type factors

This approach is based on the belief that each type of expense raises different problems. Therefore, it is advisable to go through the list of expenses and consider each in turn.

Supplies. You can estimate the cost of supplies along the same lines as you estimated material purchases. You take net trade price, less the cash discounts you expect to claim. The items involved are very varied and if they are not particularly large amounts, do not spend too much time preparing individual estimates. You may as well adjust last year's figure for the general budget factor unless there are special circumstances. For example, if Pergon Ltd paid £1,200 for supplies in 1985, a 15 per cent adjustment would give £1,380 expense for 1986.

Freight and carriage. These costs can be affected by the level of business activity but if new suppliers and customers are being served, may rise disproportionately because of an increase in the area served. The price charged by outside contractors may also rise.

For example, the Charnock Mining Company uses the services of Destour Transport to deliver quarry stone. In 1985, the price was £15 per hour but this is expected to rise to £15.50 per hour in 1986. In addition, the tonnage delivered will rise from 300,000 tons to 400,000. In 1985, Charnock calculated delivery time as 1 hour per 100 tons but the wider area served in 1986 will mean this rises to 1 hour 15 minutes per 100 tons. You can calculate the budget expense (Table 4.3).

Table 4.2

Business activity

				Estimate for 1986 budget
Company A	Sales £3,750,000			
	Freight 10% of sales revenue			Freight £375,000
Company B	Warehouse expected to handle 40,000 cartons			Warehouse
	Wages 50p per carton			wages £20,000
Company C	Ore to be mined 300,000 tons			Mining
	Royalties £2 per ton			royalties £600,000
Company D	Sales of books by A. Plumkett			
		1,500 at £10 =	£15,000	A. Plumkett
		2,200 at £ 4 =	8,800	Author royalties: £3,750
		Total cash receipts	23,800	
		Royalty	£ 3,750	
	Royalty 15% on cash receipts			
Company A	Sales		£3,750,000	
	Average invoice amount		£150	
	No. of invoices in year:			
	$\dfrac{\text{Sales}}{\text{Average invoice amount}}$	= $\dfrac{3,750,000}{150}$ =	25,000 for year	
	Invoice cost 60p. per invoice: 25,000 × 60p			Invoicing cost £15,000

Table 4.3

Charnock Mining Co. transport expenses

1985	Destour Transport	
	3,000 hours @ £15 per hour	£45,000
1986	Destour Transport	
	$\text{Time} = \dfrac{400,000}{100} = 4,000$ hours	
	Rate £15.50 per hour	
1986 Transport expense 4,000 × 15.50		£62,000

Personnel. Salaried personnel may be on scales which move up annually and you should adjust the amount for this factor as well as any general increase. If merit awards are given you can use an average figure.

For example, clerical salaries for Manson Motors in 1985 were £8,500,000 for 1,000 employees. This is an average of £8,500 p.a. The salary scale increases in steps of £250 from £6,500 to £10,000 per annum. For 1986, the company forecasts no clerical staff turnover, a general wage rise of 10 per cent and that individual merit awards will be given, totalling 5 per cent of the clerical salaries bill. You can calculate the 1986 expense as shown in Table 4.4. Note that you should make the adjustments in the order in which the various awards are made.

Table 4.4

Manson Motors

	£
1985 clerical salaries, 1,000 persons	8,500,000
Move up salary scale 1,000 @ £250	250,000
	8,750,000
Merit increases, average 5%	437,500
	9,187,500
General wage rise 10%	918,750
1986 clerical salaries, 1,000 persons	10,106,250

The figure you take for any wage or salaries awards should be realistic but you should remember that, if it is disclosed to negotiators, the figure could be taken as evidence for the real intentions of the firm, so you should not broadcast it.

It is possible that your wages and salaries may be influenced by selling and production levels. In this case, you can budget for them as a percentage of sales revenue. For instance, Hilal Hotels expect wages to be 60 per cent of sales revenue. It is expected that 1986 sales will be £693,000. The wages expense for the year can therefore be forecast as £415,800 (£693,000 × ·6).

It is the gross cost of salaries and wages which is relevant for cash budgeting. Although the gross amount is not necessarily payable in one instalment because deductions, such as PAYE, are paid to third parties it is often accurate enough to treat the gross cost as a single expense. You can also use a percentage to forecast the employee-related expenses, or the amount may be a flat rate per employee. For instance, Manson Motors expect that employer contribution to the superannuation fund will amount to 10 per cent of salaries and, in addition, national insurance, luncheon vouchers and other fringe benefits amount to £1,500 per employee per year. The employee-related costs will be as shown in Table 4.5.

Table 4.5

Manson Motors

	£
1986 clerical salaries estimate, 1,000 persons	10,106,250
Employee-related expenses	
Employers' contribution to superannuation fund 10% of salaries	1,010,625
National insurance, luncheon vouchers, etc., £1,500 per employee	1,500,000
1986 employee-related expenses	2,510,625

Fuel and power. The pricing intentions of fuel and power suppliers are often announced well ahead. So, you can get quite accurate estimates of the prices likely to be paid. The usage of fuels is a major determinant of what the total bill will eventually be and you should make allowance for the influence of business activity. A contingency amount may also be provided for additional heating costs in case of a cold winter. For instance, heating and lighting of Hilal Hotels is entirely by electricity and cost 5p per unit in 1985 when consumption was 144,000 units. Occupancy is expected to rise by 10 per cent in 1986 and the Electricity Board have announced price increases of 15 per cent on tariffs. The hotel usually provides for a contingency rise of 10 per cent to allow for bad weather. The expected bill is forecast as in Table 4.6.

Services. You may need to review charges for services in detail if considerable use is made of them. A general budget factor adjustment can be surprisingly useful in producing a realistic estimate.

Table 4.6

Hilal Hotels

		£
1985	Electricity consumption 144,000 units @ 5p per unit	7,200
1986	Consumption increase 10% $144,000 \times 1.1 = 158,400$ units Price increase 15% $5p \times 1.15p$ Cost $158,400 \times 5.75$	£ 9,108
	Add contingency 10%	911
	Forecast electricity bill for 1986	£10,019

For instance, Hilal Hotels used the Doclean Laundry Service at a cost of £23,000 in 1985. The general adjustment factor for activity and price increases in 1986 is 15.5 per cent. The laundry expense may be forecast as £26,565.

Maintenance. You should be able to find out the agreed charges for contracts and the expense of scheduled overhauls as a known programme of work. For instance, Delicatessen Meats paid £30 per annum for maintenance on each of three slicing machines in 1985 and it is known that the 1986 contract price will be £32 per machine. The firm employ a general handyman who proposes to overhaul the sausage machine in 1986. He believes that new parts will cost not less than £100 and not more than £300. The estimated costs could be calculated as in Table 4.7.

Table 4.7

Delicatessen Meats

Maintenance	£
3 slicers @ £32 each	96.00
Parts for slicer overhaul	200.00
1986 maintenance expense	296.00

In this case, the estimate for parts is mid-way between the higher and lower estimates from the handyman. That is purely a matter of judgement – an optimist might plump for the low £100 and a pessimist for the high of £300 (or more!).

Hire/lease/rent. These payments are usually fixed by contract but some lease arrangements also include a usage charge which should be based on expected activity. The Surrey Nursery Farm Ltd are hire purchasing a tractor on five annual payments of £4,000. Two further payments remain. In addition, the farmer is renting a slurry plant at £3,500 per annum plus £5 per ton for slurry processed. In 1986, it is expected 400 tons will be processed. The farm is rented under an agricultural tenancy for £1,500 per annum (Table 4.8).

Table 4.8

Surrey Nursery Farm Ltd – rentals and lease of equipment

	£
HP on tractor	4,000
Rent on slurry plant £3,500	
Plus 400 tons @ £5 per ton £2,000	
	5,500
1986 equipment rentals and lease	9,500
1986 farm rent	1,500

Of course, the legal position with regard to these payments is different but that is irrelevant from a cash point of view. Both involve cash payments which total £9,500.

Travel. Travel costs can be estimated by a general budget factor but if special travel plans are involved, it may be useful to obtain estimates from a travel agent who may, in any case, be willing to offer discounts for handling all the travel business.

For example, the managing director of Delicatessen Meats had a travel allowance for visits to customers in 1985 of £1,500. This is to be adjusted upwards for price and activity levels by 20 per cent in 1986 but, in addition, the firm is contemplating opening a new shop in Toronto in 1987. To prepare for this, the managing director expects to spend a total of twelve days over three trips to Toronto in 1986. His cousin, a travel agent, can arrange such trips at a package cost of £830. The managing director estimates that incidentals would amount to £100 per day. The travelling allowances for 1986 could be estimated as shown in Table 4.9.

Security and insurance. The expense of security services should take account of the demand for services and the fees being paid. If Delicatessen Meats employ a security firm for two hours each Friday to collect the payroll at £150 per hour, they can budget £300 for each pay day. Over the year the cost may be calculated as £15,600. For a plant

Table 4.9

Delicatessen Meats

	£
1985 normal travel	1,500
1986 normal travel Cost increased 20% £1,500 × 1.20 =	£1,800
Canadian visits 3 visits at £830 = 2,490 12 days at £100 p.d. 1,200	
Cost of Canadian visits	£3,690
1986 travel budget	£5,490

which closes down completely for holidays, there may not be 52 pay days in the year.

Insurance premiums need to be reviewed to ensure that losses are adequately guarded against. Buildings are usually insured at replacement cost and many insurers provide an automatic revaluation annually. Some premiums may need increasing in line with business activities, e.g. insurances against stock losses or loss of profits. Car premiums may rise if no claims bonuses are lost because of accidents during the current year.

Lancashire Leadweight Ltd has a building insured at £1 per £100 on a valuation of £100,000 but has been informed that the current replacement cost is £120,000. The company insures against stock losses at £2 per £100. Stocks are expected to average £30,000 in 1986. The managing director's Jaguar comprehensive insurance will be £800 in 1986 but he currently enjoys no claims discount of 60 per cent. At the time the estimates are being prepared, he has had an accident and it is likely his bonus will fall to 40 per cent in 1986. Insurance expenses will be estimated as in Table 4.10.

Table 4.10

Lancashire Leadweights Ltd – insurance expenses

	£
Building insurance £120,000 @ £1 per £100	1,200
Stock loss insurance £30,000 @ 20p per £100	600
Car insurance Premium £800 less 40% NCD 320	480
1986 insurance expense	£2,280

The employer's contributions to superannuation and pension fund may be calculated on the gross payroll. Beware of double counting if contributions are made both by the employee and employer. Suppose clerical employees in Manson Motors have 6 per cent deducted from their salaries for the pension scheme and the employer matches this by a further 12 per cent. The expense to the employer will be £1,212,750.

The employees will also contribute 6 per cent of £10,106,250 that is, £606,375, so that a total of £1,819,125 will be paid into the fund. With large sums like this, it would be desirable to budget cash according to the actual pattern of payments, especially if contributions are remitted to the fund periodically, say half-yearly or quarterly in arrears.

Manson Motors pay clerical employees monthly and superannuation contributions quarterly. In January and February 1986, there will be four pay days each month and in March, five. The contributions are payable to the fund at the end of March. The clerical salary expenses and the superannuation fund contributions will appear in the cash budget as in Table 4.11.

Table 4.11

Manson Motors — extract from cash budget 1986

Clerical salaries		January 4 weeks £	February 4 weeks £	March 5 weeks £
Gross	£194,350 p.w.			
less 6%	£ 11,661			
Net payment per week	£182,689			
Net wages payment		730,756	730,756	913,445
Superannuation fund 18% of £194,350 × 13				909,558

Taxes, licences and duties. At this stage, you can include VAT, customs and excise duties in purchase costs and sales revenues. You can include income or corporation tax payments if they fall due in the period. Base the expense of licences on the amount to be paid in the budget period.

Royalties. Royalties are a variable expense. The amount you will pay will depend on the general level of the royalty basis. Look at Pirate Publications Ltd. They pay 15 per cent royalties to authors on 80 per cent of cash received from sales. Pirate Publications Ltd expect to receive £940,000 from sales in 1986. The royalties to authors will be £112,800 $((\cdot 8 \times 940{,}000) \times \cdot 15)$.

Advertising and selling. The amounts budgeted for advertising and selling may be calculated as a percentage on sales, after these have been forecast for the year. Hilal Hotels spend 5 per cent of sales by value on advertising each year. The estimate would be £35,650 (5 per cent of £693,000).

In other cases, you can estimate the expected costs of specific campaigns from the marketing plan.

Establishing the timing of expenses

In general your cash budgeting is very much affected by the timing of receipts and payments and it is important that your forecast dates for receipts and payments are accurate.

Supplies

Supplies are normally paid within 30 to 45 days unless an earlier payment is made to obtain cash discount. You will usually not have a great problem in postponing payment if this is convenient for you because most supplies are subject to fierce competition.

Freight and carriage

You will usually pay these expenses monthly in arrears when regular contractors are used. Otherwise, you may occasionally find they have to be paid in advance.

Personnel

Net wages are normally paid weekly and salaries monthly. However, the deductions and employee-related expenses may be payable monthly, quarterly or even annually. You need to get the timing right because these are usually large expenses.

Fuel and power

Energy supplies in various forms are normally paid monthly or quarterly in arrears.

Services

Some services are paid in cash or even in advance, such as postages. Many are invoiced monthly or quarterly in arrears or, like the telephone, a mixture of arrears and advance payments.

Maintenance

Contracts are often payable annually or quarterly in advance. Variable costs may be paid in arrears or on a monthly basis.

Hire/leases and rentals

These are usually payable annually in advance although quarterly or monthly payments may be arranged, usually at higher cost.

Travel costs

These are mixed, some in advance, some in arrears, although use of credit cards for these expenses can lead to higher costs if bills are not settled within six weeks.

Security

Payments for these services, if used regularly, may be monthly. Otherwise, advance payment may be requested.

Insurance

Insurance is payable in advance although most insurers will arrange quarterly or monthly premiums at higher cost.

Taxes

PAYE tax withheld is payable monthly. Duties are payable at the time of the underlying transaction. VAT is paid quarterly and income taxes are generally payable in two instalments in January and July. Corporation tax is due nine months after the end of the accounting year.

Licences

Most licences are payable in advance, annually.

Royalties

Royalties are normally payable in arrears. Industrial royalties may be payable monthly or quarterly but others, such as authors, are paid annually.

Advertising and selling

Some fees are payable in advance but other expenses are paid on a monthly basis as they arise. An important consideration is that advertising campaigns are mounted in order to increase sales, so the money may be spent some time before the returns are realised. The time delay may not be long if you are advertising customer goods on TV but if you are trying to persuade industrial customers to use a new aero engine or a new material such as carbon fibre, the delay can be considerable.

The broad brush

A golden rule in cash forecasting is to avoid excessive detail. The variations of individual expenses, which we have just considered, may not be significant in practice. If many small items are put together, the odds are that they won't all come due at the same time. And if you are budgeting cash, you will have time to manoeuvre so that you can avoid an excessive delay on any one payment.

You can treat any group of items which together account for less than 10 per cent of the total cash funds available as one and you can group individual items amounting to less than 5 per cent together. For example, the monthly expenses of Alan Thomas Ltd for 1985 were as shown in Table 4.12.

Table 4.12

Alan Thomas Ltd – monthly expenses

		£	% of total
1	Salaries and wages	11,816	15
2	Insurance	5,514	7
3	Materials	39,385	50
4	Supplies	1,575	2
5	Freight	790	1
6	Electricity	2,362	3
7	Telephone	788	1
8	Maintenance	3,150	4
9	Royalties	9,452	12
10	Advertising	3,939	5
		78,770	100

Table 4.13

Alan Thomas Ltd – monthly expenses

		£	%
1	Salaries and wages	11,816	15
2	Insurance	5,514	7
3	Materials	39,385	
4–8	Supplies, freight, phone and electricity	8,665	11
9	Royalties	9,452	12
10	Advertising	3,939	5
		78,770	100

Consider the percentages for a moment. There are five items, nos 4–8 which are individually below 5 per cent. They could be taken together, in which case they add up to 11 per cent of the total expenses, and the list would be reduced (Table 4.13).

This leaves advertising, at 5 per cent of the budget, as the smallest item. If you are not happy about the items being grouped in this particular way, there is a wealth of possibilities. For instance, the items could be combined with larger items, one by one, with, for instance, freight going with insurance, supplies with materials, electricity and phone with maintenance.

Case study – Tregallion Production Ltd

Tregallion Production Ltd bottles table water in Weston-super-Mare and markets the product through an associated company Tregon Water Ltd which takes all production at a standard price of £3.70 per case of ten 1-litre bottles on monthly terms. Sales in the quarter May–July 1986 are expected to be:

> May 100,000 cases
> June 150,000 cases
> July 200,000 cases

Salaries are expected to be £25,000 per month but wages vary with production at £2 per case. A royalty of 7.5p per litre is payable quarterly in arrear and because he has found this substantial sum difficult to raise in the past, John Tregallion, the managing director, has decided to prepare a cash budget for the three months May to July. On 1st May, John expects the cash float to be £18,000 at the bank and £700 cash in hand.

Tregallion water comes from a pure natural source and the Tregallion factory is situated alongside the plot of land on which the spring emerges. The factory is rented for £16,000 per annum, payable quarterly on quarter day (the next payment is due on 21st June). The rates for 1986/7 are 140p in the £ on a rateable value of £5,500 and are payable on 15th May. The factory machinery and equipment is insured at a replacement value of £250,000 at a premium of £1.50 per 1,000 and the company pays this in two instalments, on 1st January and 1st July.

Maintenance of equipment is done under contract for £100 per month, plus charges for parts. John usually allows £30 per month for this. He expects to pay £100 per month for office supplies, £250 per month for telephone and electricity and lighting £40 per month. Telephone bills are paid quarterly. The next is due in June. Postage amounts to £80 per month. Delivery of water is made by Dragon Transport Ltd who charge 50p per case to pick up at the factory and deliver to the warehouse of Tregon Water Ltd. Payment is made on monthly terms. Electric power is expected to cost 20p per case of water bottled. Electricity bills are paid quarterly. The next is due in July.

Budgeting for expenses

All three companies are family concerns under the management of three brothers, as follows:

Tregallion Production Ltd   John Tregallion MD
Tregon Water Ltd   Champrey Woods-Tregallion MD
Dragon Transport Ltd   Fred Tregallion MD

Although there are interlocking shareholdings and each brother is a director of all three companies, the firms are run as independent profit centres for which each managing director is fully responsible. Terms of trade are clearly specified and strictly adhered to. Ebenezer Tregallion is chairman of all three companies.

List of expenses

In collecting together data for the cash budget, John decided first to make a list of expenses. The following list follows the order in which they are mentioned above (Table 4.14).

Table 4.14

Tregallion Production Ltd – list of expenses

Salaries
Wages
Water royalties
Factory rent
Rates
Insurance of machinery and equipment
Maintenance of equipment
Office supplies
Telephone
Heating and lighting
Postage
Water delivery (Dragon)
Electric power

Amount of expenses

John then went systematically down the list estimating the amount payable for each expense in the three months, with the results shown in Table 4.15. John decided to keep these calculations as part of his working papers, which are Table 4.19.

The timing of expenses

John next considered the timing of each expense, as shown below (Table 4.16). As he did so, he also noted the conditions applicable, if any.

Table 4.15

Tregallion Production Ltd – amount of expenses

Salaries	£25,000 per month		
Wages	£2 per case	May:	100,000 × £2 = £200,000
		June:	150,000 × £2 = £300,000
		July:	200,000 × £2 = £400,000

Water royalties production in litres
(10 litres per case)

		£
	May:	1,000,000
	June:	1,500,000
	July:	2,000,000
Total production for quarter		4,500,000
Royalties @ 7.5p per litre		£ 337,500

Factory rent
    £16,000 p.a. £4,000 per quarter

Factory rates
    £5,500 @ £1.40 = £7,700 per annum

Insurance
    £250,000 @ £1.50 per 1,000 = £375 per annum
    £187.50 on 1 January and 1 July

Equipment maintenance
    £100 per month + £30 for parts per month

Office supplies
    £100 per month

Telephone
    £250 per month

Electric heating and lighting
    £40 per month

Postage
    £80 per month

Water delivery (Dragon)
    50 per case: May: 100,000 @ 50p = £ 50,000
                                  June: 150,000 @ 50p = £ 75,000
                                  July: 200,000 @ 50p = £100,000

Electric power
    20p per case: May: 100,000 @ 20p = £20,000
                                 June: 150,000 @ 20p = £30,000
                                 July: 200,000 @ 20p = £40,000

Table 4.16
Tregallion Production Ltd

	Timing of expenses	Conditions
Salaries	Monthly, as incurred	—
Wages	Monthly, as incurred	—
Water royalties	In arrear: next three months payable at end July	—
Factory rent	21 June (one quarter)	
Factory rate	15 May (full amount)	
Insurance	1 July (half amount)	
Equipment maintenance	Monthly	Amounts for parts estimated
Office supplies	Monthly	Estimated
Telephone	Three months payable in June	
Electric heating and lighting	Next quarter due in July	
Postage	Monthly	
Water delivery (Dragon)	Monthly	
Electric power	Next quarter due in July	

The broad brush

At this stage, without going too deeply into the monthly expenses, John could see that some were not particularly large and he decided to amalgamate wages, water, delivery and electric power because these were all calculated on the production level and calculated monthly. He calculated the rate to be £2.70 per case. He decided against including the water royalties in this rate because that amount is payable quarterly in arrears.

The next group amalgamated were all estimated amounts which, although payable in different ways, did not, in total, amount to a big proportion of expenses and John believed there would be sufficient flexibility to meet any 'lumpiness' in the demands for payment.

Table 4.17 shows the final calculation which John included in the working papers, the final data sheet (Tables 4.18 and 4.19) and the cash budget in Table 4.20.

Table 4.17
Tregallion Production Ltd

	£
Office supplies	100 per month
Equipment maintenance	130 per month
Telephone	250 per month
Electric heating and lighting	40 per month
Postage	80 per month
Miscellaneous expenses	£600 per month

Table 4.19(a)
Tregallion Production Ltd – working papers for cash budget

Prepared by: J. Tregallion
Date: 20 April 1986

List of expenses	Amounts		Timing	Conditions and flexibility
Salaries		£ 25,000	Monthly	
Wages				
£2 per case May:	100,000 =	200,000		
June:	150,000 =	300,000		
July:	200,000 =	400,000		
Water royalties	Litres			
May:	1,000,000			
June:	1,500,000			
July:	2,000,000			
Total production for quarter	4,500,000			
Note 1 @ 7.5 per litre		337,500		
Note 2 Factory rent		16,000	£4,000 per quarter due 21 June	
Note 3 Factory rates £5,500 R.V.@£1.40 = p.a.		7,700	15 May	Could be paid by instalments
Note 4 Insurances £250,000@£1.50 per 100 = p.a.		3,750		
		1,875	Due on 1 July	
Equipment maintenance				
Contract		100	Monthly	
Parts		30	Monthly	
Office supplies		100	Monthly	
Telephone		250	Monthly	
Electricity, heating and lighting		40	Monthly	
Postage		80	Monthly	
Water delivery (Dragon) 50p per case:				
May 100,000 cases		50,000		
June 150,000 cases		75,000		
July 200,000 cases		100,000		

Table 4.18

Tregallion Production Ltd – data sheet for cash budget

Budget period: 3 months May – July 1986
Budget basis: Monthly
Prepared by J. Tregallion
Date: 20 April 1986

	Items	Amount		Timing	Conditions and flexibility
		£			
Section 1	Opening float				
	Cash in hand	700			–
	Cash at bank	18,300			–
Section 2	Receipts	Cases			
	Sales	100,000	370,000	May	£3.70
		150,000	555,000	June	per case
		200,000	740,000	July	
Section 3	Payments				
	Salaries	25,000		Monthly	–
	Wages, water delivery and electric power	270,000		May	£2.70
		405,000		June	per case
		540,000		July	
	Water royalties	337,500		Payable end July	(Note 5)
	Factory rent	4,000		Payable 21 June	(Note 1)
	Factory rates	7,700		Payable 15 May	(Note 2)
	Insurance	187.50		Payable 1 July	(Note 3)
	Miscellaneous expenses	570		Per month	(Note 4)
					(Note 6)

Table 4.19(b)

Tregallion Production Ltd – working papers for cash budget

Prepared by: J. Tregallion
Date: 20 April 1986

	Amounts	Timing	Conditions and flexibility
	£		
Electric power 20p per case			
May 100,000	20,000		
June 150,000	30,000		
July 200,000	40,000		
Note 5			
Wages £2 per case			
Water delivery .50 per case			Combined into a single rate
Electric power .20 per case			
Wages, delivery			
and power £2.70			
Cases	£		
100,000 May	270,000		
150,000 June	405,000		
200,000 July	540,000		
Note 6 Miscellaneous expenses	£		
Office supplies	100	Monthly	
Equipment maintenance	130	Monthly	
Telephone	250	Monthly	
Electric heating and lighting	40	Monthly	
Postage	80	Monthly	
	£600	per month	

Table 4.20

Tregallion Production Ltd – cash budget

Prepared by: J. Tregallion
Date: 20 April 1986

Budget for period: May – July 1986
Budget basis: Monthly

	May £	June £	July £
Section 1			
Cash float at start of month	19,000	85,730	206,160
Section 2 Receipts			
Sales	370,000	555,000	740,000
Total cash available	389,000	640,730	946,160
Section 3 Payments			
Salaries	25,000	25,000	25,000
Wages, water delivery and electric power	270,000	405,000	540,000
Water royalties	–	–	337,500
Factory rent	–	4,000	–
Factory rates	7,700	–	–
Insurances	–	–	1,875
Miscellaneous expenses	570	570	570
Total cash needs	303,270	434,570	904,945
Section 4			
Cash float at end of month	85,730	206,160	41,215

5
Budgeting for stocks

The effects of stocks on cash management can be considerable and, sometimes, unexpected. Cash flow is affected by the timing of payments for stock and the timing of receipts from sales. Cash receipts and payments are in turn affected by the levels of stock held, the rate of stock usage and the recording levels.

Cash float

The cash float at any time will be the result of combining the inflows and outflows. These are influenced by several interrelated factors such as stock holding policy; the terms of trade obtained from suppliers and offered to customers; the level of business activity on both the production and the selling sides; and so on.

Because the resulting cash float is impossible to guess by intuition, these factors must be carefully forecast. If they change, you should be ready to revise your cash forecasts.

At the end of 1982, British industries were holding stocks valued at £75,567 million. Most of these stocks, nearly 60 per cent were held by the manufacturing and energy industry, but stocks are also an important, if not decisive, element in wholesaling and retailing, which, between them held £19,411 million in stocks, that is, 26 per cent of the total.

Business forecasters use stock levels as an indicator of economic confidence. In times of economic growth, stocks rise and in recession, they fall. That is fine, for the economy as a whole, but when you look at an individual business, efficiency in controlling stock can have a big impact on the demand for cash and profitability. The UK retail stocks at the end of 1982 were 12 per cent of sales for 1982, that is 44 days.

Marks and Spencer, at the end of March 1983, were holding £163 million in stocks, which is 6.5 per cent of their sales, or 23 days. At the other extreme, the National Health Service held stocks of £240 million for issues which cost £500 million, which is 48 per cent or 173 days!

One may argue that the consequences of the NHS running out of surgical instruments are more catastrophic than if M & S run out of men's socks, but experts in the NHS have pointed out that stocks could easily be halved without loss of service. In some cases, stocks could be reduced to 10 per cent or less. Even halving NHS stocks would release £120 million for other uses. Authorities are also looking for reductions in prices by more efficient ordering. A 10 per cent reduction in prices would give a saving of £5 million which could be put to other uses in patient care.

Stocks are held in many diverse forms, ranging from raw materials to finished goods.

Raw materials

These are natural resources such as timber, stone, gold, copper and they usually are acquired for treatment or use in manufacture. At the end of 1982, 31 per cent of the stocks of manufacturing industry in the UK were in the form of raw materials and fuel.

Finished goods

Finished goods, products which have been completed and are ready for sale, account for 30 per cent of the stocks of manufacturing industry. For industry as a whole, the proportion of finished goods is nearer 50 per cent because of the stocks in distribution, with wholesalers and in retail outlets.

Work-in-progress

Work-in-progress is any product or service on which work has commenced but is not yet completed. Work-in-progress is an intermediate stage through which work passes before the final product is completed and ready for sale. Work-in-progress may take the form of parts, components and sub-assemblies which have been completed to the required standard but are made or bought in for use in making a final product. Sub-assemblies, similarly, are sections of a final product which have been made and/or assembled ready for incorporation into a final product. Sub-assemblies, also, may be bought in. Work-in-progress accounts for nearly 40 per cent of the stocks of manufacturing industry.

In manufacturing, raw materials are issued into production. Labour and expenses are incurred as the materials are adapted from their raw state. Parts, components and sub-assemblies may be created or bought in and used in the final product.

In construction, work-in-progress may include an element of profit, if progress payments have been received. The balance sheet of Trafalgar House at 30th September 1983 disclosed gross work-in-progress of £2,014 million reduced to £126 million net after progress payments were deducted.

In service industries, labour and expenses are incurred on a job. So long as the job is incomplete, then, at best, all we have is cost of work-in-progress. Examples are architects preparing a proposal for a development, accountants working in an audit, or a central heating firm installing a system. A work-in-progress cost arises from the use of labour and services. Material costs will be a relatively minor cost in service provision. Some expenses, such as computer usage or information service, may be major.

The two things all these forms of stock have in common is that they are costly to get and costly to keep. On the other hand, we must have them. If a manufacturing or retailing firm does not have finished goods to hand when they are needed, sales may be lost. If professional and service firms are not prepared to work on projects before they are paid, then they won't be in business. So, stocks must be controlled, hard as that often is, and the watchword must be neither too little nor too much.

Too little stock may lead to interruptions of production or loss of sales. Too much stock incurs additional costs of carrying and there is greater risk of waste, loss and obsolescence.

Stocks are buffers, provided at key points in the chain of production and distribution to absorb differences in demand and supply (see Figure 5.1).

These buffers absorb mistakes and unforeseen changes. Stocks allow production and demand to meet smoothly together. The cycle of cash inevitably flows through the various forms of stock (Figure 5.2).

From the cash budgeting viewpoint, cash is used to buy raw materials and to pay for labour and expenses. Added together, these flow into work-in-progress and then, after a time delay for completion, into finished goods stocks. Stocks may be sold for cash or to customers, so that the time delay gives rise to debtors.

Since expenses and raw materials may be obtained on credit, creditors arise and the operating cycle of cash flow is completed when these are paid – at a later date, of course.

Stock costs

The costs of stocks can be looked at in three categories.

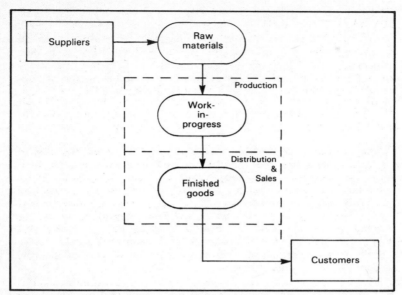

Fig. 5.1 Stocks as buffers in the chain of production

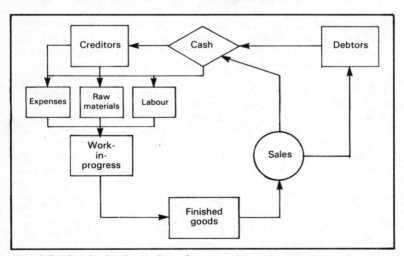

Fig. 5.2 Stocks in the cash cycle

Acquisition costs
These are the net trade price plus the costs of transportation and handling. We have already discussed these costs under trade credit and expenses.

Ordering costs

These are the administrative costs of placing orders with suppliers and with production (for finished goods). These costs will be included in expenses. It's worth noting that the number of orders processed may be a useful measure of business activity when estimating the expenses involved, such as accounting wages and cost of supplies.

Carrying costs

These are the costs involved in holding stocks. Some are easier to measure than others. Storage of stocks may require the possession of suitable buildings and equipment such as racking or trucks. During handling, stocks may be damaged and deterioration may occur. These are fairly easy to monitor.

But holding stocks also ties up capital, so there is an imputed cost of capital. To this may be added insurance against various risks such as theft, fire and flood. Over-ordering can mean that stocks become obsolete. These costs are not so easy to monitor. Many of them will appear as cash expenses, but the cost of capital does not.

Economic order quantity (EOQ)

If we assume that stocks are ordered in batches, but used at a steady rate, and that we can establish both the cost of placing an order to purchase and the annual cost of carrying one unit of stock, then it is possible to calculate the best amount to order. Stocks could be ordered once a year or at the other extreme, once a day. The economic order quantity (EOQ) is the size of order that should be placed if costs are to be minimised and implicit in this is the frequency of ordering.

Many firms use EOQ in their stock control procedures. For instance, if a firm uses 10,000 components every week, it could place a weekly order for 10,000 or order 40,000 every fourth week, or 130,000 every quarter. In the first case it would place 52 orders each year, in the second 13 and in the third, 4.

When to order

EOQ shows how often to order and what size of order to place but other factors determine when the order is to be placed. The level of a stock will decline steadily if usage is steady. Gummer Plastics use 20 kilos of powder per day and place 200 kilos in stock at the start of each ten day period; the pattern of stocks held would be a 'sawtooth' as shown in Figure 5.3.

This assumes that every order for 200 kilos is placed and met in time.

Budgeting for stocks

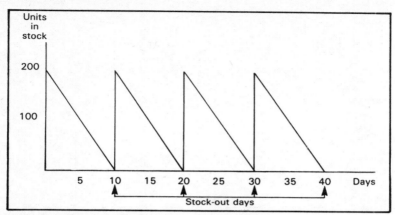

Fig. 5.3 Gummer Plastics – stock levels

Stock-out time

The day when the stock is zero is the stock-out day which is day 10 in the example.

Lead time

The time taken to make out an order, for it to be received and filled by the supplier and for the goods to be placed in store is the lead time. It is the waiting time between the time when a need for replacement stock is identified and the time when the stock actually comes available for use.

Re-order level

This is the level of stock at the beginning of the lead time. If replacement stock is ordered at this level, then the replacement will arrive in time to replenish the stock and avoid any losses due to interruptions of supply, always assuming that the rate of usage is as expected. If Gummer Plastics find the suppliers need seven days to fill an order, then the re-order level will be at 140 units, as shown in Figure 5.4.

Re-ordering would be necessary on the third day of each 10-day period. The time is found by counting backwards from the stock-out day, 10. The quantity can be read off the chart, or simply calculated as:

$$\text{Lead time} \times \text{daily usage} = \text{re-order level}$$

For Gummer Plastics:

$$7 \text{ days} \times 20 \text{ units} = 140 \text{ units}$$

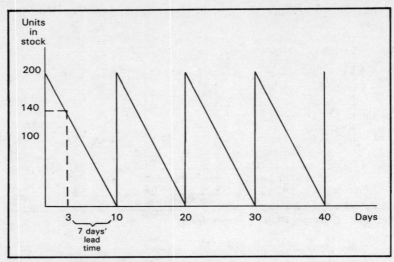

Fig. 5.4 Gummer Plastics – re-order level

Safety minimum

The risk of stock-out can be reduced if a minimum safe level is established for each major item of stock. After all, the lead time can never be known with absolute certainty, nor can the rate of usage. The

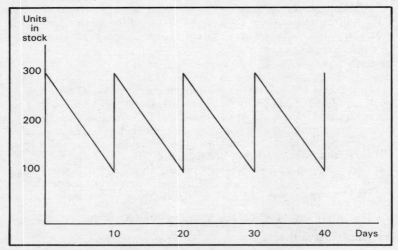

Fig. 5.5 Gummer Plastics – minimum safety stock

Budgeting for stocks

re-order point should be readjusted by adding on the required safety stock.

For example, if Gummer Plastics decide that a minimum safety stock level of 100 kilos should be maintained, the 'sawtooth' will be moved upwards, as shown in Figure 5.5.

The lead time remains the same, but the re-order level is now:

Lead time × daily usage + minimum stock = re-order level

For Gummer Plastics:

7 days × 20 kilos per day + 100 kilos = 240 kilos

Average stock

The average stock held can be calculated from

$$\frac{\text{Opening stock} + \text{closing stock}}{2} = \text{average stock}$$

For Gummer Plastics:

(a) No minimum stock

$$\frac{200 + 0}{2} = 100 \text{ kilos}$$

(b) Minimum stock 100

$$\frac{300 + 100}{2} = 200 \text{ kilos}$$

You will notice that setting a minimum stock adds the corresponding amount to the average, so it is important not to set minimum too high.

If Gummer Plastics pay £100 per kilo for the powder, then the average investment in stock rises with the minimum stock from £10,000 at no minimum to £20,000 on 100 kilos minimum.

The effects of stock on cash

In a steady state, the cash required for stock holding will reflect the 'sawtooth' pattern but the fact that selling prices are normally higher than purchase prices gives a sharper fall to the back edge of the tooth. Suppose Gummer Plastics use a plastic powder which costs £100 per kilo and that they sell the product for £300 per kilo. No weight losses occur in processing. The cash needed for this process will be the result of putting together two patterns, one the cash demand and the other, the cash supply. The cash demand is a series of pulses.

The timing of these pulses depends upon the timing of re-orders and the terms of trade: their magnitude depends on the size of order placed which in turn reflects the rate at which stocks are being used in production. The receipts represent pulses of cash in the opposite direction and represent the terms of trade which actually operate and the rate and pattern of sales which may be very different from those of production. Both receipts and payments may be made up of many small frequent pulses. In this case, the flows will appear continuous for practical purposes. Gummer Plastics spend £50 per kilo on processing plastic powder and they sell the product at £300 per kilo. If they process and sell at the rate of 20 kilos per day, there will be an additional continuous demand for cash at the rate of 20 kilos @ £300 = £1,000 per day. The net result is a continuous inflow of £5,000 per day.

Cash float

The key question is what is the cash float which results from the sales and stock levels decided upon.

Gummer Plastics, in 1985, was run on a cash basis. The proprietor purchased plastic daily at £100 per kilo and employed casual employees to process it at £50 per day. Sales were made for cash at the factory gate at £300 per kilo. Production and sales in January and February were 20 kilos per day on 45 working days (9 weeks @ 5 days p.w.). In this case, the flows are positive, daily and cash will accumulate steadily.

				£
Cash sales £300	× 20 kilos	=		6,000
Less materials £100	× 20 kilos	=	2,000	
labour £50	× 20 kilos	=	1,000	3,000
Net positive cash flow				£3,000

By the end of February, the firm will hold cash of £135,000 (45 × 3,000).

The position of Gummer Plastics may be very different in 1986 if the terms of trade change, even if all activity factors remain the same. Assume that in 1986, labour is now paid on a weekly (5 days') basis but suppliers allow 10 days' credit and customers are allowed 30 days. Labour is paid 20 × 50 = £1,000 per day, so the weekly wages bill will be £5,000. No payment is made to suppliers until the tenth day when the payment will be £100 × 10 = £1,000. Thereafter, that amount will be paid every two weeks. Both these pulses are negative.

The first receipts will be at the end of four weeks (because the 30 days is assumed to be on a calendar basis), when £300 × 20 × 20 days = £120,000 will be received. Notice there are 20 working days in the 30 calendar day period. The data can easily be handled by preparing a cash budget on a weekly basis for the first nine weeks, January and February, of 1986 (Table 5.1).

Budgeting for stocks

Table 5.1
Gummer Plastics – cash budget (in £000's) 1986

	January				February				
Week	1	2	3	4	5	6	7	8	9
Cash float at start of week	0	−5	−30	−35	−60	−35	−30	−5	10
Receipts from debtors	–	–	–	–	30	30	30	30	30
Total cash available	0	−5	−30	−35	−30	−5	0	25	30
Payments to:									
Suppliers	–	20	–	20	–	20	–	20	–
Wages	5	5	5	5	5	5	5	5	5
Total needs	5	25	5	25	5	25	5	25	5
Cash float at end of week – deficit	−5	30	−35	−60	−35	−30	−5	0	–
– surplus	–	–	–	–	–	–	–	–	25

Under these conditions Gummer Plastics will need to find £60,000 to finance stocks and labour until the end of the week when the first receipts from debtors begin to appear. From then on, receipts will be at the weekly rate of £300 × 20k × 5 days = £30,000 per week because sales are continuous and the cash needed begins to decline. You will notice that it is not until the final week that the ending cash float is positive. Gummer are likely to be in the red for the first eight weeks of 1986! It is instructive to look at the cash float in the form of a graph (Figure 5.6).

This does bring out the symmetrical pattern which the cash float takes on its way up to and down from the peak cash requirement of £6,000 at the end of week 4. A study of the patterns taken by cash float should improve your intuitive feeling for what is likely to happen if circumstances change. For example, what would be the effect on cash if Gummer Plastics agreed to sell all their production, to a single customer, if deliveries were made at the end of each four-weekly period on 30-day terms?

The effect is to make the cash position much worse, since the first delivery would not be made until the end of week 4 and the first cash would not be received until the end of week 8. The amount received would then be:

$$£300 \times 20 \times 20 = £120,000$$

Table 5.2 shows the resulting cash budget and Figure 5.7 is a graph of the cash float. These show quite dramatically the way in which the firm's cash need has now shot up to £95,000 at its highest point in week 7 and how this need is completely eliminated by the one receipt from debtors of £120,000 the following week.

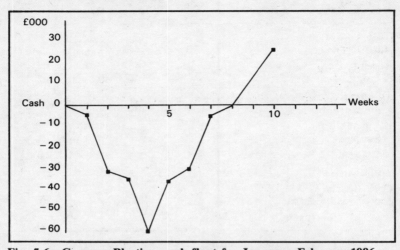

Fig. 5.6 Gummer Plastics – cash float for January—February 1986

Table 5.2

Gummer Plastics – cash budget (in £000's) 1984

	January			February					
Week	1	2	3	4	5	6	7	8	9
Cash float at start of week	0	−5	−30	−35	−60	−65	−90	−95	
Receipts from debtors	—	—	—	—	—	—	—	120	
Total cash available	0	−5	−30	−35	−60	−65	−90	25	
Payments to: suppliers	—	20	—	20	—	20	—	20	
wages	5	5	5	5	5	5	5	5	
Total needs	5	25	5	25	5	25	5	25	
Cash float at end of week -deficit -surplus		−5	−30	−35	−60	−65	−90	−95	0

Budgeting for stocks

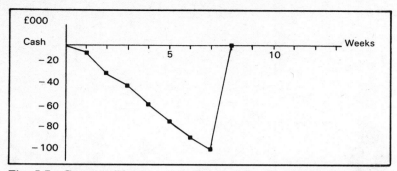

Fig. 5.7 Gummer Plastics – cash float for January—February 1986

6
Budgeting for long-term needs

The distinction between long- and short-term needs is convenient but misleading. What begins as a long-term possibility eventually becomes a short-term certainty. In cash planning the focus of your attention is first on operating cash flows and the circulation of cash into operating capital and back again to cash. Survival matters, but it is a mistake to ignore long-term needs on which you need to spend very large amounts of cash on projects in which the spacing between receipts and payments is very wide. Therein lies the danger. If you ignore long-term trends it may be a long time before you pay the consequences, but then, they can be devastating. Equally if you anticipate strategic changes in good time, you can vastly improve the profitability of your business and smooth your path to success.

Investment appraisal

In this book we do not deal with the theory and practice of investment appraisal. For that, you should refer to *Managing Money and Finance* by G. P. E. Clarkson and B. J. Elliot (third edition by Alan Johnson) published by Gower, or to any other good text on financial management. The emphasis in financial management is on the appraisal of profitability using discounted cash flow techniques. Here we are concerned with planning and management of cash. However, you should make long-term forecasts in a form which is useful, also, for appraisal of the investment.

The long-term cash cycle is discussed on pages 6 to 7 and the sequence of flows is shown in Figure 1.5. You need cash to invest in fixed assets and provide basic working capital. The sources of this cash are owners who receive dividends and exercise the rights and privileges of control, and lenders who receive interest and, eventually, repayment of capital.

We saw earlier that economists use investments in stock as an indicator of economic activity. Another measure is the rate at which industry is investing in fixed assets. Expenditure on fixed assets for UK manufacturing industry fell from £7,200 million in 1978 to £4,500 million in 1982, a decline of 40 per cent. A similar decline occurred in construction, but in the distribution, shipping and financial sectors, investment rose by 35 per cent to £10,000 million. Overall, government data show that large firms invested £30,000 million in 1982. As well as fixed assets, the firms were obliged to provide more working capital because their current assets rose 40 per cent from £4,100 million to £6,800, but the amount they borrowed in the short term rose only 13 per cent, from £6,000 million to £6,900 million. Current assets rose from 72 per cent of current liabilities to 100 per cent. Indeed, in 1983, working capital continued to demand cash. Current assets rose to £9,800 but current liabilities only moved up to £8,201, so current assets were then 118 per cent of current liabilities. Between 1980 and 1983, large firms had to find an extra £3,500 million to finance working capital, even though their short-term borrowing increased by over £2,000 million.

Table 6.1 is a simplified form of the aggregated balance sheets of a group of large UK companies in 1982 which we looked at in Table 1.1. In this presentation, the bank loans are included in borrowing and the facts are arranged to show the long-term financial structure of the companies. You can see that the net working capital of £64,300 million is 43 per cent of the net assets, and fixed assets are 57 per cent.

Nearly 30 per cent of the total funds provided to the companies is borrowed, 18 per cent from banks and 12 per cent by means of debentures and mortgage loans. Although most bank loans are technically short-term borrowing, in practice they are a major source of business finance and are here looked at as long-term borrowing. The table shows that shareholders are the major source of the long-term funds provided to companies. Shareholders provide capital when a company is first set up and the company may issue new shares from time to time as funds are needed, but new issues are not currently a major source of new funds for UK industry. In 1982, less than £1,000 million of the £30,000 new funds were raised through share issues. A much larger amount, £16,000 million, was generated internally by the companies. Of this, nearly £6,500 million was retained earnings. The rest is mainly depreciation allowances.

Table 6.1

Aggregated balance sheet of a group of large UK companies, 1982

		£ million	%
Current assets		122,600	
Less current liabilities		58,300	
Net working capital		64,300	43
Fixed assets		85,800	57
Net assets		150,100	100
Provided by:			
Bank loans	£27,200		
Long term debentures and mortgage loans	15,700		
Borrowing		42,900	29
Shareholders' equity		107,200	71
Total funds provided		150,100	100

The asset structure

The balance sheet in Table 6.1 is useful because it draws attention to the two elements of long-term needs: for working and long-term capital. On page 15 we described the asset structure as one of the major determinants of the cash flow cycle.

Working capital

The provision of basic working capital is a long-term need. Although part can be obtained from trade creditors, it is dangerous to place too much reliance on outside sources for the provision of working capital. Sufficient working capital must always be available to keep operations going and this cannot be guaranteed if it is all provided by outsiders.

Fixed assets

The more obvious long-term need is in providing fixed assets. These assets, such as plant equipment, buildings, land and so on involve massive outlays of cash. Their purpose is to provide the basic facilities of the business. The life of these assets is measured in years but the cash to buy them must be found at the start of that life.

The term 'fixed' refers to the relatively permanent nature of the asset, in contrast to the working capital assets which are constantly circulating and re-circulating in the operating cycle.

Looking at the long term, however, the term 'fixed' is misleading. The large UK companies have fixed assets of £85,800 million in their balance sheets, on which they allowed about £10,000 million in depreciation in 1982. But the companies put £30,000 million to use in that year of which about £25,000 million was spent on new fixed assets. So, fixed asset investment goes through a cycle of acquisition, use and replacement, too.

For a typical plant asset, there is a cash outflow when it is acquired. Then there is a long period of use. Finally, the asset is scrapped and sold off for what it will fetch. For the typical going concern, there are a number of investments in fixed assets which at any one time will be at different stages in their life. Every year some assets will be scrapped and sold off. Every year some new fixed assets will be acquired to continue, expand or support the changing nature of the business operations.

British American Tobacco (BAT) Industries spent £278 million on fixed assets in 1981 and this rose to £341 million in 1982. Despite the company's strong efforts to diversify, 49 per cent of the 1982 spending was on tobacco products but 25 per cent was on their retailing activities and 18 per cent on paper packaging and printing.

Imperial Metal Industries PLC spends much less on fixed assets, less than £30 million in 1982 and their spending fell 4 per cent in 1982. Even so, they increased spending on some of their products, like heat exchangers and as a result spending fell on other product groups, such as engineering (-18 per cent), metals (-14 per cent) and building (-13 per cent). This group is facing the problem that whilst tangible assets increased nearly 50 per cent from £229 million in 1977 to £338 million in 1982, the return fell from 16.5 per cent to 9.7 per cent. This is not necessarily bad management, even if it is bad business. The period was a difficult one for manufacturing industry.

Imperial Chemical Industries PLC spent £760 million on fixed assets in 1979 and this fell to £292 million in 1982. At the same time their return on assets fell from 16.4 per cent to 7.4 per cent.

Capital expenditure proposals

If you manage a successful going concern you should find that you are faced with periodic proposals for capital expenditure. There should be time to work out the implications of these proposals for your profitability and cash position and you should avoid hurried decisions based on 'hunch'.

You need to work out the effects of capital expenditure on cash flows very carefully because the normal pattern is that heavy initial outflows will be followed by a stream of smaller receipts extending over a period of years.

Net cash flow from operations

The future cash receipts should follow from the benefits to your business as a result of the capital spending. You are urged to spend on some proposals because they will equip your business to make and sell new products or enter new markets or expand your existing operations. You need to estimate carefully the net cash flow which will be added to your annual returns if you decide to go in for the new proposal. We looked at the use of the income statement for this purpose in Chapter 2. The main point is that you must confine your predictions to cash flows. Your gross receipts will be from the volume of sales at the predicted prices. From this must be deducted the cash payments for materials, labour and expenses. To be realistic, you must also deduct income, corporation or other taxes to which you are liable. Another important point is that you do not deduct depreciation from your cash receipts.

Life of the project

You should base your calculations on the economic life of an asset. You invest in the asset in order to sell a product or service. The question is, how long will you be able to continue selling that product or service or, more accurately, how long will your customers continue to buy it?

Your assets may be built to last 20 or 100 years, but if the market will only take the product for four years, then that is the economic life. In that time you need to get back your capital expenditure and sufficient extra to cover all your costs and leave you with a profit.

Types of project

Not all products involve you in making new products, improving designs and meeting expansion of demand. Some proposals for spending arise from the need to replace worn-out assets or to improve their efficiency. The wise manager should be wary of these. As far back as 1866, the First Lord of the Admiralty put his finger on the problem: 'If we must need keep up an old fleet, we cannot expect a new one too. We have plenty of ships which would have been very useful in 1846, but we have taken such care of them that we have had little to spare for the substitutes which present times require. Happy the nation which had no money ten years ago! That is what has sent the Americans so far ahead. Every sixpence of their expenditure has been on vessels of real and immediate efficiency'.

You should make sure that promises of efficiency improvement are realised and that the cash from improved sales or reduced costs will more than recoup your capital expenditure. Otherwise, spend your money on new ventures or keep it in the bank. Another category of capital spending is on welfare projects. In some cases, these arise out of statutory requirements and you have no choice about whether to heat your offices, take adequate safety precautions or provide sanitary facilities. From a cash point of view, the questions are: can you find the cash at the time when it is required? and what is the cheapest way to meet your obligations?

Some welfare projects do not offer you tangible returns which can be traced in cash. You may still consider them worthwhile. In that case, you must be sure that you can find the money and that you can afford to do without it.

Long-term data sheet

For long-term cash planning, then, you need to start with a data sheet with three sections. The long-term data sheet is similar to the short-term form but you will probably need to split it into sections because of the large amount of data.

Section 1   Capital expenditure

In this section you list the fixed assets which you will have to obtain at the start of the project. You need to estimate the cost and record the timing and conditions which will apply. You must also record the expected proceeds from disposal of the assets at the end of the economic life. An example is shown in Table 6.2.

Section 2   Working capital

In this section you list the various current assets you will require to support the project, including stock, trade debtors and cash reserves. You also need to estimate the funds you can obtain from trade and expense creditors. Then you can calculate the difference, which is the net working capital requirement. An example is shown in Table 6.3.

Section 3   Net cash flow from operations

In this section you calculate the volume and prices of sales for each year of the economic life, to get the gross receipts. Then you have to calculate the cash operating payments from the cash costs of materials expenses and taxes. Again you should note timing conditions and flexibility. An example is shown in Table 6.3.

Dyfed Hughes has proposed that J. B. Jones Ltd open a new factory on 1st January 1987 to assemble visual display units (VDUs). The building will cost £2.5 million, plant £1.5 million and equipment will cost £1 million. Dyfed estimates that 40,000 VDUs per year can be made and sold for £300 each. At the end of ten years, the equipment will be sold for £250,000 scrap and the building and plant are expected to bring in

Table 6.2

J.B. Jones Ltd – long-term proposal data sheet (Section 1)

Name of proposal: VDU Factory, Gwyned
Name of proposer: D. Hughes
Prepared by:
Date:

Item	Amount	Timing	Conditions and flexibility
	£		
Section 1			
Capital expenditure			
(i) Buildings: Site 7, Dragon Road, Gwyned		start on 1.1.86	
(a) Site clearance and foundations	200,000	1 month	Progress payments 90% on 1.1.86
(b) Main factory	1,700,000	8 months	(£2.25 million)
(c) Offices and administration	500,000	2 months	
(d) Landscaping, lighting and roads	100,000	1 month	
Total	2,500,000	12 months to build	
		6 months after completion	10% (£250,000) on 1.1.87. Contract already placed. Completion due 1.1.87.
(ii) Plant			
(a) Air conditioning	800,000	2 months	Installed after offices and administration building complete
(b) Compressed air	700,000	1 month	In factory when completed. Payment on 1.1.87
	1,500,000		
(iii) Equipment			
(a) Main chassis manufacture	350,000		First items can be installed after completion of factory. Should be paid for by 1.1.87
(b) Screenmaking	450,000		
(c) Minor components and assembly	200,000		
Scrap value 1997		Life 10 years	
Building and plant	1,000,000	Sold on 31.12.96	Estimate obtained from Theo D. Lite & Tape, Surveyors
Equipment	250,000		

£1m. On average, stocks will be 10 per cent of cost of sales, and debtors 5 per cent of sales turnover. A cash float will be maintained to keep a minimum balance of £500,000 plus 25 per cent of creditors. It is estimated that each VDU will cost £240 to assemble, of which £120 will be materials, parts and sub-assemblies, £60 labour, £10 administration and £20 overheads. Corporation tax will average 30 per cent of the profit. Creditors will average 10 per cent of annual cost of materials, parts and sub-assemblies. The results are shown in the data sheets in Tables 6.2 and 6.3 and the long-term budget in Table 6.4.

The long-term cash budget

We have already suggested you should draw up a long-term cash budget in a form which makes it suitable, also, for appraisal of the proposed spending. Table 6.4 shows a suitable form. It differs from the short-term cash budget in a number of ways.

You should not draw up your long-term budget for particular calendar dates. It is better to work on a time scale in which Time 0 is the reference point, that is, the time at which the capital facilities are completed and operations can begin. You can then work forward in calendar years although, by convention, you will usually conduct your appraisal of profitability on the assumption that all receipts and payments come in or go out at the end of the period.

Using a Time 0 reference means you can show the period during which the capital facilities are being prepared as negative time from Time 0, year −1, year −2 and so on. This format facilitates use of discounted cash flow appraisal (DCF) methods. You will see that £2.25 million of the building cost is shown as being paid in 1986 and £250,000 at Time 0 on 1st January 1987.

Once a project gets under way, you can enter actual dates and times for each period as shown in Table 6.4. Another feature of the long-term budget is that you should not make it cumulative, so you do not need to calculate the float.

For long-term planning and appraisal, it is better to work on the net cash outflow or inflow at the end of each year or at Time 0. If you are using DCF, it will then be easy to calculate the discounted value for each year. You will also notice that the long-term cash budget lists each item as an inflow or outflow. Do not use + and − signs until it is absolutely necessary, when you work out the net effect for each period. You will find it simpler.

A final point is that the example in Table 6.4 shows the kind of pattern we normally expect of proposals for capital expenditure, that is, a year or two of net spending, followed by some years of net receipts and, in the final year, additional receipts as fixed assets are sold off and working capital released. In practice, the patterns of cash vary enormously. In some cases, returns start low and increase, in others they start high and then decline. Yet others may require refurbishing of assets at an

Table 6.3

J.B. Jones Ltd – long-term

Name of proposal: VDU Factory, Gwyned
Name of proposer: D. Hughes

Item	Amount
Section 2	£
Working capital	
(a) Cash	
25% of £720,000 = £180,000	
Plus minimum 500,000	680,000
(b) Stocks	
10% of £240 × 40,000 =	960,000
(c) Debtors	
5% of £300 × 40,000 =	600,000
Current assets	2,240,000
(d) Creditors	
10% of £180 × 40,000 =	720,000
Net working capital	1,520,000
Section 3	
Net cash flow from operations	
(a) Sales	£12m
(b) Costs of sales:	
Materials, parts and sub-assemblies	4,800,000
Labour	2,400,000
Overheads	800,000
	400,000
Total costs	8,400,000
Operating profit	3,600,000
Corporation tax	1,080,000

intermediate stage, giving a dip in net receipts or even a negative cash flow.

Cash payback

Whether you consider our example a good investment or not depends on the method of appraisal you use. One method of appraisal which is proposal data sheet (Sections 2 and 3)

	Prepared by: Date:
Timing	Conditions and flexibility

Timing	Conditions and flexibility
March 1987	Production assumed to start in February
February – March	
March – April	2 months' credit terms
February – March	1 month term from suppliers
Annually	Price of £300 Sales 40,000 units
Annually	£120 per unit
Annually	£60 per unit
Annually	£20 per unit
Annually	£10 per unit
Total	£210 per unit
Annually	Sales of £12 million less costs £8.4 million 30% of operating profit

widely used, although it is also widely criticised, is the cash payback. This is the length of time in which the net cash returns from a project equal the initial cash investment. Where the net cash returns are at a uniform rate, as in our example, the calculation is:

$$\frac{\text{Initial cash investment}}{\text{Annual net cash returns}} = \text{payback in years}$$

Table 6.4

J.B. Jones – factory project cash budget, £ million

	Year −2 1985	Year −1 1986	Time 0 1.1.87	Year 1 1987	Year 2 1988	Year 3 1989	Year 4 1990	Year 5 1991	Year 6 1992	Year 7 1993	Year 8 1994	Year 9 1995	Year 10 1996	Year 11 1997
Cash inflows														
Sales:														
of products				12	12	12	12	12	12	12	12	12		
of plant and buildings													12	
of equipment													1	
Working capital released													.25	
Gross inflows	−	−		12	12	12	12	12	12	12	12	12	1.52 14.77	
Cash outflows														
Investment:														
building		2.25	.25											
plant			1.50											
equipment			1.52											
working capital				8.4	8.4	8.4	8.4	8.4	8.4	8.4	8.4	8.4		
Costs of products				1.08	1.08	1.08	1.08	1.08	1.08	1.08	1.08	1.08		
Corporation tax														
Gross outflows	−	2.25	3.27	9.48	9.48	9.48	9.48	9.48	9.48	9.48	9.48	9.48		
Net inflow + Outflow −	−	−2.25	−3.27	+2.52	+2.52	+2.52	+2.52	+2.52	+2.52	+2.52	+2.52	+2.52	+5.29	

Budgeting for long-term needs

For J. B. Jones, the total investment if £5.52 million and the annual net cash returns are £2.52 million after tax.

The payback is therefore:

$$\frac{£5,520,000}{£2,520,000} = 2.19 \text{ years}$$

This can be expressed in days or months by multiplying by 360 or 12, which gives a result of 789 days or 27 months.

Payback (also known as payout) tells you how soon you will get your money back if your predictions are correct. After that, you start making profits.

Long-term borrowing

Long-term borrowing is usually for periods of more than five years and is often in the form of a debenture or mortgage. An annual rate of interest is payable on the loan. The legal conditions in the debenture or loan document state the annual rate of interest payable whether it is to be paid monthly, quarterly, half-yearly or annually and the dates on which payments are to be made. The arrangements for repayment may provide for some flexibility. For instance, the balance sheets of ICI PLC at 31st December 1982 showed a total of £1,536 million in loans at rates of interest ranging from as low as 3½ per cent in Swiss francs to as high as 22¼ per cent. US dollar bonds of £232 million had repayment dates between 1983 and 2003, and rates from 8⅞ to 11 per cent. About one-third of the loans were wholly repayable within five years, so the company had £522 million to find for this purpose within the fairly short term. Clearly, a financing structure of this complexity must be carefully managed or disaster may follow.

In the UK and most other countries, the payment of interest is regarded as a business expense for tax purposes and the effect of this is that the cost of interest is reduced by the company's marginal tax rate.

If Eureka PLC has a 12 per cent loan of £800,000 and a marginal tax rate of 40 per cent, then the cost of the interest payments is:

Gross interest payable:	£
12% on £800,000	96,000
Less tax at 40%	38,400
Net cost of interest	57,600

Since the company is liable to pay the net cost of interest to the lender, the cash flow expense is £57,600, the net cost of interest.

Debentures are sometimes issued at a discount, for instance at a price of £97. This indicates that a unit of the debenture can be obtained for £97 but the debenture certificate will be made out for £100 and that £100 will eventually be repaid. The interest is also calculated on the nominal price of £100.

If J. B. Jones Ltd do not have the £5 million required for their new factory, they may decide to raise new finance. Suppose they are thinking of issuing 20,000 10 per cent debentures, 1994-97, at 98 and there are other issue costs of £260,000. The corporation tax rate is 30 per cent and interest is payable annually.

The net proceeds from the issue and annual costs will be as in Table 6.5.

Table 6.5

J. B. Jones Ltd – debenture issue on 1 January 1984

	£
Nominal value 20,000 @ £100 =	2,000,000
Issue price 20,000 @ £98	1,960,000
Less issue costs	260,000
Net proceeds of issue	1,700,000

	£
Annual interest costs £2m @ 10%	200,000
Less tax £200,000 × 30%	60,000
Net annual interest costs	140,000

The relevant cash flows will be as shown in Table 6.6.

This is a typical pattern for a loan. A large initial receipt is followed by a stream of payments which are terminated by a final interest payment and repayment of the capital.

At the end of March 1983, Marks and Spencer PLC had four debenture loans repayable after 5 years or more, at 1985/1990, 1989/1994, 1993/1998 and 1995/2000. The company stated that it planned to repay

Table 6.6

J.B. Jones Ltd – cash budget

	1984	85	86	87	88	89
Inflows						
Issue	1,700					
Outflows						
Interest	140	140	140	140	140	140
Capital repayment						

each loan at par during the later of the two years shown in each case.

The pattern of loan finance can vary but not all that much. Some loans work on a constant repayment in which the interest element is large at the start and then declines with the repayment of capital; conversely, small at the start and large at the end. Most mortgages work in this way.

Arrangements can be made for an interest 'holiday' for part of the loan period or for repayment of capital and accumulated interest.

Times interest covered

The purpose of a loan is to finance profitable investment. From a cash viewpoint, it is useful to compare the receipts from an investment with the payments on the money borrowed to finance that investment.

Take the case of J. B. Jones Ltd who are considering taking a loan of £1,700,000 which involves net interest payments of £140,000 a year for a minimum of ten years depending on when the company chooses to repay the debenture. This period is more or less the same as the life of the factory which they are proposing to build for £5 million. The factory will generate £2,400,000 net cash receipts annually. Comparing these we can calculate the number of times the interest is being earned each year:

$$\frac{\text{Net cash generated}}{\text{Interest charges}} = \text{times interest earned}$$

For J. B. Jones Ltd:

$$\frac{£2,520,000}{£140,000} = 18 \text{ times}$$

So, for every £1 of net interest, the project is generating £18. This is, in fact, a very high rate of cover compared to the loan interest. There should be no difficulties in meeting the interest payments each year.

If the forecast cash flows are reasonably realistic, things would have

for debenture issue, £'000

90	91	92	93	94	95	96	97
140	140	140	140	140	140	140	140
							2,000

to go very badly before J. B. Jones Ltd ahd difficulty in paying the interest.

In fact, there is so much more money expected in than is to be paid out under the ten-year loan that it would be better to consider shorter-term borrowing, which is often cheaper than long-term, anyway. Suppose £2m can be borrowed from a bank for 2 years at 8 per cent. The net cash cost of interest would be as in Table 6.7.

Table 6.7

J.B. Jones Ltd — bank loans

		£
Annual interest cost £2m × 8%	=	160,000
Less tax £160,000 × 30%	=	48,000
Net annual interest cost		112,000

This interest would be payable at the end of each of the first two years and the capital sum would then be due for repayment, also (Table 6.8).

Table 6.8

J. B. Jones Ltd

Bank	Payments	Receipts
	£	£
January 1984 loan		2,000,000
End of 1984 net interest	112,000	
1985 final interest and repayment	2,112,000	

The best way to consider the cash liability of these two propositions is to combine the receipts from the project with the payments on the loan in each case and calculate the cash float in the same way as in the short-term cash budget. It is only necessary to look at the earlier years.

It can be seen from Table 6.9 that there are ample funds to pay off the bank loan within two years and since the rate of interest on the short-term loan is also lower, the bank loan is to be preferred. You may well ask why any firm should borrow long-term when the long-term rates are often higher than the short-term. The simple answer is that if you are working on a tight cash margin, the long-term loan is less risky. If J. B. Jones were only expecting to sell 4,000 VDUs per year, the net cash flow would be £252,000, the long-term interest cover would fall to 1.8 times and the short-term loan would not be practical because there would be no way in which the company could repay the capital at the end of the two years.

Table 6.9
J.B. Jones Ltd – paying off a loan, £'000

	1984	85	86	87	88	89	90	91	92	93
Bank loan										
Opening float	0	2,408	2,816							
Add receipts	2,520	2,520	2,520							
Available cash	2,520	4,928	5,336							
Deduct payments	112	2,112	–							
Closing float	2,408	2,816	5,336 Plus £2,520 p.a. thereafter							
Debenture '84									1994 – 7	
Opening float	0	2,380	4,760							
Add receipts	2,520	2,520	2,520							
Available funds	2,520	4,900	7,280							
Deduct payments	140	140	140						2,140 (final)	
Closing float	2,380	4,760	7,140 Plus £2,380 p.a. thereafter							

Capital

The prime source of funds to any business is the investment of the owners. This is true whether the owners be shareholders, partners or a single person. Potential lenders usually want to see that the owners have sunk a substantial part of the necessary capital into the business first, before money is borrowed. Equally, most owners are reluctant to borrow too heavily.

Some owners never borrow but even those who do generally like to keep their borrowing within limits which can be easily managed. In our examples here we shall deal with the case of shareholders in a company but the general principles are equally applicable to the one-owner business and the partnership.

Contributed capital

The primary way in which owners invest capital in a business is by providing new capital. This is invariably the method used at the start of a business but it is sometimes used at later stages, too. At the time of writing a popular method of raising capital for companies is a 'rights issue'. Under this arrangement, existing shareholders are given the right to subscribe for new shares in some stipulated ratio to their existing holding.

For example, if J. B. Jones Ltd was originally formed in 1960 with 500,000 £1 ordinary shares the shareholders' capital contributed would be:

   500,000 £1 ordinary shares fully paid £500,000

If the company needed more capital in 1970, this could be raised by issuing more shares and they could do this by offering existing shareholders rights to subscribe for one share for every one held. If all the shares are taken up, the contributed capital would rise to 1,000,000 shares as follows:

    1,000,000 £1 ordinary shares fully paid   £1,000,000

Retained earnings

The secondary way in which shareholders invest in a business is when the directors retain earnings, that is, do not pay out profits as dividends. A large group of UK firms retained 25 per cent of their earnings in 1981 and 1982. Dividends and interest took about 30 per cent of earnings. If J. B. Jones Ltd earn £200,000 after interest and tax in the first year after formation and they pay a dividend of 10 per cent, the dividend will be £50,000 (10 per cent on £500,000 ordinary share capital). There will then be £150,000 of retained earnings and the shareholders' equity shown in the balance sheet will increase by that amount (Table 6.10).

Table 6.10

J.B. Jones Ltd – income statement 1960

	£
Earnings after interest and tax	200,000
Less 10% dividend	50,000
Retained earnings	£150,000

Balance sheet at end of 1960 (extract)

	£	£
Shareholders' equity – contributed capital	500,000	
Add retained earnings	150,000	
		650,000

Now, if J. B. Jones Ltd carry on the same rate of earnings for the next 20 years and the same dividend payment, the retained earnings will accumulate at £150,000 per year which is £3m over 20 years! The shareholders' equity will then appear in the balance sheet as £3.5 million (Table 6.11).

It may be noted in passing that although the £50,000 dividend will still be quoted as 10 per cent on £500,000 it has now declined to 1.4 per cent on the £3.5 million of capital invested in the business by shareholders.

Table 6.11

J. B. Jones Ltd – balance sheet at end of 1980 (extract)

Shareholders' equity		
	£	£
Contributed capital	500,000	
Add retained earnings	3,000,000	
		3,500,000

7
Credit management

If you, as a businessperson, accept a delay between the times you deliver goods or services and the time your customer pays, then you are granting trade credit.

Normally you give trade credit on open account, without a formal contract and without much thought. That is a mistake. Trade credit needs to be actively managed because it has a big impact on your cash needs.

UK stockbrokers Phillips & Drew (P & D) base their industry forecasts on a sample of companies representing all the sectors of British industry. Their statistics show that for industry as a whole trade creditors exceed trade debtors. In 1972, UK companies obtained 3 per cent of their assets by taking more credit than they gave. This proportion has risen steadily, up to 10 per cent in 1982, when it actually exceeded the amount borrowed from banks.

For individual firms, the trade credit position varies. Marks & Spencer owed £79 million to trade creditors, against trade debtors of £18 million at the end of 1983. That reflects the fact that they largely sell for cash. The debtors represent less than 1 per cent of sales. Cadbury-Schweppes had trade debtors and creditors of £137 million in 1978 but by 1982, creditors were £295 million and 23 per cent higher than trade debtors. ICI are one large company for which debtors of £1.5 billion exceeded creditors, but only by 8 per cent.

Large firms keep their trade creditors at a higher level than their trade debtors by squeezing suppliers for better terms on one side and dealers for early payment on the other. Many small firms have to give customers credit. This ties up their funds and squeezes cash liquidity.

Suppose your product sells for £100. Giving a month's credit will tie up £100 of capital for that period. If you get a month's credit from your supplier, the amount of credit you obtain depends on the proportion of bought-in materials and components in your product. If we suppose that is 60 per cent you will then obtain £60 of credit to offset the £100 you have given. The balance of £40 has to come from some other sources. If your sales total £120,000 you will on average grant £10,000 credit, obtain £6,000 and have to find £4,000 of extra capital. Admittedly part of that extra capital will be the profit which might be £10 per unit, £12,000 per year. In the first year £4,000, or one-third, will not be available for dividends or drawings by the owner.

A 1974 British Institute of Management report opened with the words: 'There is probably no more neglected area of financial management in the UK than credit control and management'. Readers are recommended to consult the *Credit Management Handbook* edited by H. Edwards and published by Gower for an authoritative introduction to the whole field. Here we shall concentrate on the significance of credit management for the management and forecasting of cash flows.

Why give credit?

From a cash point of view, there is a simple answer: if you don't have to, then don't.

Unfortunately most firms have no real choice. Trade credit is a way of increasing sales; it is a marketing device. To the customer, the attraction is obvious: take the goods or services now, pay later. To the supplier, the attraction is that giving credit helps to make a sale.

Other things being equal, the buyer will naturally place orders with firms which offer credit because it eases his or her cash flow problems. If things are not equal, customers will consider quality, delivery, price and credit terms, but not necessarily in that order. If the economy is booming and supplies are short, then credit will lose importance. Customers will buy wherever they can, even if they have to pay cash on the nail. In these circumstances the seller may be able to reduce or even eliminate trade credit. Slow-buying customers may find it difficult to have their orders filled. Cash customers will be given priority.

When the economy is in recession, supply exceeds demand and the seller is fighting to keep the order book full. Customers become more choosy and the availability of credit becomes more important. Of course, the quality, delivery and price are also important but profits will be squeezed and cash will be in short supply. Sellers will offer larger terms for settlements and as a result, accounts receivable rise. The seller now has some difficult problems in managing trade credit. As we saw from the P & D statistics, cash can be found by persuading suppliers to extend their credit and this may be more than enough to meet the rise in accounts receivable. The chances of bad debts also rise and if trade credit is not actively managed, cash flows will get out of control. The result may be disaster.

Credit management

The purpose of credit management is to maximise the overall profitability of trading. That sounds sensible, but it is rarely the way credit management is seen in practice.

Some firms simply grant credit to all and sundry without worrying too much until times turn hard and they suddenly find they are short of cash. Many firms have a system of credit control but this is often confined to taking up references on customers and then instituting procedures for collecting overdue accounts with the hope of avoiding bad debts.

Credit policy

Effective credit management must take a wider brief based on a clear credit policy. This policy must cover four aspects:

1. *Credit standards.* These define the maximum acceptable risk in granting credit.
2. *Credit period.* This is the time allowed for payment.
3. *Terms of trade.* These are the prices to be changed in relation to credit periods.
4. *Collection policy.* This lays down the procedures for making sure customers pay up on time.

Credit standards

There are several costs associated with defining the maximum acceptable risk when granting credit to a customer.

Default costs. First, there is the cost if the customer fails to pay. This can be fairly measured by the value of the sale lost. We supply goods priced at £2,000 and a customer eventually fails to pay. What you lose is the full £2,000 because it is more likely that, if you had refused credit, you would have sold the product to a customer who *would* have paid. Thus, the level of bad debts shows the default costs.

To evaluate the credit risk, managers normally consider the five C's:

Character is the probability that the customer fully accepts the obligation to pay and will faithfully try to honour obligations.

The cash *capacity* of the business is the available cash plus the level of additional funds which could be available from borrowing.

Capital, in the form of net owners equity or net worth of the business, is important because it determines the total level of borrowing which the firm can enter into and, therefore, influences the cash capacity.

The volume of assets which may be offered by the customer as security for borrowing is *collateral*. This is not normally used in trade credit.

The conditions, or the economic influence to which the customer's market is subject, affect your willingness to grant credit. The risk on debtors may be expressed as a probability of non-payment that is of a bad debt, and it is possible, then, to classify customers according to their risk class. Suppose we establish five classes then the associated risks of loss might be as shown in Table 7.1.

Table 7.1

Risk class	Probability of payment, %
1	100
2	99
3	98
4	95
5	90

These probabilities may change over time as credit conditions improve or deteriorate. Also, the rating of a particular customer may get better or worse.

From the level of debtors in each risk class, the expected value of cash receipts may be calculated by multiplying the money amount of sales by the probability of payment, as shown in Table 7.2.

Table 7.2

Risk class	Sales value	×	Probability		Expected value
	£		%		£
1	50,000		100	=	50,000
2	70,000		99	=	69,300
3	80,000		98	=	78,400
4	60,000		95	=	57,000
5	10,000		90	=	9,000
	270,000				263,700

Thus, although the face value of the debtors is £270,000, the realised value is probably going to be £263,700.

If the probabilities are drawn up by an experienced manager, they can give an expected value which is a much more reliable guide to future receipts than the face value of debtors. The probabilities are global factors which are easily applied to large sums. The alternative may be to wade through large numbers of debtors' accounts, deciding for each one whether it will be paid or not. Life rarely allows the time for such an exercise unless there are only a handful of debtors.

The idea of expected value can be used in cash forecasting, but in a slightly different form, as shown later.

Investigation costs. There is a cost of investigating credit worthiness before granting credit. In larger firms a credit manager with supporting staff may be employed and part of the costs of such staff will arise from their activities in credit investigations. Similarly, if you run your own business it will cost you time and money to manage credit.

This cost may be justified in two main ways. The first is that the level of ultimate collections can be improved because the risks of each type of business are known and an acceptable level established.

For example, by accepting a lower probability of payment, monthly sales can be increased, but expected value increases at a lower rate. Take the facts shown in Table 7.3.

Table 7.3

Risk class	Sales value, £'000	Probability, %	Expected value, £'000
1	50	100	50
2	70	99	69.3
3	80	98	78.4
4	60	95	57
5	10	90	9
6	20	80	16
7	30	70	21

A policy of offering credit to all comers would mean that £50,000 more sales could be made to customers in risk areas 6 and 7 but the expected value would only increase by £37,000. Put the other way round, by establishing the cut-off point at risk class 5, the credit manager saves a loss of £13,000 in bad debts.

Working capital cost. By extending credit, funds are tied up and more working capital must be found.

The amount of working capital depends on the level of credit sales authorised. For example, if only risk classes 1 to 3 are acceptable and the terms of credit are monthly, then the debtors at the end of each month will amount to £200,000. If the annual rate of interest is 12 per cent, then the monthly cost of working capital is £200,000 × 1 per cent = £2,000.

Credit period

The longer the time which you give customers to pay, the more debtors you will have. This may or may not be worthwhile. Suppose you can increase your monthly sales from £200,000 to £300,000 by allowing two rather than one months' credit. Debtors will rise to £600,000, an increase of £400,000 and at 12 per cent p.a., that will cost you £4,000 extra.

If, however, your profit rate on the increased sales is 10 per cent you will have an extra profit of £10,000, so you are £6,000 better off. The other factor is the probability of collection, which decides the level of default. If you increase sales you are pushed down the risk classes as shown in Table 7.3. You can obtain £200,000 of sales from the first three risk classes and the bad debts would only be £2,300. To get £300,000 of sales, you would need to go down through the risk classes and into class 7 and the penalty would be that the bad debts would rise by £11,000. Lengthening the credit period brings extra profit of £10,000 but, extra capital cost of £4,000 and extra bad debt losses of £11,000. Thus, you would be £5,000 worse off!

Terms of trade

Trade credit is normally on an informal basis so it is all the more important for you, as a seller, to lay down clearly when and how customers are to pay. There is a wide range of possibilities and you, the seller, must make clear to the buyer which ones apply to your mutual business. Cash settlement may be geared to delivery: cash with order (CWO), cash in advance (CIA), cash before shipment (CBS), cash on delivery (COD), net payment on delivery and cash next delivery (CND). Credit is geared to time after delivery, and may be weekly, half monthly, monthly and so on.

You need to be familiar with the terms advanced by your business so that you can make accurate cash forecasts. For instance, half-monthly credit may have a different meaning in different trades. It may mean that deliveries made in days 1–15 of one month are payable on one specified day in the following month and deliveries from day 16 on another specified date. Or it may mean what it says – all deliveries paid for after a half calendar month.

Many firms only send invoices for part of the month, say 20 days. This leaves a variable number of days during which queries are settled and overdue debtors chased up. For this purpose, payment may be required on specified days of the month, for instance, the 7th, 10th, 15th, 25th or last working day. Firms directly serving retail outlets require payment to the representative or van salesman for supplies delivered or ordered on the last call. Cash discounts may be allowed for prompt settlement, for instance 2 per cent/10 or M30 means the buyer may deduct 2 per cent if settling within 10 days. Otherwise the full amount is to be paid in 30 days. The basic effect of cash discounts on cash flows was dealt with in Chapter 3.

Collection policy

Collection policy is the set of procedures laid down for the collection of cash from customers, but clearly, the policy must incorporate decisions on the other factors, such as the credit policy, credit standards, credit periods and terms of trade. Also implicit in your policy is the amount of working capital you will have available and the level of sales and debtors which you can finance. The essential feature of collection is then a routine. An example is shown below:

Invoicing. Invoice to be sent within 24 hours of delivery.

Statements. Statements of accounts should be sent within five days of the month end.

First reminder. A first reminder should be made seven days after the statement.

Second reminder. The second reminder should be made 14 days after the statement.

Final reminder. The final routine reminder should be given 28 days after the statement.

The reminders are of increasing severity and the final reminder is merely the last *routine* reminder. Phone calls are better than letters. Thereafter, the account is regarded as overdue and will be followed up by phone or personal contact. Some of the overdue accounts will turn out to involve disputes and these are separately classified whilst efforts are made to settle differences.

If genuinely overdue accounts are not paid, the account should be passed to a more senior manager. Eventually, they may be handed on to a collection agency or solicitor.

Key factors in effective credit management

A survey of medium-sized companies in the UK showed that there were eight significant factors which combined together for effective credit management.

1 *Prompt despatch of invoices and statements.* Good firms get these off within three days.
2 *Standard collections procedures.* These procedures are used by 60 per cent of good firms and rigorously adhered to. Bad firms were constantly changing procedures.
3 *Delinquency.* Failure to pay on time resulted in stoppage of supplies and legal action by the effective firms, even though they faced tough competition.
4 *Evaluation of new customers.* Nearly 80 per cent of the effective firms invariably checked the credit standing of prospective customers with the bank, trade from sales or from agencies. Dun and Bradstreet was widely used.

5 *Review of customers' credit rating.* Over half of the good firms made regular reviews of how customers were performing on payments and nearly 85 per cent of them kept good records of the payments' history, manually or on computer.

6 *Performance measurement.* The good firms produced a number of key figures for credit control:

Days sales outstanding: (DSO) 95 per cent used
Aged debtors analysis: 95 per cent used
Cash collection targets: 63 per cent used

The use of these figures at the budgeting stage was lower but still significant for DSO and cash collection targets:

Days sales outstanding (DSO): 63 per cent
Aged debtors analysis: 16 per cent
Cash collection targets: 58 per cent

7 *Professionally qualified credit manager.* About 70 per cent of the good firms employed credit managers with accounting or chartered secretary qualifications. Strangely enough, only 4 per cent of the sample were members of the Institute of Credit Management.

8 *Departmental relations.* Nearly 70 per cent of the good credit management firms said that relations between sales and credit management departments were good, whereas 16 per cent of the poorly managing firms said it was 'adverse'.

Preparing a debtors' (cash collections) budget

Cash will be collected from sales after a time delay. Ideally, the time delay is laid down in the terms of credit but, in practice, the process is more complicated. Certain stages in the selling and collection prices can be identified.

Debtors

Sales are made on credit. As a result, trade debtors (accounts receivable) are recorded for the full amount of the sales, including VAT where applicable. When making annual budgets, the closing debtors will often be expressed as a percentage of sales for the year.

$$\frac{\text{Closing debtors}}{\text{Annual sales}} \times 100 = \% \text{ debtors to sales}$$

So, if Cramont Ltd expects to make sales in 1985 of £1,920,000 and the closing debtors are expected to be £326,400 then this can be expressed as a percentage. For Cramont Ltd:

$$\frac{£\ 326,400}{£1,920,000} \times 100 = 17\%$$

This is a convenient way of calculating working capital requirements. It will normally be used in conjunction with similar percentages for cash stocks and trade creditors.

Suppose the percentages for Cramont Ltd are 8 per cent cash, 17 per cent debtors, 25 per cent stocks, less 20 per cent trade credit, then the net working capital requirement is 30 per cent of sales for the year, as shown in Table 7.4. These percentages can be used to gauge the effect of different levels of sales on working capital, for example, if Cramont Ltd normal sales rise from £1,920,000 to £2,160,000 the working capital requirements would rise proportionately, from £576,000 to £648,000, as shown in Table 7.4.

Table 7.4
Cramont Ltd forecast

		£ (a)	£ (b)
Sales		1,920,000	2,160,000
Working capital	%	£	£
Cash	8	153,600	172,800
Debtors	17	326,400	367,200
Stock	25	480,000	540,000
	50	960,000	1,080,000
Less trade creditors	20	384,000	432,000
Working capital	30	576,000	648,000

This is a useful approach when the firm is considering the level of sales for which sufficient working capital can be found.

Days' sales outstanding

For effective credit control it is more useful to express the debtors in terms of the number of days' sales which they represent. The days' sales outstanding (DSO) can be obtained by multiplying the number of days in the period by the proportion of debtors to sales. In the case of Cramont Ltd, the proportion of debtors to sales is 17 per cent, so DSO is 108 days in both cases (0.17×360). You may well ask what is the advantage of using DSO rather than the percentage. The answer is that DSO is most useful when sales change.

Annual sales are made over the whole year: the closing trade debtors represent the amounts not yet paid by customers for sales in the closing weeks of the year. For Cramont Ltd, the DSO of 62 days represent two months' credit taken — or does it?

Credit management

The answer is, only if sales are at a uniform rate throughout the year. If sales are rising, the DSO will show that the same level of debtors represents better credit management than if sales are steady or falling. Take Cramont Ltd as an example. Sales figures for the last three months could be steady, rising or falling. Whilst the percentage debtors to annual sales would be the same, the DSOs would differ. Suppose the sales patterns are as shown in Table 7.5.

Table 7.5
Cramont Ltd

		£'000		
	No. of days	October 30	November 30	December 30
Steady sales		160	160	160
Rising sales		150	180	200
Falling sales		150	140	130
Closing debtors (all cases) £326,400				

In each case, working back from the end of December, the sales represented in debtors differ and, therefore, the number of days outstanding (DSO) differ, as in Table 7.6.

Table 7.6
Cramont Ltd

	Steady	Rising	Falling
Debtors represented by	£'000	£'000	£'000
December	160	200	130
November	160	126.4	140
October	6.4	–	56.4
Sales equal to debtors	326.4	326.4	326.4

The number of days' sales represented in each incomplete month is calculated:

$$\frac{\text{Sales in month}}{\text{Sales required (to equal debtors)}} \times 30 = \text{No of days' sales}$$

Notice that the year is assumed to have 12 months of 30 days each. The calculations for each condition are given in Table 7.7.

Table 7.7

Cramont Ltd

Steady / October	$\dfrac{6.4}{160}$	× 30	=	1.2 (say 1 day)
Rising / November	$\dfrac{126.4}{180}$	× 30	=	21 days
Falling / October	$\dfrac{56.4}{150}$	× 30	=	11.28 (say 11 days)

The DSOs are as shown in Table 7.8.

Table 7.8

Cramont Ltd – days' sales represented by debtors (DSO)

	Steady	Rising	Falling
December	30	30	30
November	30	21	30
October	1	–	11
Days' sales outstanding (DSO)	61	51	71

On a constant amount of closing debtors and annual sales, the DSO discloses a very different picture of credit management. The firm with rising sales has a low 51 DSO and is more in control than the other two firms, especially the firm with falling sales and a DSO of 71. At the planning stage, the annual sales figure can be turned into a sales per day figure and this can then be used to calculate the debtors at the end of each period on the planned DSO.

DSO expresses the credit terms and can be calculated from the proportion of debtors outstanding for each period, multiplied by the number of days outstanding.

For example, if 10 per cent of debtors pay within 30 days, 40 per cent within 60 days and 50 per cent within 90 days, the calculation would be:

$$
\begin{aligned}
.1 \times 30 &= 3 \\
.4 \times 60 &= 24 \\
.5 \times 90 &= \underline{45} \\
\text{DSO} &= \underline{72} \text{ days}
\end{aligned}
$$

Don't worry about the different number of days in the month: treat them all as having 30 days.

Credit management

For instance, annual sales of £1,920,000 represent sales per day of £53,330, and the budgeted debtors for the last three months of the year on a DSO of 60 would be £320,000 each month.

However, experience may show that at certain times of year DSO will rise or fall, in which case a different DSO may be used for each month, giving a different level of debtors.

Table 7.9

Cramont Ltd

	October	November	December
		£'000	
Sales	160	160	160
Debtors	347	373	400
DSO	65	70	75

If Cramont Ltd DSO tends to rise towards the year end, the budget might look as in Table 7.9. Control would be based on the comparison of actual DSO to planned DSO because this gives a better insight into the position. For example, what are we to make of the figures for December shown in Table 7.10.

Table 7.10

Cramont Ltd

	October	November	December
		£'000	
Budgeted sales	160	160	160
Actual sales	160	170	160
Budgeted debtors			400
Actual debtors			410
Budgeted DSO			75

Superficially, sales were on budget for December, but actual debtors were higher than the amount budgeted. Does this imply bad credit management? We can answer a firm 'No' to this question by calculating the actual days' sales outstanding:

	Days	Sales
		£
December	30	160
November	30	170
*October	15	80
Amount of debtors		410

$$*\text{October DSO} = \frac{80}{160} \times 30 = 15 \text{ days}$$

The DSO is 75, exactly as planned. The debtors are higher because of the higher sales in November.

Cash discount

A proportion of debtors pay promptly in order to take advantage of cash discounts. This fact affects the amount of cash we can actually expect to collect from the debtors. The more effective the cash discount is in encouraging debtors to pay early, the more serious the effect on cash flow. At the end of each period, therefore, it is advisable to calculate the amount which will be lost. This can be done:

Amount of debtors × proportion taking cash discount × % cash discount = loss due to cash discount

If Cramont Ltd expect 40 per cent of debtors to take advantage of a cash discount of 5 per cent/10 days, then the budgeted cost of the discount will be as shown in Table 7.11.

Table 7.11

Cramont Ltd

	October	November	December
Budgeted debtors	342,000	368,000	395,000
Less cost of cash discount	6,840	7,360	7,900
Net cash from debtors	335,160	360,640	387,100

The percentage cost is:

Proportion taking discount × percentage discount allowed = percentage cost of cash discount

In the example for Cramont Ltd:

.4 × .05 = .02 (i.e. 2%)

For forecasting purposes, this may be expressed as a 98 per cent probability of collecting the debtors eligible for cash discount. For example, debtors not yet outstanding for 10 days amount to £65,280. Cramont Ltd expect 60 per cent to claim a 10 per cent cash discount then the percentage cost of cash discount is .6 × .1 = .06, i.e. 6 per cent and the probability of collecting the amount is 1.00 − .06 = .94. The expected value of these debtors is then £65,208 × .94 = £61,295. The key figure here is the proportion of debtors expected to claim cash discount. If it is estimated by an experienced person after careful study of past experience, it can be surprisingly accurate.

The ageing schedule

Debtors pay their accounts at various times, according to their circumstances and the energy with which their suppliers enforce the terms of trade. Those debtors who still have time to pay according to the terms of trade are current. Those who have taken credit beyond the reminder times are overdue. As the time taken by the customer rises, so do the risks of non-collection. For this reason you should prepare an ageing schedule of debtors. The schedule is prepared for each individual customer and these are totalled. Both forms are useful. An ageing schedule for Cramont Ltd is shown in Table 7.12.

Table 7.12

Cramont Ltd – debtors' ageing schedule

	Total	\multicolumn{5}{c}{Days outstanding}
		0–10	11–30	31–60	61–90	91 and over
	£	£	£	£	£	£
Debtors at 31.12.1984	326,400	65,289	81,600	114,240	39,170	26,110
Percentage		20%	25%	35%	12%	8%
Probability of collection		.94	1.00	1.00	.98	.90
Expected value	319,022	61,295	81,600	114,240	38,387	23,500

The figure in expected value may be useful in assessing the cash capacity at a particular moment in time. Cash capacity was earlier defined as cash or equivalent plus borrowing power. The expected value of debtors could be added to other monetary resources as a cash equivalent.

The debtors' ageing schedule is useful in credit management, especially if the percentage of debtors outstanding in each period is carefully monitored. An individual schedule for each customer is used to identify particular invoices which have not been paid and every effort made to collect these. Customers who fail to pay after 60 days should have further supplies stopped.

Whilst the ageing schedule is not directly used in cash forecasting it can be an important influence on the collection rate.

Overdue and disputed accounts

In theory, any account which has been outstanding for longer than the period allowed in the credit terms is overdue. For instance, if we assume that the terms of trade of Cramont Ltd are 10/10 per cent or M30, that is, 10 per cent cash discount if paid within 10 days or net invoiced amount after 30 days, then the overdue debtors shown in Table 7.12 total £179,520 (114,240 + 39,170 + 26,110) which is 55 per cent.

On average, debtors very rarely conform to the terms of trade, so it may be more useful to base your calculation of overdues on the planned DSO, which would give £65,280 (39,179 + 26,110) in the example, i.e. 20 per cent.

It is the *proportion* overdue that is of most concern for credit management, rather than the absolute amount although you must bear in mind that a rise in the amount will require working capital support, so from a cash planning point of view it is the absolute figures which will be used.

In considering overdues, you should separate out those accounts which are in dispute. It is not uncommon for a small proportion of accounts to give rise to disputes about whether the goods invoiced were actually delivered, what their quality and condition was, and so on. There is no point in trying to collect these amounts until the dispute has been thoroughly dealt with and, in most cases, settled amicably. It may be possible to establish norms for disputed accounts, too, which would give a probability of eventual receipt of the amounts invoiced and, thus, an expected value.

Bad debts

Almost inevitably some accounts turn into bad debts. In some cases this will be after they have been in dispute and in others it will be after they have been overdue and all collection efforts fail. All the procedures of credit management which we have discussed are designed to avoid bad debts, but not absolutely. It might be possible to avoid bad debts entirely by restricting credit to A1 firms or by trading entirely for cash, but the penalty could be the loss of potential sales. We have already suggested that a better policy is to identify the level of risk of bad debts which is acceptable in relation to the sales which can be achieved. This does not mean that you should adopt a supine attitude to doubtful debts! Whatever level of risk you use during credit appraisal or in planning cash receipts, you should still make every effort to collect all debts when they become due and, with increasing vigour, if overdue.

Predicting cash flows from sales

The best way you can predict the timing of cash which will flow from sales is to use a data sheet on which is calculated the proportions of cash which will result from sales in each period. These proportions can then be applied to the sales for each period to show the cash receipts in each

Credit management

period and also the debtors outstanding. Table 7.13 is a suitable data sheet. Each item is listed in a logical sequence and against each columns are used to show:

> (i) *Proportion.* This is the percentage of sales for the first two calculations and of credit sales for all others.
> (ii) *Calculations.* This shows how the proportions are used, that is the figure to which the proportion is applied.
> (iii) *Period.* This column identifies the period in which a collection will occur or a loss will be recognised.
> (iv) *Example value.* There is no need to have this column once you are familiar with the calculations. Just check each item on the sheet.

Table 7.13

Data sheet for credit budgeting

Budget period   Prepared by:
                         Date:

	(i) Pro. %	(ii) Cal.	(iii) Period (days)	(iv) Example value £
Item				
A Sales			0–30	1,250
B Cash sales	20	A×B	0	250
C Credit sales	80	A×C	See D–K	1,000
	100			1,250
Credit sales analysis				
D Taking cash discount	20	C×D	0–10	200
E Paying in month 1	40	C×E	11–30	400
F Paying in month 2	30	C×F	31–60	300
G Paying in month 3	5	C×G	61–90	50
Proportion collected	95			950
Losses Rate				
H Cash discount 5% × 20% =	1%	D×H=I		
I Cash discount cost	1%	C×I	0–10	10
J Disputes	1.5%	C×J	31–60	15
K Bad debts	2.5%	C×K	61–90	25
Proportion lost	5%			50
Summary				
L Collections				
During month 1	60%	D+E	0–30	
During month 2	30%	F	31–60	
During month 3	5%	G	61–90	
Debtors				
M At end of month 1	39%	C−(D+E+I)		
N At end of month 2	7.5%	M−(F+J)		
P At end of month 3	0%	M−(G+K)		

A Sales

This is the starting value for all subsequent calculations. It is the total sales in a period — £1,250 in the example.

B Cash sales

The proportion, B, of total sales made for cash. The value is obtained by multiplying A × B. In the example 1,250 × .2 = £250. This amount will be collected as sales made.

C Credit sales

This is the balance of total sales, and the value is obtained from A × C. In the example 1,250 × .8 = £1,000. Obviously, B and C must equal A. D to K are all calculated as proportions of the credit sales.

D Customers taking cash discount

This is the proportion of customers expected to pay in time to take advantage of cash discounts, if offered. The value is obtained from C × D. In the example £1,000 × .2 = £200. This is the net cash collected from customers. The cost of the discount is calculated in H and I under the losses, below.

In the period column enter the period within which the payment must be made to claim the discount. In the example it is 0–10 days.

E Paying in month 1

This is the proportion of customers who pay in month 1, even though they do not claim cash discount. The value is obtained from C × E in the example 1,000 × .4 = £400. The payment period will be the rest of month 1 after the cash discount limit — in the example 11–30 days.

F and G Paying in months 2 and 3

You may need further items of payments spread over more than 3 months. In each case the value is obtained by C × F; C × G and so on; in the example £1,000 × .3 = £300; £1,000 × .05 = £50. Items D to G, or further if longer payment periods are experienced, give the total proportion of debtors collected. These, together with the losses must account for 100 per cent of credit sales.

Losses

In this section, each type of loss must be listed and the basis of calculation worked out. The specimen lists three types of losses commonly experienced.

H and I Cash discounts

The rate of discount multiplied by the proportion of debtors taking advantage of it gives the cost of the discount as a proportion of the debtors, i.e. $D \times H = I$. In the example, $20\% \times 5\% = 1\%$.

This factor, I, is then multiplied by the total creditors to give the value: $C \times I =$ expected loss. In the example, $1,000 \times 1\% = £10$. This cost is incurred in the first ten days.

J Disputes

This is the expected loss on disputed accounts, as a proportion of total debtors, so that $C \times J =$ expected loss. In the example, $£1,000 \times 1.5\% = £15$. The timing of this loss will depend on your circumstances. The example assumes it will occur in the second month.

K Bad debts

This is the expected loss from debtors which turn out to be uncollectible, i.e. $C \times K =$ expected loss. In the example, $1,000 \times 2.5\% = £25$. This loss is usually recognised in the final credit period on the assumption that all efforts to collect are made before the loss is admitted. Arguably, the loss occurs when the credit is granted to a bad customer but if we knew that at the time we wouldn't grant credit, anyway! Again, the proportions lost should be totalled and checked to make sure 100 per cent of the sales on credit is accounted for either as collections or as losses.

Summary

The final section of the data sheet summarises the data to show the proportional collections and debtors, by period.

L Collections

Remember to add the debtors taking cash discount (D) to those paying in month 1 but not taking discount (E) to get the total proportion collected in month 1, i.e. $D + E =$ total collected in month 1. In the example $20\% + 40\% = 60\%$. Otherwise, the proportions are those calculated above.

Notice that the losses are ignored in this method. If the proportion and timing of losses is significant, then sections D to G should account for 100 per cent of the credit sales. The net collections would then be these proportions less the losses in each period. If this method were used, the calculations in the example would be as shown in Table 7.14.

M & N Debtors

The outstanding debtors are the proportion of credit sales which have

Table 7.14

	Expected collections %		Losses %		Net collections %
D	21.0	− I	1.0	=	20
E	40.0		−	=	40
F	31.5	− J	1.5	=	30
G	7.5	− K	2.5	=	5
	100%	−	5%	=	95%

not yet been collected less any losses which have been recognised. Whilst sales collections occur in a constant stream a debtors' figure is related to a particular moment in time. The data sheet shows how to calculate the amounts at the end of each month.

Starting from the sale, debtors are increased by the full sales value. In the cash discount period the value is reduced by the amounts collected *plus* the cash discounts allowed, i.e. $C - (D + E + I) = M$. In the example, $100\% - (20\% + 40\% + 1\%) = 39\%$. The next period starts where the first ended, and the proportion of debtors outstanding is reduced by the proportion collected plus any losses recognised, i.e. $M - (F + J) = N$. In the example, $39\% \ (30\% + 1.5\%) = -7.5\%$. Similarly for each subsequent period, i.e. for the period: $N - (G + K) = P$. In the example, $7.5\% - (5\% + 2.5\%) = 0\%$.

Preparing the cash forecast

Using the data assembled, the preparation of cash collections budget is straightforward. Table 7.15 is an example.

Table 7.15

Cash collections budget for November and December

		% of sales	% of credit sales		August	September	October	November	December
							£'000		
1	Sales	100			175	187.5	200	225	250
2	Credit sales	80		100	140	150	160	180	200
3	Collections		Month 1	60	84	90.0	96.0	108.0	120.0
4			Month 2	30		42	45.0	48.0	54.0
5			Month 3	5			7.0	7.5	8.0
6				95					
7	Credit sales collected						148.0	163.5	182.0
8	Cash sales collected		20		35	37.5	40	45	50
9	Total	100%					168.0	208.5	232

Credit management

The aim is to prepare the collections budget for October, November and December, as shown in Table 7.15.

Taking the sales for each month from August to December on line 1, the proportion of credit sales is calculated on line 2, for each month. The cash sales can be calculated now, although the figures are entered on line 8.

Notice that the example gives columns for showing the percentages, first of sales and then of credit sales, purely as a cross-check from the data sheet. On line 3, the percentage of credit sales which will be collected is shown, in the example 60 per cent, and this is then applied to the credit sales figures for each month. In the example, the amounts rise from £84,000 in August to £120,000 in December.

The next line, 4, is staggered by a month. Thus, 30 per cent of August credit sales, £42,000, is collected in September. Similarly, line 5 is staggered a further month, showing that 5 per cent of August sales, £7,000, is collected in October, and so on, until each period is covered. Thus, we need sales figures for August and September if we are to forecast the collections from credit sales in October. On line 9, the total of collections in each month is obtained from adding lines 3−8.

Debtors and days sales outstanding (DSO)

A schedule showing the expected level of debtors at each month end can be prepared from the sales data and the data sheet for credit budgeting. Table 7.16 shows the results for the example.

Table 7.16
Debtors at month end

	%	August	September	October	November	December
Sales on credit		140	150	160	180	200
Outstanding at						
end of month 1	39		58.5	62.4	70.2	78
month 2	7.5		10.5	11.25	12.0	13.5
month 3	0		−	−	−	−
	Total		69	73.65	82.2	91.5
Days sales outstanding (DSO)				14	14	14

It will be seen that the DSO is constant at 14. This reflects the application of standard credit expectations to the sales figures:

	% of debt outstanding	×	no. of days	=	days sales outstanding
Month 1	39	×	30	=	11.7 days
Month 2	7.5	×	30	=	2.25 days
					13.95
					14 days app.

8
Cash control of projects

F. L. Harrison defines a project as 'a non-routine, non-repetitive, one-off undertaking, normally with discrete time, financial and technical performance goals'. Readers who are interested in the management of projects are recommended to read Mr Harrison's book *Advanced Project Management* (also published by Gower).

Examples of projects are the development of an aircraft or weapons system, the construction of oil and chemical plants, the building of bridges, research into and development of new technology, designing and manufacturing a heating and ventilation system, putting on an exhibition, promoting a pop concert, or launching a new product. What projects have in common is that each venture is, to a large extent, unique. True, projects could not be undertaken if the skills to work on them were not available, but projects are not routine, repetitive activities. There is always some new skill, knowledge or material which must be developed or, at minimum, a new way of combining existing skills if the project is to be successful. For this reason, it is difficult to predict what a project will cost and when it will be completed. In one case, a new hospital was predicted to cost £11 million and to take two years to build. It actually took four years to build and cost more than £50 million. That is not an isolated example.

One way in which the uncertainty on the time required and cost of projects can be handled is to identify the stages through which each project will pass. Six can be identified.

Project development and preliminary engineering

This stage carries out a fairly broad, but careful analysis of the likely project design. For this, some preliminary engineering would be done so that a broad idea of the work to be done in later stages can be obtained. On this are based calculations of likely cost and resources needed to complete by target date. Fairly substantial allowances are made for contingencies. For instance, if the client's completion date is 31 December 1987, commencement on 1 January 1985, the estimates of resources needed might be drawn up on the basis of completion by 30 June 1987, thus allowing two-and-a-half, rather than three years for the work and giving a time allowance for contingencies of six months. This earlier completion might automatically push up costs, but suppose the estimated costs were then £10 million, a further allowance for cost overruns of 20 per cent might be allowed, giving an estimated cost of £12 million.

On projects costing millions, this stage may well cost hundreds of thousands and any particular project might not be proceeded with. If possible, the costs of abortive projects will be recovered from the successful ones or charged against profit, which amounts to the same thing.

Bidding and contract negotiation

The price bid for any contracts must depend on the state of the opposition, how desperately the work is needed and the likely costs. In the long run, the prices obtained should be sufficient to recover all costs including unsuccessful tenders, administration and overheads and to leave a satisfactory margin of profit. In the short run a low price may be bid to obtain work to keep the organisation intact or to exclude competitors but a low price needs to be compensated for when a boom comes along by setting high prices which partially recover past losses or provide for possible future losses.

In preparing the final bid, the tenderer will want to negotiate on various aspects of the contract which can have a considerable effect on the final cost. These negotiations could be concerned with the precise siting of a power station, the use of new materials in place of traditional iron or steel, the methods of fabrication or assembly, the proportion of work to be done off site and the standards of performance. A small change in specification can have a dramatic effect on costs and, therefore, price. For example Biddle and Weekes PLC construct chemical plants. On average, they obtain 25 per cent of the work they tender for and the cost of preparing a tender is £100,000. Allowing for contingencies, the cost of construction of a plant for Hanlon Chemical Ltd is estimated at £12 million, and a 10 per cent profit margin is aimed for. The target tender price would be as in Table 8.1. The target tender price is a reference point. If work is in short supply, a minimum tender of £10 million would leave no cover for contingencies, tendering costs and profits. If work is plentiful, a price of £15 million might be asked.

Table 8.1

Biddle & Weekes PLC – target tender price for Hanlon Chemicals Ltd

	£
Estimated cost	10,000,000
Plus contingencies	2,000,000
Plus tendering costs	400,000
Plus target profit 10% on £12 million	1,200,000
Target tender price	13,600,000

Engineering design

At this stage, the detailed engineering design is done and drawings produced, preferably in the sequence in which they will be used in later stages. Attention should be given to designing to cost so that the project meets required performance objectives at or below the predetermined cost. This stage of the project should considerably reduce the uncertainty about the cost and completion time of the later stages.

Purchasing and procurement

Once the engineering designs have been completed, the necessary materials, parts, components and sub-assemblies can be ordered from suppliers. Orders may also be placed for various services. As well as meeting cost objectives, purchasing must meet delivery dates, arrange for inspection and control of materials on site and progress chase suppliers' commitments.

This stage of a project feeds forward to the previous stage since realistic estimates and designing to cost must be based on up-to-date information on suppliers and sub-contractors.

Construction and manufacture

This is the key stage in which the project is made in accordance with the preliminary plans and the actual conditions met on site. Good planning in the previous stages will minimise uncertainty, leaving site managers to concentrate attention on unexpected variations in site conditions, weather and so on. A net work diagram or bar chart may have been developed for use in the monitoring progress, with critical path analysis. These will show the relationships between various activities, and site management requires detailed effective knowledge of these.

There is often a sequence in which materials arrive on site and there is a gradual build-up of labour and efficiency. Then, as completion approaches, there is a tendency for efficiency to fall as labour leaves and those remaining pace the work to bridge the gap between projects. Delays may be very costly in lost efficiency but also in cash terms because the bulk of the capital cost is tied up in the project and is incurring interest charges or loss of profits.

Completion and commissioning

As far as possible plant should be commissioned in stages, as it is completed. This may allow work to be certified and interim payments of cash to be made by the client. If not, the cash flow implications are considerable because all the costs of construction are incurred and any delay in commissioning leads to high interest charges. A project costing £12 million at a time when interest charges are 20 per cent per annum incurs a charge of £2,400,000 per annum, which is £6,575 per calendar day, or £46,027 per week.

If Biddle & Weekes PLC complete a chemical plant at a cost of £12 million for which they have agreed a tender price of £13 million, then six months' delay in payment will wipe out their profit through interest charges on the expended cost alone.

Cash forecasting on projects

Cash forecasting for projects is concentrated on forecasting the amount and exact timing of payments. As these accumulate, so will the cash tied up in the project. In some cases, there may be interim receipts from the client based on a certificate of the amount of work completed. The value of work certified is based on the value of the work to the client but the full amount is usually reduced by a percentage which is retained by the client until final completion. Usually the contractor will need to provide sufficient cash to meet the differences between payments and receipts. It is rare for these receipts to exceed cash at any stage, but it is not uncommon for contractors to fail because they have run out of cash partway through a project.

Forecasting project cash expenditures

In project management, the estimates for cash expenditures can be obtained in two ways and each may be used at the appropriate stage.

Analysis of global estimates

An estimate of cash expenditure can be obtained from the estimates of total cost if these are analysed into the sequential stages of the project. This method is particularly useful at the project development and preliminary engineering stage. Indeed, at that stage it is the only method which can be used, but it can be used throughout the project, and especially in bidding and contract negotiation.

Synthesis of detailed estimates

An estimate of cash expenditure can be built up from the analysis of work packages and activities which have yet to be performed. This method is particularly useful at the closing stages of the project when management will usually conduct a detailed survey of the work required to completion, as a means of expediting completion, commissioning and final cash settlement. This method is also useful at the engineering design, purchasing and procurement and all stages of construction and manufacture when many diverse contributions may be made to the project from various departments, such as purchasing, design and engineering and from sub-contracts both on and off the site. At these stages, work may get out of sequence and the project manager will be alert to the dangers of loss of co-ordination and slippage in key work. He must also closely monitor the cash flow in case that, also, slips badly and begins to escalate demands for capital.

Contingency allowances

Having made an allowance in the costs for the unforeseeable — the contingency allowance — how should this be allowed for in the cash forecasts? The most conservative approach would be to assume that all contingency money would be required as soon as the project gets under way. The cash would then be available to the site manager, to be drawn on as required and the calculation of maximum cash need would allow for the worst possible situation.

An alternative is to allow for contingencies as a percentage of expenditures, as they are incurred. The effect of this is that the contingencies allowance builds up as the project proceeds. If it is not drawn upon, the full amount would have accumulated by the end of the project. A third possibility is to leave the contingency allowance out of the cash forecasts, so that the cash budget shows the demand for cash under normal circumstances. Then, any contingency would have to be provided from another budget.

The method used may depend on the management style of the firm and the extent to which site managers are empowered to handle contingencies. It may also depend on the relative importance of the project. A large firm might have a number of projects under way at any one time, a small firm only one. From a purely financial point of view, if contingency allowances are centralised in the hands of the treasurer, the financial costs to the firm will be minimised. Of course, this may not minimise other costs.

Certified work and retention money

The work certified may be calculated in various ways. First, the *global estimate method* is one in which an expert estimates the percentage of the final work completed and allocates the value accordingly. Second, the *synthetic method* is based on an analysis of the tasks completed. The value put on each task reflects the proportion of estimated costs which it represents. However, it should be noted here that the estimator responsible for certifying the work is working for the client and will not necessarily have access to the cost records and estimates of the contractor. Indeed, in Defence contracting the Government Inspector certifying the work may be working on a formula which bears little relationship to the costs of the contractor. The contractor's cash forecasts must be based on the value which the client is expected to put on the work, not on his own costs.

As an example of forecasting based on global figures Webb Builders are tendering for the building of a factory outside Bournemouth which they estimate will take 16 weeks to build. The total costs and tender price are estimated to be as in Table 8.2.

Table 8.2

Webb Builders – factory contract

	£
Materials	100,000
Labour	220,000
Site management	80,000
Contingencies	40,000
Estimated cost	440,000
Target profit	44,000
Tender price	£484,000

Materials will go on to site at the rate of £10,000 per week for the first ten weeks. Labour will be £10,000 for the first four weeks and £15,000 per week thereafter. The site management services will cost £5,000 per week.

The client accepts the tender price of £484,000 and agrees to make an interim payment of the value of work certified less retention of 10 per cent at the end of each four-week period, with the retention monies paid at the end of a further 12 weeks. It is expected that the value of work certified will be:

week	4	25%
	8	45%
	12	60%
	16	100%

In preparing the cash budget, the receipts can be calculated as follows (Table 8.3).

Table 8.3

	Week 4	8	12	16	Total
Proportion certified	25%	20%	15%	40%	
	£	£	£	£	£
Value (proportion of £484,000)	121,000	96,800	72,600	193,600	484,000
Less 10% retention	12,100	9,680	7,260	19,360	48,400*
Cash to be received	108,900	87,120	65,340	174,240	435,600

*To be received at end of week 28.

The cash budget is shown in Table 8.4. The cash flows will be altered if the contingency allowance is included. Allowing the full £40,000 at the start increases the payments to £140,000 and results in a net deficit throughout, until the final payment is received, whereas allowing it as a percentage of cost spreads the £40,000 over the full period of building (Table 8.5).

Table 8.4

Webb Builders – factory contract, cash budget

Weeks	1–4	5–8	9–12	13–16	17–24	25–28
	£	£	£	£	£	£
Payments						
Materials	40,000	40,000	20,000	–		
Labour	40,000	60,000	60,000	60,000		
Site management	20,000	20,000	20,000	20,000		
Total payments	100,000	120,000	100,000	80,000		
Less receipts	108,900	87,120	65,340	174,240		48,400
Net payments/ receipts	+8,900	-32,880	-34,660	+94,240		
Cash float						
surplus	+8,900			+35,600	35,600	84,000
deficit		-23,180	-58,640			

Table 8.5
Webb Builders – factory contract

Allowance for contingency	Weeks					
	1–4	5–8	9–12	13–16	17–24	25–28
(a) Allowed at start	-40,000					
Cash float						
surplus						+44,000
deficit	-31,000	-63,980	-98,640	-4,400	-4,400	
(b) Allowed as % of cost	-10,000	-12,000	-10,000	-8,000		
Cash float						
surplus						+44,000
deficit	-1,100	-45,980	-90,640	-4,400	-4,400	

Notice that once the contingency allowance of £40,000 is deducted, the expected closing cash balance goes down from £84,000 to £44,000, which is the expected profit. Cash forecasts built up by the synthetic method can often be based on the S curves.

The S curve

An S curve is a graph showing the cumulative value of one variable against another. The S curve has a variety of applications in project planning and control. For instance, an S curve can be drawn showing the cumulative man-hours required for each work package, over time. The curve tends to assume an S shape because most tasks start slowly, build up to a higher rate and then slow down towards the end, but the shape can be a straight line if a steady rate is maintained throughout. For example an S curve for design work might look as in Figure 8.1. This work commitment arises as in Table 8.6.

Table 8.6
Hanlon Projects PLC – design work package hours, project 4392

	Man-hours incurred	Cumulative total man-hours
Week 0–16	1,000	1,000
Week 11–20	3,000	4,000
Week 21–30	2,000	6,000
Week 31–40	2,000	8,000
Week 41–50	1,000	9,000
Week 51–60	500	9,500
Week 61–70	500	10,000

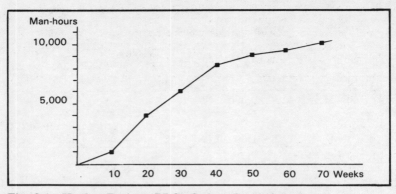

Fig. 8.1 Hanlon Projects PLC–S chart for design work, project 4392

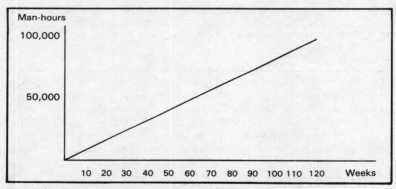

Fig. 8.2 Hanlon Projects – security man-hours, project 4392

By contrast, if the site is fenced and patrolled from the time work commences to the time the plant is handed over to the customer, the S curve might be drawn as in Figure 8.2.

This represents a coverage of 5 men, 24 hours a day, 7 days per week for 120 weeks. Since there are 168 hours in the week, if each man works 40 hours per week 21 men will actually be needed, working in shifts, to keep a constant patrol of 5 men.

Cost curves

If the cost per unit of a resource is known, then it is relatively simple to convert the S curve into a corresponding cost curve. If the cost per unit is constant the shape of the curves will be the same. For example if the rate for design work is £20 per hour and that for security £10 per hour, the costs can be calculated and the cost curve will have the same shape as the S curve. If costs change, the cost curve will differ. For example, if design costs are expected to rise to £30 per hour and security to £15 per hour at the end of week 40, the costs curves will be as in Figures 8.3 and 8.4.

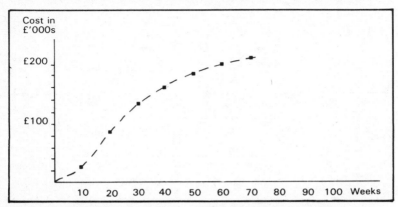

Fig. 8.3 Hanlon Projects PLC – cost curve for design work, project 4392

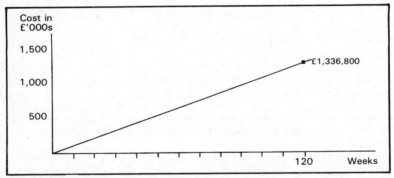

Fig. 8.4 Hanlon Projects PLC – cost curve for security

Several S curves are often plotted on the same graph to show the sequence of operations which often overlap. Figure 8.5 is an example.

These disparate curves are the detailed activity curves which underline the S curve for design shown in Figure 8.1.

It is not usually meaningful to combine S curves unless they do represent a common activity, but in the case of cost and cash flow, money is a common denominator. All the curves can be added to give the total pattern of cash flows for the project.

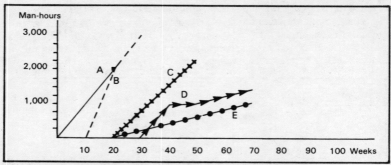

Fig. 8.5 Hanlon Projects PLC – design activities, project 4392

On-going cash control

Once a project is under way cash control will be based on two main factors, the master budget and the actual results.

The master budget

The first is the original estimate which, having been agreed with the client, then becomes the master budget. A master budget is a managerial plan expressed in financial and quantitative terms. It may be broken down in various ways so as to provide the individual budgets for each activity, each department, each organisation (such as consortium members and sub-contractors) and also each phase of the project. The financial aspect will be summarised in the cash budget which will show the capital demand (or supply) arising as the result of the interaction of payments and receipts over time. Thus, the budget incorporates a schedule of performances in terms of time. So, in agreeing a price of £484,000 for their factory contract, Webb Builders also agreed for its own purposes a master budget involving costs of £440,000 and a time schedule of 16 weeks from start to completion. From these forecasts, we produce the cash budget shown in Tables 8.4 and 8.5.

Cost and time are very interdependent: if the time required for completion were cut to 12 weeks, no doubt the costs, and therefore the price, would be higher. If Webb were allowed 20 weeks to complete, they might well be able to quote a lower price.

Also implicit in the budget is an assumed efficiency in performance, which is partly a matter of cost, partly a matter of time taken, but each of these related to the amount of work to be performed. In the cash budget, the interim receipts from clients will be based on the work certified, less any retention monies. Again, these budgeted receipts will be estimated at the start of the project and the amount will only be modified if changes to the contract are agreed by the client.

The cash budget will depend on the treatment of the contingency allowance. Assuming that it is allowed as a percentage of cost, the starting cash budget for Webb Builders may be summarised as in Table 8.7.

Table 8.7

Webb Builders – factory contract, cash budget (including contingency)

Weeks	1 – 4	5 – 8	9 – 12	13 – 16	17 – 20	21 – 24	25 – 28
	£	£	£	£	£	£	£
Opening cash float	0	– 1,100	– 45,980	– 90,640	– 4,400	– 4,400	– 4,400
Payments	– 110,000	– 132,000	– 110,000	– 88,000	–	–	–
	– 110,000	– 133,100	– 155,980	– 178,640	– 4,400	– 4,400	– 4,400
Receipts	+ 108,000	+ 87,120	+ 65,340	+ 174,240	–	–	48,400
Closing cash float	– 1,100	– 45,980	– 90,640	– 4,400	– 4,400	– 4,400	+ 44,000

Budget changes. So, the cost estimate sets the budget. Normally, the budget is fully determined at the start of the contract. However, the budget may be modified if changes are agreed with the client. These changes may change the contract price, the costs and the expected completion date. Only fully authorised changes may be used to change the budget. Once agreed, a new revised budget follows and is used thereafter for control purposes.

Suppose, after the first four weeks into building the factory, Webb Builders have already carried out additional foundations work at a cost of £20,000 for which the client has agreed a price of £22,000, which is included in the first certification. Additions to the final work will cost £44,000 for which a price of £48,000 has been agreed with the client. It has been agreed that this additional work will be completed by week 20. The cash budget must be amended to take account of these changes (Table 8.8).

Table 8.8

Webb Builders – factory contract cash budget after changes

					Date: End of week 4 Prepared by:			
Weeks	1 – 4	5 – 8	9 – 12	13 – 16	17 – 20	21 – 24	25 – 28	29 – 32
	£	£	£	£	£	£	£	£
Opening cash float	0	– 1,300	– 46,180	– 90,840	– 4,600	– 5,400	– 5,400	– 5,400
Payments	– 130,000	– 132,000	– 110,000	– 88,000	– 44,000	–	–	–
	– 130,000	– 133,300	– 156,180	– 178,840	– 48,600	– 5,400	– 5,400	– 5,400
Receipts	128,700*	87,120	65,340	174,240	43,200	–	–	55,400
Closing cash float	– 1,300	– 46,180	– 90,840	– 4,600	– 5,400	– 5,400	– 5,400	50,000

*£108,900 + £19,800 = £128,700

The changes in the work certified and retention money are as in Table 8.9.

Table 8.9

Webb Builders – factory contract, cash budget after changes

	Week 4	Week 20	Total
	£	£	£
Value of work	22,000	48,000	70,000
Less 10% retention	2,200	4,800	7,000
	19,800	43,200	63,000

The cost and profit of the contract are now modified (Table 8.10).

Table 8.10

Webb Builders – factory contract

			£
Estimated costs £440,000 + £64,000	=		504,000
Target profit £ 44,000 + £ 6,000	=		50,000
Tender price after changes £484,000 + £70,000	=		554,000

These figures are now the budget to which the project team will be working. Notice that extending the duration of the work by four weeks has postponed the expected receipt of all the retention money to week 32.

A further point is that the proportion of the work to be certified at each stage has changed, as follows (Table 8.11).

Table 8.11

Webb builders – factory contract, proportion of work to be certified

	% time		Amount	% of total	Original budget, %
Week 4	20	121,000 + 22,000 =	143,000	25.8	25
Week 8	40		96,800	17.5	20
Week 12	60		72,600	13.1	15
Week 16	80		193,600	34.9	40
Week 20	100		48,000	8.7	–
			£554,000	100	100

This information will be useful as the project develops.

The actual

The second main factor used in project cash control is the actual levels of spending and receipts. The record of what has been spent and received from the client will show the current cash position, that is, the size of the deficit or surplus: the amount of working capital tied up in the project or generated by it. This is useful information, especially if the actual position is compared to the budgeted position.

However, the financial information must be put in perspective and this can only be done if the level of performance achieved is also measured. The meaning of the current cash position, whether surplus or deficit, can only be understood if we can compare this to the performance actually achieved and the performance expected at the particular stage of time.

These points can easily be met. For example, Webb Builders, at the end of week 4 might prepare the following comparison of budget to actual performance (Table 8.12).

Table 8.12

Webb Builders – factory contract, cash budget report

Date: End of week 4
Prepared by:

Total value of contract £554,000

	Budget	Actual	Variance	
Value of work certified to date				
% of total	25.8%	23%	2.8%	U
	£	£		
Value certified	143,000	127,420	75,580	U
Less retention money 10%	14,300	12,742		
Cash receipts	128,700	114,678	14,022	U
Payments	130,000	117,278	12,722	F
Cash requirement				
Increase	1,300	1,300		
Decrease				

This statement shows that exactly the right amount of cash has been required, £1,300, as was expected under the budget. However, the detail shows an unfavourable variance on the cash receipts from work certified, offset by lower costs than expected. Is it a good performance? The temptation is to say it is, because the project manager has kept cash demands to exactly the level expected. However, the project is not on target because only 23 per cent of the work has been performed instead of the 25.8 per cent budgeted for. We can, in fact, get a deeper insight into the position by using the cost performance index.

Cost performance index

Once a project is under way, the efficiency of performance in cost terms can be measured by comparing:

(a) ACWP – the actual cost of work peformed to

(b) BCWP – the budgeted cost of work performed

The cost performance index (CPI) is calculated as follows:

$$\frac{\text{Budgeted cost of work performed}}{\text{Actual cost of work performed}} = \text{Cost performance index}$$

or

$$\frac{\text{BCWP}}{\text{ACWP}} = \text{CPI}$$

For example, firms Clapton Ltd and Denton Ltd bid £1 million for two similar contracts and each is awarded one of them. Both firms have similar cost estimates which give them an expected profit of 20 per cent of contract price. Each contract is to be completed at the end of one year.

At the end of six months, the actual results for each firm are as follows (Table 8.13).

Table 8.13

C & D Ltd – data at end of six months

	C Ltd £	D Ltd £
Actual cost of work performed (ACWP)	350,000	450,000
Budgeted cost at completion (BAC)	800,000	800,000
% of work completed	50%	40%

From these data, the budgeted cost of work performed can be calculated.

Budgeted cost at completion (BAC) × % work completed = BCWP

For Clapton Ltd £800,000 × 50% = £400,000

For Denton Ltd £800,000 × 40% = £320,000

The cost performance index for each firm is:

For Clapton Ltd:
$$\frac{BCWP}{ACWP} = CPI$$

$$\frac{400,000}{350,000} = 1.14$$

$$\frac{320,000}{450,000} = 0.71$$

Obviously, if the firms are up to target, then, CPI = 1.0. Our example shows that Clapton Ltd is ahead of target with a ratio of 1.14 and Denton Ltd is behind target with a ratio of 0.71. If we return to Webb Builders, their performance is as in Table 8.14.

Table 8.14

Webb Builders – factory project

End of week 4	£
Actual cost of work performed	117,278
Budgeted cost of work performed (23% of £504,000)	115,920
$\frac{BCWP}{ACWP} = CPI \frac{115,920}{117,278} = .988$	

Here we see that Webb are behind target with a CPI of .998, although that is not a serious shortfall.

Cost to complete

The cost performance index can be applied to the cost data to give a new estimate of the cost to complete. Here we expect the level of performance to date to continue through to the end of the project. In the example, Clapton Ltd has achieved above the expected level: this is expected to continue. Denton Ltd has fallen below the level of performance originally set: the method expects Denton Ltd to continue in the same way.

The first step is to calculate the original budgeted cost of the work which remains to be completed (BCWR), as follows:

Budgeted at completion – budgeted cost of work performed
= budgeted cost of work remaining

or

$$BAC - BCWP = BCWR$$

For Clapton Ltd:

$$£800,000 - £400,000 = £400,000$$

For Denton Ltd:

$$£800,000 - £320,000 = £480,000$$

For Webb Builders:

$$£504,000 - £115,920 = £388,080$$

The likely actual cost which we forecast can be obtained by dividing the budgeted cost of work remaining by the cost performance index:

$$\frac{\text{Budgeted cost of work remaining}}{\text{Cost performance index}} = \text{estimated cost to complete}$$

or

$$\frac{\text{BCWR}}{\text{CPI}} = \text{ECTC}$$

For Clapton Ltd:

$$\frac{400,000}{1.14} = £351,000$$

For Denton Ltd:

$$\frac{480,000}{0.71} = £676,000$$

For Webb Builders:

$$\frac{388,080}{.988} = £382,790$$

The estimated final cost will be the combination of the actual cost to date and the estimated cost to complete:

Actual cost of work performed + estimated cost to complete
= estimated final cost

For Clapton Ltd:

$$£350,000 + £351,000 = £751,000$$

For Denton Ltd:

$$£450,000 + £676,000 = £1,126,000$$

These figures show that on a fixed price of £1 million, the efficient firm can expect to make a profit of £249,000 (£1m − £0.751m) and the inefficient firm a loss of £126,000 (£1m − £1.126m). In each case, the budgeted profit was £200,000. Considering the date for Webb Builders, the calculations are:

$$£117,278 + £392,790 = £510,068$$

Thus, we can see that Webb Builders are likely to finish up with total costs of £510,000 and, with a revised contract price of £554,000, they can expect a profit of £44,000, not £50,000.

Cash control of projects

It follows that the cash forecast for the remaining duration of the project should now be revised but before doing that we need to consider a further aspect of the performance and to try to work out when the firm can expect the contract to be completed.

Scheduled performance index

Is the project on schedule, in advance, or behind? We can obtain an index of the performance against schedule by comparing the budgeted cost of the work completed to the budgeted cost of the work scheduled:

$$\frac{\text{Budgeted cost of work completed}}{\text{Budgeted cost of work scheduled}} = \text{schedule performance index}$$

or

$$\frac{\text{BCWP}}{\text{BCWS}} = \text{SPI}$$

For Clapton Ltd:

$$\frac{400{,}000}{400{,}000} = 1.0$$

For Denton Ltd:

$$\frac{320{,}000}{400{,}000} = 0.8$$

For Webb Builders Ltd at the end of their first four weeks, the calculation is:

$$\frac{\text{Budgeted cost of work completed}}{\text{Budgeted cost of work scheduled}} = \frac{127{,}420}{143{,}000} = .89 \quad \text{SPI}$$

Notice that the SPI could also be calculated from the percentages i.e.

$$\frac{\%\ \text{work completed}}{\%\ \text{work scheduled}} = \frac{23}{25.8} = .89\ \text{SPI}$$

The budgeted cost of the work scheduled can be built up in a synthetic fashion by checking the estimated costs of all the work expected to be completed by the point in time at which the exercise is carried out or in a global fashion by multiplying the budgeted total cost by the time elapsed, divided by the total time scheduled:

$$\text{Budgeted total cost} \times \frac{\text{Time elapsed}}{\text{Total time scheduled}} = \text{Budgeted cost of work scheduled (BCWS)}$$

For Clapton Ltd and Denton Ltd:

$$£800{,}000 \times \frac{6\ \text{months}}{12\ \text{months}} = £400{,}000$$

The scheduled performance index can then be used to forecast the likely completion date, in much the same way as the cost performance index was used to forecast the estimated final cost. The time remaining is the scheduled completion time less the actual time elapsed:

$$\text{Scheduled completion} - \text{time elapsed} = \text{time remaining}$$

For both Clapton Ltd and Denton Ltd this is six months. For Webb Builders, under the agreed budget after changes it is:

$$\begin{array}{ccccc} \text{Completion scheduled} & - & \text{time elapsed} & = & \text{time remaining} \\ 20 \text{ weeks} & - & 4 \text{ weeks} & = & 16 \text{ weeks} \end{array}$$

The estimated time for completion can be obtained by dividing the time remaining by the scheduled performance index:

$$\frac{\text{Time remaining}}{\text{Scheduled performance index}} = \text{estimated time to complete}$$

or

$$\frac{\text{TR}}{\text{SPI}} = \text{ETTC}$$

For Clapton Ltd:

$$\frac{26 \text{ weeks}}{1} = 26 \text{ weeks}$$

For Denton Ltd:

$$\frac{26 \text{ weeks}}{0.8} = 32.5 \text{ weeks}$$

For Webb Builders, the calculation is:

$$\frac{16 \text{ weeks}}{.89} = 18 \text{ weeks approx}$$

This calculation now allows us to proceed to the preparation of the cash budget for the remaining period of the project. Using the CPI, we have forecast the likely eventual level of costs and using the SPI, the likely eventual completion time. These two calculations open up the possibility of preparing an up-to-date and more realistic forecast of receipts and payments from an interim stage in the project up to final completion and receipts of final settlement.

The current cash position can be obtained from the actual cost of work performed (ACWP) and the budgeted cost of work performed (BCWP) although the latter figure will be reduced by the retention percentage.

From a practical point of view, it is probably as well to maintain the division of the actual expenditures into the budget periods used, e.g. weekly, four-weekly, monthly, quarterly, although from a cash viewpoint the divisions of past expenditures are no longer significant: it is the forecasts which matter.

In the case of Webb Builders, the position at the end of week 4 is that ACWP = £117,278 and the receipts will have been:

$$BCWP - 10\% = £115{,}920 - £11{,}592 = £104{,}328$$

The estimated cost to complete (ECTC) is £392,790 and the estimated time to complete (ETTC) is a further 18 weeks, that is week 22 from the starting date, instead of week 20.

Deciding how costs and receipts will be distributed over the forthcoming period is not easy. The obvious way is to assume the costs will be incurred at a steady rate, in which case, the estimated costs to complete can be divided by the number of periods to complete to give the cost per period.

For Webb Builders this would be:

$$\frac{ECTC}{ETTC} = \frac{£392{,}790}{18 \text{ weeks}} = £21{,}820 \text{ per week}$$

The payments for four weeks would be £87,280. Similarly the receipts could be calculated from the budgeted value of the project less the budgeted value of the work already certified, divided by the ETTC to give the expected weekly certified value. This is reduced by the retention rate to give the expected receipts per period.

For Webb Builders, this would be:

£554,000 − £127,420 = £426,580 value of work to be certified

The weekly rate is:

$$\frac{£426{,}580}{18} = £23{,}700 \text{ per week}$$

This calculation assumes that, as 23 per cent of the work has already been performed, the 77 per cent remaining will be completed and certified at the rate of

$$\frac{77\%}{18 \text{ weeks}} = 4.28\% \text{ per week}$$

or 17% approx. per four-week period.

The expected rate of receipts at the end of each four weeks would be:

	£
Value of work certified 4 × £23,700	= 94,800
Less 10% retention	9,480
	85,320

Since the project now extends over 18 weeks, the final period would have payments of £43,640 and receipts of £42,660. In the cash budget (Table 8.15) these have been rounded to £43,670 and £42,642. Working on this basis, the cash budget for the remaining period can be prepared.

The receipts and payments can be summarised as follows (Table 8.16).

Alternatively, the estimate of receipts and payments can be built up

Table 8.15

Webb Builders – factory project, cash forecast

Date: End of week 4
Prepared by:

Position to date	Week 4	5–8	9–12	13–16	17–20	21–24	25–28	29–32	33–34
Opening float	0	–2,600	–4,560	–6,520	–8,480	–10,440			11,468
Payments	117,278	87,280	87,280	87,280	87,280	43,670			
	117,278	89,880	91,840	93,800	95,760	54,110			11,468
Receipts	114,678	85,320	85,320	85,320	85,320	42,642	—	—	55,400
Closing float:									
deficit	–2,600	–4,560	–6,520	–8,480	–10,440	–11,468	–11,468	–11,468	
surplus									43,932
% work performed	23%	40%	57%	74%	91%	100%			

152

Table 8.16

Webb Builders – factory project, payments and receipts

	Payments	Receipts
	£	£
Weeks 1–4	117,278	114,678
5–22	392,790	383,940
Total costs	510,068	
Total progress receipts		498,600
Week 34 retention money		55,400
Value of contract		554,000

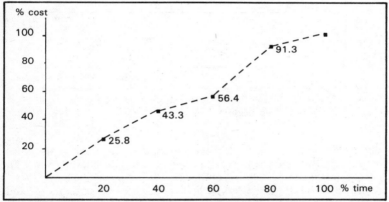

Fig. 8.6 Webb Builders – factory project, cumulative % cost/time chart

from an analysis of the work remaining and the revised work schedules. Sometimes, a project is controlled in terms of 'milestones' which are definite points at which separable sections of the work are brought to a conclusion. The estimates could be based on these milestones. Yet again, in theory, it would be possible to assume that the pattern of completion of the work will be same as in that envisaged in the original budget. This can be shown on a chart plotting percentage cost against percentage times. The data for Webb Builders are in Figure 8.6.

A similar chart could be prepared for the cumulative receipts. The curves differ because of the retentions. Notice that as the project advances, it is the remaining portion of the curve which applies, i.e. at the end of week 4 in the case of Webb Builders, the 23 per cent of the budgeted work has been performed. The curve followed by the new expected cost to complete will be the curve of the remaining 77 per cent

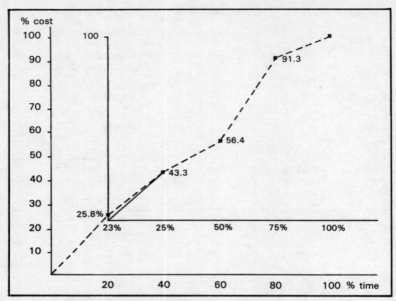

Fig. 8.7 Webb Builders – factory project, cumulative % cost/time chart with modified scale

of the work. In effect, a fresh scale is applied to the curve as the work completed grows and the proportion uncompleted declines (Figure 8.7).

The original curve is plotted on the AO'A' axes and the axes BO'B' are drawn at the end of week 4 when 80 per cent of the orginal time and 77 per cent of the original cost remain. Axis BO' scales 100 per cent of the revised cost to completion and axis O'B' 100 per cent of revised time to completion. The method to be used is largely a matter of judgement, bearing in mind that the purpose of the forecast is to produce a realistic estimate of the cash which will be required to finance the project to commissioning and final settlement.

Causes of cost and time over-runs

There may be a number of reasons why costs on a project run ahead of budget.

Inefficiency

Failure to control the use of materials: failure to deploy labour effectively; interruptions and delays; bad general or site management may all give rise to cost escalation.

Changes

It is quite common for changes to be made to the specifications and performance requirements while a project is in progress. These changes should result in a renegotiation of the contract price. If this aspect is overlooked, the result will be loss of profit.

Uncertainty

Uncertainty about the job and the resources required to do it is a prime characteristic of projects. In plain words, estimates are at best inspired guesses and often they will be wrong. By the law of large numbers the differences should cancel out but most project managers have more faith in Murphy's law which says that everything that can go wrong, will.

Price level changes

The prices of resources may change during a project. The longer the project takes, the more likely it is that prices will also change. Some price changes are the result of general price level changes – inflation – but others may result from competition. Prices do not always rise; nor do all prices always go in the same direction at the same pace. Even during the headiest times of inflation in the 1960s and 1970s, the prices of agricultural products tended to fall, as did the price of computers. Over the same period, the cost of some products went up at a much higher rate than the general rate of inflation (as indicated by the Retail Price Index).

Type of contract

The form of contract negotiated for a project can influence the control of costs. A common form is the cost-plus contract in which the client agrees to reimburse the contractor for the costs incurred plus an additional percentage to cover general overheads and profits.

This type of contract is used where technology is completely new or in circumstances in which an early start of work is needed, before a full tender and contract price have been agreed.

The difficulty for the client is that the contractor has no motive to control his costs, in fact, quite the opposite: the higher the costs, the higher the profit.

This problem may be met by a contract based on cost plus a fixed fee and there are many different variations and combinations.

The incentive to control costs is greater when a fixed price is negotiated for a contract. The contractor then increases profit by any costs saved. The problem, however, is that standards might be cut in order to save on costs.

9
Cash control of standard operations

Many firms are concerned with repetitive, routine operations in which those involved in the organisation do the same thing over and over again. These operations are often analysed down to fine detail in terms of method and time taken so that reliable and predictable standards of performance can be applied to the materials required for and work done on any product.

These producers turn out large quantities of each item they make and for all practical purposes, each item is the same as any other. True, the organisation may produce a range of items but the range is normally limited, and, even then, different items may still incorporate standard elements. For example, a range of cars may all be built around one engine design modified to meet the needs of each model in the range.

Because the products are standardised and largely uniform, common goals can be aimed for. These goals include the time needed to produce an item, the costs of production and the technical performance. The selling prices of items are also strictly controlled, according to the market into which the products are to be sold. It is quite common for the planning of production to start with the price at which the product will reach the ultimate customer and then work backwards to the prices for dealers, the cost at the factory gate, the cost of each component, function and the capital investment which can be justified. In this way, the profit margin expected from each product sold can be calculated according to the market – retail or wholesale, home or overseas – into which it is to be sold. The main purpose is to ensure the profit of the producer but the method does also determine the profit margins of the dealers who buy the product in order to sell it again.

The long chain between the producers and the ultimate customer means that, as production rises, so the amount of cash needed to invest in stock rises, too.

An example is the De Lorean car factory in Northern Ireland. Construction of the car factory began in 1978 and full-scale production started in February 1981. First shipment of cars was made in April 1981. By January 1982, the British government had provided £77 million in finance and by that time, only 8,333 cars had been produced. Of these, 7,401 had been shipped to the USA, 5,114 sold to dealers but only 3,347 sold to the public. In February 1982, the company went into receivership. The average cost to the British government of each car sold was £23,000!

Mass production firms may be involved in making parts which are assembled into components and then into final products as in car making or they may be involved in an analytic process by which a natural resource passes through various processes which give off finished or intermediate products, as in oil refining or gold mining. A key concept in this type of production is high volume of production coupled with a low profit margin on each item. The Mini was reported to give only 5 per cent of the ex-factory price in profit to the manufacturer, but the expectation was that the large number sold would nevertheless give an adequate return on capital.

Budgeting

Budgeting in the standard operation firm is a key method for planning activities. The starting point is normally a prediction of the sales volume and prices which can be aimed for in the coming period, usually a year or a season. At the start of the budgeting process, broad goals are set by top management and then each department works out the implications of those goals for its operations.

A 10 per cent growth in sales revenues may be coupled with the launch of new products or the opening up of new markets. The sales department will need to work out in detail the effects of these targets on the number of each product that can be sold, the prices which may be charged and the salespersons needed to obtain the required sales levels. Following from this, the sales expenses can be calculated. For production, the number to be sold must be produced at the lowest possible cost and in advance so that there is time to distribute stocks to the markets in which they will be sold. New plant and equipment will need to be commissioned, people need training or retraining, new staff must be recruited or redundant staff placed outside the operation.

Forecasting of both costs and revenues is highly developed in the mass production firm. Production is undertaken at a standard cost to meet a standard price for each product, so that the development of budgets from standards is a fairly straightforward, detailed, process.

Formal organisation

The formal organisation is, also, highly developed. The duties of each manager and, eventually, each operative are clearly laid down, following a hierarchy flowing down from the president or managing director. Authority flows down from the top and work is divided progressively into smaller and smaller components which define the authority and the responsibility of each department, section and operation.

Going with the authority to perform certain duties goes the responsibility for the efficient discharge of the duties and, since the organisation is highly complex, each person is accountable for efficient performance. The budget states in financial and physical terms the plans for each part of the firm: sales, revenues, production, expenses and costs.

The accountant is usually involved in turning all targets and plans into money terms but the main process of budgeting should be carried on by the managers who will have to implement the budgets, the sales manager and selling force, the production manager and production workforce and so on.

The particular contribution of the accountants is to develop the financial budgets, that is, the budgeted profit and loss account, the budgeted balance sheet and the cash budget. These are derived from the other budgets.

The budgeting process is a complex one because the implications of change on a large organisation are complex and often surprising.

The master budget

Working on the broad goals set by the Board, management will spend several months turning these into budgets which are realistic in all aspects: revenues, costs, profit margins, required investment and expected cash flows. The final product is called the master budget which, once agreed, forms the basis for future operations.

Control

All activities during a period in which a master budget applies are controlled by comparing the actual to the planned performance. If your sales target for April is £130,000 and you actually sell £120,000 of products, there is an unfavourable variance of £10,000. If your costs for £120,000 sales should be £100,000 and your actual costs are £95,000, there is a favourable variance of £5,000.

Cost behaviour

The mass production firm aiming for high-volume output of standard products at low profits per unit invests a great deal in assets. The firm also has high overheads arising from the services which develop to support the manufacturing or processing operations. Because of this, it is important to divide costs into two categories for budgeting purposes.

Fixed costs. These are costs which do not vary in proportion to changes in operational activity.

Variable costs. These are costs which vary directly with operational activity. Variable costs can be looked at in two ways, as total costs or as costs per unit.

The mass production firm normally has high fixed costs in total but small variable costs. The small production firm usually has low fixed costs and high variable costs, in total. Table 9.1 shows two examples.

Table 9.1

Fixed and variable costs for a mass production and small production firm

	Product A	Product B
	£'000	£'000
Fixed costs	800,000	32,000
Variable costs	200,000	48,000
Total costs	£1,000,000	£80,000
Production	100,000 units	4,000 units
	£	£
Fixed cost	8	8
Variable cost	2	12
Cost per unit	10	20

Unit cost

The differences between these cost structures can be seen in the graphs in Figure 9.1.

If you produce A you will get a shallow sloping total cost curve by investing heavily in equipment and services. Fixed cost is relatively high. By contrast, if you produce B, you will get a steeper variable cost curve but your fixed costs will be relatively low.

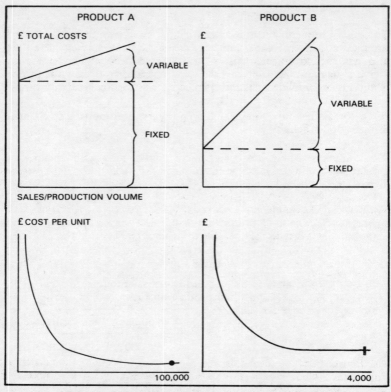

Fig. 9.1 Fixed and variable costs for a mass production and small production firm

For each unit, the variable cost will be constant, at £2 per unit for A and £12 per unit for B. The fixed cost, however, is spread over the number of units produced, so that the fixed cost per unit falls as production rises. The formula is:

$$\frac{\text{Fixed cost}}{\text{No. of units}} + \frac{\text{variable cost}}{\text{per unit}} = \text{cost per unit}$$

For ten units:

$$\text{Product A} \quad \frac{800,000}{10} + 2.00 = £80,002$$

$$\text{Product B} \quad \frac{32,000}{10} + 12.00 = £3,212$$

Production of 100 would cost £8,002 per unit for A and £332 for B. At

4,000 the cost of product A is down to £20 per unit, still less than B which costs £202. On the other hand, at 100,000 units, the cost of product A can be reduced to £10 per unit.

Notice the advantage of the product with low fixed costs if demand is low. Up to production levels of just below 45,000, you would obtain lower costs from product B! Above that level, you would be able to achieve much lower costs per unit by investing in production of A.

Measures of activity

Two main types of measures of activity can be used. Physical and financial.

Physical. For many purposes the best measure of activity is output and this can often be calculated in numbers produced and sold. In some cases, however, the best measure may be by weight, for instance, the tonnage of coal mined or steel smelted. In other cases, area may be the best measures, as, for instance, when a chipboard producer or paper manufacturer records the area produced in square metres. Certain products may be sold in a standard unit of quantity, such as a roll of newsprint or carpet. If a firm is extruding plastic rails the measure of product could be length (meterage or mileage produced, for instance) in standard units, e.g. metre, 1.2 metres, 1.5 metres and so on. Other physical measures of output are volume and compound units such as the ton/mile:

The number of persons employed in a function may also be used as a base.

Financial. The obvious financial measures of revenue cost and capital investment may be used as measures of activity but only with caution. A revenue or a cost may be made up, implicitly or explicitly, from a measure of quantity and a price.

You could budget for sales of 10,000 units at a price of £13 and if your sales only reach £120,000 you might have sold 10,000 at £12 or 9,231 at £13, or any other combination.

You may want to find out the true situation, although sometimes the broad financial measure is satisfactory.

Contribution

A powerful concept in planning and control is the idea of contribution. This is what is left after variable costs have been deducted from sales revenue, or price. The idea is simple enough. If you sell product A, your contribution per unit will be £18: on B, it will be £8.

Break-even point

The break-even point is the number of units which must be sold to cover the fixed costs, i.e.

$$\frac{\text{Fixed costs}}{\text{Contribution per unit}} = \text{break-even point}$$

For product A the break-even level of sales is 44,445 units (800,000 ÷ 18) and B is 4,000 units (32,000 ÷ 8).

Target profit

If you know the profit you need to make, you can calculate the level of sales which will give it: The formula is:

$$\frac{\text{Fixed costs} + \text{target profit}}{\text{Contribution per unit}} = \text{no. of units to meet target}$$

If you need to make £200,000 on product A, then you must sell 55,556 units ((800,000 + 200,000) ÷ 18). If you must make £12,000 profit on B, then you must sell 5,500 units ((32,000 + 12,000) ÷ 8).

The master budget

A master budget is a forecast and planned statement of revenues and expenses covering the whole of a business. The master budget is broken down in various ways. The breakdown by responsibilities reflects the organisational structure and enables line and staff managers to compare actual to planned performance. The breakdown by products provides the product managers with similar comparisons. Sales may be broken down by geographical location and production by function to provide efficiency comparisons.

The financial budgets

The financial controller will derive the financial budgets from the master budgets, so that they reflect managerial plans. These budgets give a forecast income statement, a balance sheet and cash budget for the budget period which is usually a financial year. The cash budget will normally be obtained by the adjusted net income method but a detailed cash receipts and payments cash budget may be produced if it seems that there may be cash flow problems at a particular time.

Case study

The case of two brothers illustrates some of the problems encountered and how they may be tackled. John Doe and his brother, Frederick, formed a business together in 1984. They manufacture and sell an RS 232 interface for use with Hazelnut computers.

At the end of 1984 John made estimates for the next year of trading, 1 January to 31 December 1985. The standard cost of the product is expected to be constant in 1985, and is shown in Table 9.2.

Table 9.2

RS 232 interface (Hazelnut)

		£
Selling price		10.00
Material cost	5.00	
Labour cost	3.00	
Variable overhead	1.25	9.25
Contribution per unit		0.75

Sales in 1985 will be 3,000 units in January and rising at 10 per cent per month throughout the year. Sales in November 1982 were 3,600 and in December 4,000 units.

The units are sold to hobby shops and departmental stores and on average the brothers allow two months' credit to be taken by customers. Production is geared to sales forecasts and two months' sales are held in stock at all times. Suppliers allow one month's credit on materials. Wages and overheads are paid monthly. Fixed overheads are £10,080 for the year, including £480 depreciation. At the start of the year, the company's balance sheet, prepared by the accountant, is expected to be as shown in Table 9.3.

Table 9.3

Doe Bros balance sheet at 31 December 1984

Current assets				Current liabilities	
	£	£			£
Cash in hand	6,000				
Debtors	76,000			Creditors	16,500
Stocks	58,275				
(6,300 units at £9.25)		140,275		Owners' equity contributed	
Fixed assets		4,800		and retained	128,575
		145,075			145,075

To the lay eye, this balance sheet looks impressive. The firm has total assets of £145,075, of which the owners have contributed £128,575. The firm has a good working capital ratio of over 8:

$$\frac{\text{Current assets}}{\text{Current liabilities}} = \frac{140,275}{16,500} = 8.5$$

The quick asset ratio is good, too:

$$\frac{\text{Current assets} - \text{stock}}{\text{Current liabilities}} = \frac{82{,}000}{16{,}500} = 4.97$$

although the acid test is not so good:

$$\frac{\text{Cash}}{\text{Current liabilities}} = \frac{6{,}000}{16{,}500} = .36$$

There is no other borrowing, so the firm probably has sufficient cash capacity to be able to finance its expansion by borrowing. But is that necessary?

Looking at the sales expected, it is clear that the company faces a strong demand for its products, but the standard cost shows that the contribution from each item is only 75p per unit. However, the fixed costs are low. How many units must it produce to break even?

$$\frac{\text{Fixed costs}}{\text{Contribution per unit}} = \frac{£10{,}080}{.75} = 13{,}440 \text{ units}$$

That is a target which should soon be reached with sales of 3,000 in January and rising by 10 per cent per month thereafter – a mere 4 to 5 months. The accountant also prepares the forecast income statement for the year and this is shown in Table 9.4.

Table 9.4

Doe Bros – predicted income statement for 1985

	£	£
Sales 64,140 @ £10		641,400
Cost of sales:		
Materials 64,140 @ £5	320,700	
Labour 64,140 @ £3	192,420	513,120
Gross profit		128,280
Expenses		
Variable overhead		
64,140 @ £1.25	80,175	
Fixed overhead	10,080	90,255
Operating profit		38,025

The rate of profit on sales is just under 6 per cent (38,025 ÷ 641,400) which seems low for a new technology company. Pre-tax profits as a percentage of sales for a sample of quoted companies were 7.6 per cent in 1972, falling to 5.8 per cent in 1982.

Over the same period, returns on opening capital employed fell from

20.2 per cent to 16.3 per cent. For the Doe Bros, the return is nearly 30 per cent (38,025 ÷ 128,600) so on that count, it looks good.

This is very encouraging and one might be tempted not to look at the cash position. After all, the company expects to sell more in 1985, the debtors take only two months to pay and the suppliers do not expect payment until after one month, so there is nothing to worry about. Or is there? In fact, there is, because of the 10 per cent increase in sales and production each month has a dramatic effect, as can be seen in Table 9.5.

Table 9.5
Doe Bros – unit sales and production, 1985

		Sales	Production	
1985	January	3,000	Two months	3,630
	February	3,300	in advance of sales, i.e.	3,990
	March	3,630		4,390
	April	3,990		4,830
	May	4,390		5,310
	June	4,830		5,850
	July	5,310		6,430
	August	5,850		7,070
	September	6,430		7,780
	October	7,070		8,560
	November	7,780		9,420
	December	8,560 (total 64,140)		10,360 (total 77,620)
1986	January	9,420		
	February	10,360		

By the end of the year, debtors will have risen to £163,400 (November and December sales 7,780 + 8,560 @ £10) and stocks to £182,965 (November and December production, 9,420 + 10,360 @ £9.25). Creditors will be £51,800 (10,360 units produced in December at £5 per unit material cost).

You can produce a prediction of cash needs by adjusting the income statement, item by item, as shown in Table 9.6. The predicted balance sheet is shown in Table 9.7.

Assuming the brothers do not have easy access to government money, how is a potential lender likely to answer a request for a loan? We saw earlier that the return on opening capital was good at nearly 30 per cent. On the closing capital employed, assuming the cash deficit can be borrowed, this has fallen to less than 13 per cent (38,025 ÷ 298,885) which is below stock brokers Phillips and Drew (P & D) industry average of 16.30 per cent. This is not good for a new technology firm. If the cash deficit can be borrowed, the long-term debt would then be 44 per cent (132,260 ÷ 298,885) of the capital employed. P & D's statistics show that even in 1972 loans and bank loans average only 33 per cent of capital employed and this fell to 28 per cent in 1982. The 44 per cent is too high.

Table 9.6

Doe Bros – cash flow from operations

Period: Year to 31 December 1985   Prepared by:
                                    Date:

Item	Income statement	Adjustments		Cash flow
	£		£	£
Sales	641,400	Add opening debtors	+ 76,000	
		Deduct closing debtors	− 163,400	+ 554,000
Cost of sales				
Materials	320,700	Add opening creditors	+ 16,500	
		Deduct closing creditors	− 51,800	− 285,400
Labour	192,420	None		− 192,420
Variable overhead	80,175	None		− 80,175
		Change in stock		
		Opening + 58,275		
		Closing − 182,965		− 124,690
Fixed overhead	10,080	Depreciation (not a cash flow)	− 480	− 9,600
		Cash flow from operations		− 138,285
		Opening float		6,000
		Deficit at end of year		− 132,285

Lenders and trade creditors would have to put in more money, £184,060, than the owners, £166,625. A more acceptable ratio of long-term debt would be 30 per cent of capital employed. The brothers need access to more equity, by issuing shares or by selling off or raising money on personal assets. The lenders might then agree maximum borrowing of £90,000. The brothers would be left to find a minimum of £42,260 in additional equity.

There would be other questions raised, such as the ability of the firm to pay the required interest. At 10 per cent net, the interest payments would be £9,000, or 24 per cent of net income. That is high, although P & D show that the percentage for British firms has been rising from 15 per cent in 1976 to 22 per cent in 1982. If the lenders stipulate a maximum interest paid of 20 per cent of pre-interest profits, this would reduce the loan to £76,000.

Table 9.7

Doe Bros – predicted balance sheet at 31 December 1983

	£	£
Use of funds		
Current assets		
Cash	–	
Debtors	163,400	
Stock	182,965	
Current assets		346,365
Current liabilities		
Creditors		51,800
Net working capital		294,565
Fixed assets		
Balance at start	4,800	
less depreciation for year	480	
		4,320
Assets employed		298,885
Sources of funds		
Required borrowing		132,285
Owners' equity		
At start of year	128,575	
Add profit for year	38,025	166,600
Capital employed		298,885

There is a range of possible adjustments to future plans which the Doe brothers could make:

1. Raise sufficient funds to finance the growth:
   (a) By borrowing and/or new equity.
   (b) By advancing receipts from debtors.
   (c) By delaying payments to suppliers.

2. Improve profitability and, thereby, cash flow:
   (a) By increasing prices. This may however, affect the quantities that can be sold.
   (b) By reducing costs without affecting quality of products and services.

3. Restrain growth to confine cash requirements within acceptable limits.

These adjustments could be combined and it would be possible to use linear programming to search for an optimum solution within the stipulated constraints.

Using a computer financial package the brothers could explore these possibilities by asking a series of 'what if...' questions. On the third point, restraint of growth, the purpose of finance is to support economic activity and the restriction of growth should be avoided if at all possible.

On the second point, it is a normal function of management and workforce to operate in the most efficient way, so the improvement of profitability should always be in the forefront of your mind. That, however, is a counsel of perfection, so, in practice, the constraints of cash may always give you a jumping-off point for efforts to improve profitability. Improving profits will always improve cash flows so long as new capital is not required.

Thus, the first point is the priority reaction to a looming cash deficit. In other words, you try to find financial solutions to the cash problem. The dramatic effect of changing financial terms can be seen if we assume that the Doe brothers are able to meet to demand for cash by advancing receipts from debtors and delaying payments to creditors by one month, all other things remaining constant. This transforms the situation! The revised balance sheet is shown in Table 9.8.

Table 9.8

Doe Bros – revised projected balance sheet at 31 December 1985

	£	£
Current assets		
Cash	–	
Debtors	85,600	
Stock	182,965	
Current assets		268,565
Current liabilities		
Creditors		98,900
Net working capital		169,665
Fixed assets		
Balance at start	4,800	
less depreciation for year	480	4,320
Assets employed		173,985
Sources of funds		
Required borrowing		7,385
Owners' equity		
At start of year	128,575	
Add profit for year	38,025	166,600
Capital employed		173,985

The significant changes are a reduction in borrowing to £7,385 and a reduction of the debtors to £85,600, because the proceeds of November sales, £77,800, will now be received in December. In the previous balance sheet, this £77,800 was included in the amount receivable from debtors. Similarly, the creditors are increased to £98,900 from £51,800.

The change in the cash required can be explained in the following way:

	£
Cash required, in first budget	132,285
Deduct extra cash from delayed creditors, £47,100	
Deduct extra cash from debtors advanced, £77,800	
Additional funds received	124,900
Cash required, in revised budget	£ 7,385

In effect, the firm is now self-financing. On the amounts of money involved, a deficit of £7,385 is one that can be fairly easily accommodated by slight adjustments affecting the cash flow. Notice, too, that the return on closing capital employed has risen to 22 per cent, now well above the industry average.

Remember, this improvement in profitability has been brought about by more efficient use of cash. The business objectives and operating efficiency are the same in both cases: all that has changed is the amount of cash required to achieve those objectives.

10
Cash control of jobbing and multiple projects

Jobbing work can be defined as the undertaking of one-off jobs with discrete time and financial goals to well established technical standards using well-known routines and operations which often recur. The jobbing firm is usually smaller than the multiple-project business and the variation between jobs is not so great as in project work. Although there may be a chargehand or foreman on each job, it will not warrant the appointment of a project manager, so the techniques of control described in Chapter 8 will not be used. Indeed, the simpler situation does not justify separate cash control. You can use the techniques described in this chapter in two types of circumstances. The first is if you undertake jobs which are not large enough to justify separate cash control for each. In practice, this also means that you, as manager, or proprietor, will control a number of jobs, indeed, perhaps all the jobs you take on.

The typical firm we have in mind here is engaged on building maintenance and small works, or in engineering sub-contracting or in jobbing printing. At any particular moment in time, this type of small jobbing firm will have a number of jobs in hand. For these, it will be necessary to estimate the amount and timing of payments and receipts. The second set of circumstances is when a large firm engaged in two or more large projects wishes to establish central cash planning to supplement the project cash management. Such a firm may regard its projects as a portfolio of investments and wish to optimise the overall use of cash. In this case, the approach will be to consolidate the receipts and payments coming from all jobs and arising from central operations so that the cash requirements will be pooled and all demands centralised. The value of this may not be obvious but it can be quite dramatic.

In both types of firms, we can assume that each project or job will be undertaken on the basis of an estimate of costs similar to that shown in Table 8.1 earlier. Your estimate will list the costs you expect for materials, labour and expenses by each section or department on sub-contracted work and bought-in parts. You may estimate the profit as a percentage on cost and this gives you an estimated price. This price is then the basis for your negotiations with the client. A higher price may increase the profit, although if it is based on a changed specification it may mean an increase in costs. In this case you need to revise your estimate before you can use it as your budget. A lower price will decrease the profit unless some relaxation of the requirements allows a reduction in costs and, again, the estimate must be revised before it is set as the budget.

The effect of consolidated cash budgeting

Consolidated cash budgeting is the key aspect of the approach. The normal basis for jobbing and project work is that the customer will not pay until sometime after the work is delivered and accepted as up to standard, so that the typical cash flow pattern is a continuous, and accumulating, flow of payments for costs followed by a large receipt which, it is hoped, repays the costs and injects cash profit. On projects, interim receipts may reduce the accumulated deficit but are rarely sufficient, after retention monies have been deducted, to turn the deficit into a surplus.

Given this pattern, the timing of the projects and the terms of settlement can have an important influence on the cash needed to finance operations. For example, the Sandall Screw Co. Ltd works as an engineering sub-contractor and they tender for the supply of 1 inch no. 8 wood screws in lots of 10,000. The estimate of costs, desired profit and price is as in Table 10.1.

Now let us assume that there are four possible customers and that each one indicates that the price must be cut to £48.00, but that a slightly milder steel costing £14.00 per 10,000 may be used. Sandall Screws may well feel they must accept the revised price and cost, in which case their budgeted costs will be reduced to £44, their price to £48 and their profit to £4.

Sandall Screws Co. Ltd have the capacity to produce 50,000 screws per week and each customer indicates that they require 200,000 per four-week period.

Table 10.1

Sandall Screw Co. Ltd

Cost estimate for 10,000 1″ × no. 8 woodscrews
Date:
Prepared by:

	£	£
Materials	15.00	
Labour	20.00	
Overheads	10.00	
Total cost		45.00
Required profit		5.00
Price		£50.00

If Sandall sell all their output to a single customer on monthly terms of trade, their cash budget for the first twelve weeks will be as shown in Table 10.2.

It is assumed that the effect of the four-week terms of trade is to delay the first receipt from the customer to the end of week 8, when £960 is received. Thereafter £960 per four-week period will be received. It can be seen also that Sandall Screw Co. Ltd will have a maximum cash need of £1,760, and this will be reduced to £800 as soon as the first payment is received from the customer. Thereafter, the cash required will be reduced progressively by the profit element of £80 as it is received at the end of each four-week period. At the end of the second period the maximum falls from £1,760 to £1,680 and the minimum from £800 to £720. It will be 22 periods before the contract ceases to need external financing.

Now let us look at the customers as a possible portfolio of jobs. Each of the firms wants the same price and has the same terms for cash settlement, but it is quite possible that they would fix, or would be willing to agree different dates for paying Sandall Screws.

If Sandall Screw Co. Ltd then arrange to supply 12,500 screws each week to each customer, the cash budget would be as shown in Table 10.3.

This simple arrangement makes a dramatic change to the cash budget. The maximum cash need is now £520 at the end of week 4, when the closing float is £280. The maximum closing float needed is £300 at the end of week 3. Under the first arrangement, shown in Table 10.2, the maximum cash need at £1,760 is three times greater than in this case.

Multiple projects

The objective of this aspect of cash budgeting is to manage the overall financing of a firm involved in a number of projects.

Table 10.2

Sandall Screw Co. Ltd – cash budget, £

For: February – April
Prepared by:

Week	1	2	3	4	5	6	7	8	9	10	11	12
Opening float	0	−220	−440	−600	−880	−1,100	−1,320	−1,540	−800	−1,020	−1,240	−1,460
Payments:												
Materials	70	70										
Labour	100	100	220	220	220	220	220	220	220	220	220	220
Overheads	50	50										
Total cash need	220	440	660	880	1,100	1,320	1,540	1,760	1,020	1,240	1,460	1,680
Receipts								960				960
Closing float	−220	−440	−660	−880	−1,100	−1,320	−1,540	−800	−1,020	−1,240	−1,460	−720

173

Table 10.3

Sandall Screw Co. Ltd – cash budget, £

For: February – April
Prepared by:

Week	1	2	3	4	5	6	7	8	9	10	11	12
Opening float	0	−160	−260	−300	−280	−260	−240	−220	−200	−180	−160	−140
Payments	220	220	220	220	220	220	220	220	220	220	220	220
Total cash need	220	380	480	520	500	480	460	440	420	400	380	360
Receipts	60	120	180	240	240	240	240	240	240	240	240	240
Closing float	−160	−260	−300	−280	−260	−240	−220	−200	−180	−160	−140	−120

It is assumed that each project is separately managed and that cash forecasts are being prepared for use in the management of each project. From the overall point of view, the cash budget will have to cover central payments for administration, research and development, marketing and other central services.

It can be assumed that all receipts from clients will come through project activities and any major receipts to the control operation will be of a capital nature, such as borrowing, and the issue of new share capital. Central payments would be required for interest, dividends, and repayment of loans. These long-term items were dealt with in Chapter 6. Another central payment would be taxation and this is dealt with in Chapter 13. A further assumption in this approach is that each project is independent in terms of demand for resources. This means that, as projects are completed, no further costs of labour, materials and equipment are incurred. Any delay in receipts of cash from the project after completion represents the application of the agreed contract terms on certification and payment for work and the holding of retention money.

Budgeting for multiple projects on these assumptions means collecting together the cash forecasts for all projects and combining them with the forecasts of central receipts and payments for the forecast period. It is desirable that the forecast period for the budget should extend sufficiently into the future to go beyond any particularly high payments and receipts so that the implications of delaying payments or advancing receipts can be fully explored. Presentation can be simplified by using − and + to indicate the direction of the cash flows.

The simplest way to produce a cash budget in these circumstances is to prepare a form on which the net payments of receipts from each project can be listed and combined with the central payments and receipts. For example, Bullet Constructors Ltd have five projects in hand. Central administration costs £50,000 per week and interest of £10,000 is due within one week, dividends of £15,000 in four weeks and a loan of £300,000 falls due for repayment in seven weeks. The controller decides to prepare cash budgets over the next ten weeks in view of the size of the loan and the imminent completion of several projects. The combined budgets are shown in Table 10.4.

It is clear from this presentation that the loan repayment falls at an awkward time, in week 7 when accumulative payments on the projects are already high. It is also clear that the position could be eased if the loan repayment were delayed or if the receipts from the completed projects could be advanced even by one week because £400,000 is due from project 1 in week 8.

Delaying the loan repayments might be easy enough if additional interest were paid. The rate might be high, say 20 per cent, but it could be lower than the alternative which is to allow the firm's overdraft to rise to £1,775,000. Interest on an overdraft is usually payable quarterly on the maximum balance outstanding at a stipulated amount over the

Table 10.4
Bullet Constructors Ltd – control cash budget, £'000

No. 491
Date:
Prepared by:

Week	1	2	3	4	5	6	7	8	9	10
Project cash flows										
Project 1	−30	−25	−20							
Project 2	−120	−120	−20	−100	−120					
Project 3	−30	−30	−30	−30	−30					
Project 4		−10	−15	−20	−40	−100	−180	+400	+900	+420
Project 5								−90	−80	−100
								−25	−40	−60
Central cash flows										
Administration	−50	−50	−50	−50	−50	−50	−50	−50	−50	−50
Interest	−10									
Dividends				−15						
Loan repayment							−300			
Net flows	−240	−235	−135	−215	−240	−150	−530	+235	+730	+210
Cumulative	−240	−475	−610	−825	−1,065	−1,215	−1,745	−1,510	−780	−570

minimum lending rate. So, even one day at the maximum carries a quarter's interest.

Advancing the receipt of cash from the projects, especially by a small amount of time like a week, might be arranged with the client without cost, but if this is not possible, the due date could be advanced by speeding up completion of the project. In this case, there could be a cost penalty.

It is useful to prepare a data sheet and a working paper to support any changes requested. From a central management point of view these changes will have a sound financial justification. For the project manager on the site who normally works away to minimise his costs and complete his contract on time, a request to complete a week early, at a higher cost, may not appear so sensible. If complaints are raised, as far as possible, affected managers should be put in the picture.

Another possibility is to delay the progress of projects to slow down the accumulation of costs and in practice this is often forced on firms which are running out of cash. However, it is generally a symptom of bad cash planning. Once a project is under way, delays due to shortages of labour and material on site are usually very costly. They also have a 'knock-on' effect and can run projects into penalties if completion dates are not met. It is probably easy enough to delay the start of a new project by a few weeks but, here again, the profit of the firm will probably be maximised if projects are started as early as possible. This alternative should therefore be regarded as a last resort.

For Bullet Constructors Ltd, the cash budget adjustment data are as shown in Table 10.5.

The working papers in Table 10.6 show the effect of each adjustment on the cash flows. For the sake of comparison the old estimated flows are noted first for each item and the effect of each change can be seen at a glance. Some items in the data sheet may not appear in the working papers. Projects 4 and 5 are omitted in the example.

Let us consider each note in turn:

Notes 1 & 2

A problem arises in allocating the increase in costs of early completion to the weeks over which completion would then take place. In the example, this has been done on the proportion of cost in each week under the old budget. If possible, the revised costs should be those agreed by the project manager.

Note 3

Again, the increase in cost has been allocated over the four weeks which the project would take on the revised terms.

Notes 4 & 5

The amount to be paid in interest and dividends is trivial compared to

Table 10.5

Bullet Constructors Ltd – cash budget adjustment data sheet

Date:
Prepared by:

Item		Amount	Timing	Conditions and flexibility
Project 1	Costs	£ 75,000	Complete by week 3	Completion could be advanced 1 week at additional £10,000 cost.
	Receipts	£400,000	Final settlement 5 weeks after completion	Client has agreed to pay after 4 weeks – no extra cost
Project 2	Costs	£360,000 £220,000 £100,000	To week 3 Weeks 4 & 5 complete by week 5 At end week 3, interim.	Completion could be advanced 1 week at additional £40,000 cost in weeks 4 & 5
	Receipts	£900,000	Final settlement 4 weeks after completion	
Project 3	Costs	£ 30,000 per week	For 5 weeks	Could be raised to £40,000 per week for 4 weeks
	Receipts	£420,000	Final settlement 4 weeks after completion	Client would settle at week 7 if completed at end of week 4
Project 4	Costs	£ 85,000	Weeks 2–5 stage I	Delay on weeks 2–5 would also delay progress payment. Delay on second stage would delay
	Costs	£610,000	Weeks 6–10 stage II	

	Receipts	£ 60,000	Progress payment on weeks 2–5 work stage I	large progress payment in week 11. There are penalties on completion, targeted for week 32
Project 5	Costs	£125,000	Weeks 8–10	Total contract costs expected to be £250,000, with £300,000 receivable in week 16
Control expenses				
Administration		£ 50,000 per week		
Interest		£ 10,000	Week 1	Could not be delayed without affecting company credit
Dividends		£ 15,000	Week 4	Could be delayed up to 2 weeks if major shareholders agree
Loan repayment		£300,000	Week 7	Can be delayed 3 weeks on payment of interest at 26% p.a.
Overdraft				
Maximum to date		£1,000,000		MLR + 3%
Minimum lending rate		8%	At week 1	Could rise 1% in next 10 weeks. Bank calculates quarterly. Next calculation week 11

Table 10.6

Bullet Constructors Ltd – cash budget working papers, £'000

Data Sheet No. 893 Date:
Central Cash Budget (revised) no. 492 Prepared by:

Note no.	Weeks	1	2	3	4	5	6	7	8	9	10	Comments
1	Project 1											
	Old: Costs and receipts	−30	−25	−20								Increased costs shared 30:25 to weeks 1 & 2
	Revised	−46	−39	−								
2	Project 2											
	Old: Costs	−120	−120	−120	−100	−120			+400	+900		Weeks 4 & 5 £260,000
	Receipts			+100			+400					Costs shared 100:120
	Revised											
	Costs − as old	−120	−120	−120								
	− raised				−118	−142						
	Receipts			+100					+900			

3	Project 3									
	Old: Costs and receipts	−30	−30	−30	−30	−30	−30			
	Revised: Costs and receipts	40	40	40	40			+420		+420 Receipts advanced 1 week by early completion + 1 week revised term
4	Old: Interest									
	Revised:	10								Delay inadvisable
5	Old: Dividends					15				
	Revised:							15		Inadvisable
6	Old: Loan repayment								−300	Interest
	Revised:									$\dfrac{.26 \times 300{,}000 \times 3}{52}$
									−305	= £4,500
										Rounded to £305,000

Table 10.7

Bullet Constructors Ltd – revised cash budget, £'000s

Data sheet no. 893 Date:
Cash budget (revised) no. 492 Prepared by:
Summary of effects on overdraft

Week	1	2	3	4	5	6	7 (Maximum)	8	9	10	Comments
Overdraft pattern	240	475	640	855	1,095	1,245	1,775	1,540	810	600	
Effect on O/D											
Project 1	+16	+15				−400		+400			Does not affect O/D max.
Project 2	+2	+2	+2	+18	+22						
Project 3						−420		−900	+900		No change
Projects 4/5									+420		Delay to week 8 from week 1 is not on
Interest							−300				Cannot delay
Dividends											
Loan repayment										+305	

182

the overdraft and there could be serious repercussions on the financial standing of the firms if they are not paid on time.

Note 6

The interest cost of postponing the loan repayment is not high but the arrangements for postponement could be delicate, since failure to meet the obligation could have a serious effect on the financial standing of the firm.

Summary of effects on overdraft

Having analysed the possible changes to cash flows which are available it is useful to summarise these, as a part of the working papers. For Bullet Constructors Ltd, the summary is as shown in Table 10.7.

The summary starts with the cumulative overdraft pattern as originally budgeted which in the example reaches a maximum of £1,775,000 at the end of week 7.

The summary next shows the net effect of each possible change. The cost increases have a straightforward effect of increasing the overdraft in the week when they occur.

The effects of a change in timing are not so obvious. For example, in project 1, it is possible to bring forward the receipt of £400,000 from week 8 to week 6.

The effect on week 6 (and, cumulatively, on week 7) is highly desirable, because the overdraft will be reduced by £400,000. By the same token, however, the effect on week 8 is equally undesirable because the overdraft at that time will be increased by the £400,000. At this point, we are looking for the minimum overdraft we can get. Seeing the usual pattern of the proposed amendments allows a search to be made for the best way to achieve this.

It seems obvious in the example that the key proposals are to advance the receipts on project 3 and delay the repayment of the loan. Together, these two measures would reduce the overdraft to little above £1m.

If one assumes that these two adjustments are made, it will be obvious that the maximum overdraft now occurs in week 8 in the example. Moreover, advancing the receipt of £400,000 from project 1 by four weeks would have the effect of increasing the overdraft in week 8 by £400,000. This, in turn, would mean that advancing the receipt of £900,000 from project 2 by one week from 9 to 8 would have to be considered. In terms of the original maximum, at week 7, this adjustment of project 2 was irrelevant. The point is that adjustments which on first inspection seem irrelevant may become relevant at a second or third stage of adjustment when the reduction of a maximum overdraft at one stage may transform the amount at another stage into the new maximum. Mathematically inclined readers will recognise that this iteration process is suitable for a linear programming solution.

Table 10.8
Bullet Costructors Ltd – central cash budget (revised)

Number: 492
Date:
Prepared by:
Data Sheet refers: 893
Working paper:

Week	Notes	1	2	3	4	5	6	7	8	9	10
Project cash flows											
Project 1	1	−46	−39								
Project 2		−120	−120	−20	−118	−142	+400				
Project 3		−40	−40	−40	−40			+420	+900		
Project 4			−10	−15	−20	−40	−100	−180	−90	−80	−100
Project 5									−25	−40	−60
Central cash flows											
Administration		−50	−50	−50	−50	−50	−50	−50	−50	−50	−50
Interest		−10									
Dividends					−15						
Loan repayment											−305
Net flows		−266	−259	−125	−243	−232	+250	+190	+735	−170	−515
Cumulative		−266	−525	−650	−893	−1,125	−875	−685	+50	−120	−635

If all those proposed changes are adopted which are not inadvisable, the revised central cash budget will be as shown in Table 10.8. This revised cash flow gives a much better pattern, which reaches a maximum of £1,125,000 in week 5 and is even £50,000 positive in week 8.

11
Cash control in product management

Probably no previous century has seen the pace and scale of economic change of the twentieth. Housing, transport, consumer goods, new technology, the global environment, have all been subject to rapid and extensive changes in which business has played a large part. Market patterns of demand for consumer and industrial products are constantly changing and there is a restless search for new markets, new outlets and new products. Radical changes in the patterns of supply, of manufacture and production have moved whole industries from one location to another and produced the relative decline of some countries such as the UK and the rise of others such as the USA and Japan.

Going with these changes has been an increasing emphasis on marketing which not merely sets selling prices and arranges advertising but which analyses customer needs both manifest and latent – and develops products to meet those needs. Because of the complexity of the processes through which products are marketed, many multi-product companies have organised a section of management along product lines which cut across the traditional organisational hierarchies.

The titles vary: product managers, marketing managers, brand managers, call them what you like, but the responsibilities are to develop a marketing plan for each product which co-ordinates the whole process from first conception of need, through research, development, test marketing, launching, product improvements and eventual demise.

Effective product management is often the key to success in marketing. For example, MFI is a UK firm which developed a lucrative market for well-styled furniture sold directly to the public in knock-down form. In 1982 they decided to extend their product range to cover electrical kitchen equipment such as fans, hobs and cookers. The result was a dramatic 38 per cent rise in profits in the second half of the year to £15.6 million. Sales rose to £136 million, an average of £45,000 per worker and £44 per square foot of selling space.

In the face of intense competition, a constant review and control of the product range is needed. Old products must be revamped or dropped, new products must be introduced if the manufacturer is to meet consumer needs as and when they arise and to maintain or increase market share. 'Competition has become more international and has focused increasingly on value' according to Adrian Cadbury, Chairman of Cadbury-Schweppes at the end of 1982, and he points out that the five largest UK multiples increased their share of the packaged grocery trade from 32 per cent in 1977 to 50 per cent by the end of 1982. Thus, even a large manufacturer is heavily dependent on a few large distributors whose enhanced buying power may put heavy downward pressures on prices so that it is difficult to maintain returns on investment. The cash implications may also be considerable. Of course, the product range must be profitable, but also the cash must be found to finance it.

The product life cycle

It is often suggested that products have a 'natural' life cycle which goes through five stages.

At the *introductory* stage sales are slow. Distribution may be limited to prestige groups who learn of the product through limited advertising in the prestige press. The price may be high and profits limited. However, the firm has the advantage of surprise and competition may be minimal.

The next stage is *market growth* in which sales take off. Demand is increased by new applications and new markets for the product are found. Marketing appeals to the mass market, using the full range of media. Competitors enter the market, so that prices fall but some firms achieve high volumes of sales and on the whole profits improve dramatically. Because many firms are attracted into the market and some are able to grow at a feverish pace, there is a great temptation to overtrade by taking lots of credit because it is possible to sell products before trade creditors have to be paid. Fortunes are made by some of the pioneers. In 1983/84, the market for microcomputers was at this stage and electronic typewriters and word processors were entering it in the UK. In the USA, the market was further ahead.

At the next stage, *maturity,* sales stabilise at a level which provides for replacement and population growth only. Firms which have been overtrading run into trouble as their lack of working capital becomes evident. The industry experiences bankruptcies and mergers but eventually settles down into a pattern of few suppliers enjoying stable sales and reasonable but not excessive profits.

The microcomputer market in the USA showed some of these symptoms in 1983/84 when even firms such as Apple and Commodore were finding difficulties in maintaining their market lead and Apple reported losses for part of 1983. Because of continuing product innovation, however, the micro market had not yet achieved full maturity. The keynote of full maturity is *saturation* and at this stage the manufacturer and seller enjoy a stability which may mislead them into believing the product will go on forever.

Markets are stable, profits are comfortable, competition is for market shares, the market is not attractive to new entrants. This full maturity leads into the next stage.

The final stage in the product life cycle is *decline*. This is the time when the product begins to lose its appeal in the face of new, better products or substitutes or changing public taste and fashion. Sales may decline gently or catastrophically. Profits will fall as the larger firms move out of the market. Some small and medium firms may survive with the product but on a reduced scale, like some bespoke tailors, or manufacturers of horse brasses. Some may eventually be relaunched, like pewter hollow ware.

At the time of writing, the manual typewriter has entered this stage, pushed out by the new electrical and electronic products. The dangerous thing is not to recognise that a product is entering decline. Firms which fail in this way may cling to the method, prices and tactics which worked well in maturity in the hope that things will get better. In the process, capital may be squandered as sales and profits fall. Bankruptcy may be staved off for a long time but when it comes, the accumulated reserves will be gone. The wise course may be to recognise the inevitable, keep prices up to a level which maintains profitability and switch the capital, as it is released, to new products in one form or another.

Because of the importance of products, many large firms are organised, in part at least, along product lines. A deliberate effort is made to maintain a portfolio of products to meet market needs and the pressure of competition. Sales of each product are carefully monitored. Declining products are redeveloped, marketed in new packing, new sizes or in different flavours. New advertising approaches may be used. Pedigree Petfoods are a British firm which is highly regarded in the grocery trade because they keep lines going in this way.

In 1982, Cadbury-Schweppes relaunched its Typhoo tea bags but although the tea and foods division increased its volume sales, margins were under great pressure. The drinks division increased sales of Pepsi by 47 per cent on the first stage of a three-year programme but the group as a whole had to spend £105 million on modernisation and devote more money to marketing in order to maintain growth. Thus, whilst UK sales rose 11 per cent to £782 million in 1982 the trading profit dropped 9 per cent to £46 million, and the trading profit on assets fell from 19.9 per cent to 14.3 per cent.

In view of their earlier success in diversifying into electrical products, the British MFI were considering, in early 1983, adding further products to their range, such as refrigerators and freezers. But such a move needs careful analysis. Will it really pay off? In some cases, new products are developed. Large firms like the European Lever Brothers are very cautious in launching new products but when they do, they tend to be successful. The firm's most successful new product in recent years is Persil Automatic washing powder which in 1984 held 30 per cent of the £300m market for washing powders. However, the first launch of such a product may take many months of intensive advertising and promotion during which time cash flows are horrendously negative. It takes great nerve to hang on as sales trickle in and the cash investment piles up.

It has been estimated that 70 per cent of new products actually fail to take off. Some take off for a while and then plummet. How many people remember the 'pot snacks' launched in the UK in the late 1970s? It looked for a while as though they would be a big market. Sales grew from £5 million in 1978 to £36 million in 1980. By 1981 half the population of the UK had tried them, but they were obviusly not too happy because the market has since declined to £18 million in 1983. Many products fail to create a significant market at all and in that case the costs must fall on the successful products in the range.

The definition of a product can be applied to various product classes such as cars or computers. The product may also be a type of product within a broad class such as the estate car or the four-wheel drive vehicle. Computers may be mainframes, minis or micros. Third, a product may be defined as a particular brand or make within the broader class, for instance the British Rover or the French Talbot car. A computer may be an IBM, a DEC, a Commodore or an Acorn. The idea of the life cycle may apply at all of these levels and be at different stages.

Cash flow and the product life cycle

A number of factors will affect the cash flows associated with a product at the various stages of its life. Actual patterns will vary, but typical effects will be as follows.

Fixed capital investment

Normally an investment of cash will be required at the start to cover research and development, test marketing and the creation of production facility.

For many products it may be advisable to start with a relatively small production facility and extend it during growth. Some plants may be replaced or refitted during the maturity and saturation phases. Firms entering the maturity phase, having expanded to meet growth, may sell off or redeploy surplus plant. Products entering decline should be carefully monitored so that capital assets can be released for alternative uses or for sale.

Contribution from sales

From a cash forecasting and budgeting point of view, attention should be concentrated on the contribution obtained in each period from each product. For example if a ROM is expected to sell 20,000 at a price of £30 and variable costs of £14 in 1985, then the contribution is £16 per unit (30−14) and £320,000 in total (20,000 × £16).

This brings out the point that for accurate cash forecasting we need to know, at each stage, the price which can be charged for the product, the variable cost which can be expected and the quantity of sales which can be anticipated. Look at each of these in turn.

Price. Prices will be high during introduction but will tend to fall as competition increases during growth. At maturity, prices will stabilise with a slight fall during saturation. Prices may go either way during decline – higher to accelerate out of decline, stable or lower to prolong it.

Variable costs. These will be fairly high during introduction but a decline may occur because of increasing scale during growth. Variable costs will be stable during maturity but tend to rise during saturation as enhancements are made to protect market share. During decline, variable costs may increase as production is scaled down.

Volume. The quantity of sales will be low at the introduction stage, high during growth and fall back to a lower level during maturity and saturation, with a falling off in decline.

General administrative costs

In addition to the variable costs, there will be many general expenses such as rent, rates and insurance which will be paid in cash at various stages of the product life. These costs are fixed in a short-term sense. That is, they do not arise directly from the level of sales and production activity. However, in the medium or long term, they should be controlled. The level should be lower, as a percentage of sales revenue, when the product is in maturity but it will tend to rise during saturation as more money is spent on marketing and promotion. Decisive action will be needed if these costs are to fall during decline, as they should. During growth, too, there is a temptation to let general costs rise on a buoyant level of sales. Trimming them down may be difficult at later stages.

General administrative costs will normally support a range of products, each one of which must generate cash to meet a 'fair share'. It is not easy to determine what is fair and what is not. Ideally, the division of general costs should reflect usage, but it is easier to share, say, rents according to space occupied than it is to share prestige advertising or top management expenses.

Whatever is included for general costs in forecasts should be carefully reviewed bearing in mind that non-cash items such as annual depreciation should be cut out. The cash flow for depreciation occurs when the relevant fixed asset is acquired.

Working capital

Cash and stocks. There will be a rising demand for working capital as production comes on stream and sales rise. The level of stocks will depend on production and sales levels. The cash float held will probably keep pace with overall capital invested. For instance, 6 per cent of the total assets may be held in cash and 20 per cent held as stocks.

Trade credit. Levels of debtors and creditors will reflect the terms of trade which will probably change over the product life cycle. At the introduction the goods are in demand and the supplier can limit the granting of credit, perhaps even trading entirely in cash terms. This policy may be difficult to maintain thereafter, and during growth maturity and saturation it will become increasingly necessary to offer normal terms. During growth, the actual terms taken may be held close to the terms offered but during maturity and saturation, the actual terms taken by customers will probably be extended. Once the period of decline is entered, it is advisable for the firm to tighten up the terms to reduce their exposure to the risk of bad debts and to release working capital for investment in new products. It may even be possible to revert to cash terms.

The effect of these patterns is that investment in working capital is required at the start of a project, when sales expand and when more credit is extended. This capital will be released at the end of the project, when sales contract and when terms are shortened.

The key points which emerge from the idea of a product life cycle are:

1 That all products have a limit on their life.
2 The life of products tends to get shorter.
3 Heavy capital expenditure on equipment and marketing in the early stages of the life of a product will lead to large negative cash flows. These can only be justified if they lead to cash returns at a later date which are large enough to leave a substantial surplus.
4 At any one time a multi-product firm should have a range of products at various stages of their product life cycles.

The cash flows for each product can be budgeted in various ways but it is likely you will find the techniques of long-term budgeting in Chapter 6 most useful for individual products. These can then be combined by groups to give the overall position. You may find it useful to incorporate the stage in the product life cycle into the time-scale of your budgets.

Tarbuck and Arbuthnot decide to design and market a 32-bit computer for small businesses, and the following estimates are made:

1. Research and development will take one year and cost £150 million.
2. Test marketing will then take six months at a cost of £3 million.
3. Production facilities are expected to cost £15 million. Construction will commence at the same time as test marketing and take 12 months to complete. During this time, initial stocks costing 20 per cent of the first year sales will be built up, at a cost of £2 million (4,000 at £500 per unit). A cash float of 10 per cent of sales revenues for the following year will be required to support production and selling, i.e. £4 million (20,000 at £2,000 × 10 per cent).
4. The product life will start as soon as production facilities are completed and stocks built up. In total, it will extend for a further seven years.

Five stages in the product life cycle are identified.

The *introductory* stage will take six months during which the product will sell 20,000 at £2,000 per unit. The variable costs will be £500 per unit so at a contribution of £1,500 per unit, the receipts from sales will be £30 million (20,000 × £1,500). It is assumed the terms of trade will be strictly cash.

The *growth* will then commence and it will last for one year, during which sales will rise giving total sales of 50,000. Prices and variable costs will be the same but terms of trade change to one month given to customers and taken on variable costs. This means that the firm will have a contribution of £75 million (50,000 × £1,500) over the twelve months but in the first six months they will collect half of this, less one month debtors, that is £31.25 million. The other seven months will be collected in the following year, £43.75m.

Maturity will last for two-and-a-half years giving sales of 30,000 per year. Prices will fall to £1,500 per unit and variable costs to £350 per unit. Terms will be extended to two months.

The cash contribution from sales will be £34.5 million per year (30,000 × (1500 − 350)). In the first six months only four months' revenue will be collected, £11.5 million. The other months will be collected at the end of this stage. As a result £34.5 is collected in year 3 and £40.25 in year 4 of the project.

Saturation will extend over two years during which sales can be maintained at 20,000 per year. Prices will fall to £1,400 and variable

Table 11.1

Tarbuck & Arbuthnot – product cash flow, £m

Product: 32 bit computer
Life:
Date:
Prepared by:

Years	-2	-1	Time 0	1	2	3	4	5	6	7
Inflows										
Contribution from sales:										
Introduction				30						
Growth				31.25	43.75					
Maturity					11.5	34.5				
Saturation							40.25			
Decline								15		5
Run down stocks									20	3.25
Release cash										2
Sales of production facilities										4
Outflows										
R & D	50									
Test marketing		3								
Investment in production		15								
Working capital stocks		2								1
Cash		4								
Net inflow + Outflow –	-50	-24	–	+61.25	+55.25	+34.5	+40.25	+15	+20	+15.25

costs will rise to £400 per unit because of intensive marketing and the need for enhancements. Terms of trade average three months. The contribution will have fallen to £1,000 (1,400 − 400) per unit and £20 million per year (20,000 × £1,000) in total. The extension of the terms of trade means that only nine months' sales, £15 million, are collected in year 5 of the project and three months' sales £5 million are collected in year 7.

Decline lasts one year. The product will drop to sales of 5,000 at a selling price of £1,000. Variable costs will drop back to £350 because there will be no further enhancements and the product will be well-known. As a safety precaution and as the product goes down market the terms of trade revert to cash. The plant will finally be sold for £1m.

Cash receipts from sales are £3.25 million (5,000 × (1,000 − 350)) and, in addition, the company recovers the initial investment in stocks and cash. The resulting long-term cash profile for the product is shown in Table 11.1.

12

The use of computers in cash planning

One of the first calculating machines ever made was designed three centuries ago by Blaise Pascal for his father, a tax accountant. Computers were first developed in a practical form immediately after World War II. Actually, a lot of the ideas on how computers could work were developed in nineteenth century Britain by an eccentric genius, Charles Babbage, but the technology of the time could not support his plans, so Babbage never built his 'difference engine'. What led to modern computers was the development of electronics and its use in wartime radar and intelligence. According to the British, the first electronic computer actually to work was at Manchester University, but the Americans claim they were first. In any case, the USA developed a lead which they have held ever since, and only in the last few years has that been seriously challenged by the Japanese.

US dominance is expressed in a variety of ways. IBM is the major computer manufacturer in most countries; all keyboards have $ signs; computer 'program' is spelt that way; the design of computers is fairly standard, though not all computers will talk to each other; all the second-line computer firms such as the Digital Equipment Corporation (DEC), Hewlett Packard, Data General, Apple and Commodore are US firms.

As computers grow up, they are going through several generations, currently the third and fourth are on the market and Japan is actively developing a major programme for the fifth generation which is expected to give you intelligent, thinking machines. At the moment you can still use IBM's famous comparison between human beings and computers. Human beings are slow, unreliable and intelligent, computers are fast, reliable and stupid, but some experts think the falling cost and physical size of computers is closing the gap. In 1950, a computer with equivalent power to a human brain would have been as big as London and a single page of working memory cost £1 million. By 1980, the computer would be the size of a taxi and the same memory cost £100. By the year 2000, the brain and equivalent computer will be same size and the working memory will cost less than 50p.

The early generations of computers were all 'mainframes', controlled by specialist programmers, operators and managers working in large organisations or as bureaux. The 'mini' computers were developed for direct use by designers, engineers and other staff without the use of specialised computer personnel. The machines were cheaper, but still powerful enough for many jobs.

In the late 1970s the 'micro' computers came on the market. At first, these were used by enthusiasts but as their power and associated facilities have improved, they have been put to many uses in industry and business. The distinction between the three types is not really hard and fast. A second-generation IBM 1300, which was a good mainframe in its day, required an air-conditioned room, at least one operator and manager and had a main memory of 16,000 (16K) bytes. A 16K third-generation micro can operate almost everywhere and costs less than £100 today.

It is estimated that more than 3 million people in the UK have computers at home of equivalent or greater power to the old IBM, many of them working through the family TV in colour and increasing numbers connected up via the domestic phone to information files and networks. Small businesses are using micros for a tremendous variety of purposes such as stock control; word-processing; labelling; payroll; statistical analysis; electronic filing and so on. A micro with 256K of main memory, associated printer and floppy discs can be had for a few thousand pounds including a spreadsheet programme which can be used for cash forecasting, among other things.

As far back as 1968, a US store of several hundred thousand spares lost 16,000 items in a fire which was quelled at midnight. By 8 a.m. the next morning the computer had corrected all the records for the losses, calculated whether it was necessary to replenish stocks and printed out 10,000 orders ready to despatch to suppliers. Today, that sort of performance is available to any firm, however small.

There are, however, snags. Remember, the computer is fast and reliable but stupid. Do not put down this book and dash out to buy a micro for your cash planning yet. If a computer is to work for you, you have to supply the intelligence to put it to work. Hasty action can result in hours of frustration or a wasted machine gathering dust in a corner. You need to know what you expect your machine to do, and you need to be sure it can do it exactly before you buy.

It sounds cynical, but many computer salesmen are selling dreams. It is not that their machines cannot do what they claim; it is more that your needs are rarely exactly what is on offer. Bridging the gap can be difficult. In principle, your computer can do almost anything but what matters is what it can actually do here and now. Many people are put off computers by the jargon. Why can't these people use ordinary words with plain straightforward meanings? It is a complaint made against all specialists. Do they really need new words, or are they just trying to pull the wool over our eyes?

The answer seems to be a bit of both. Computers are new machines, so inevitably, new words are needed for some of their parts. Computers are also very much general purpose machines, so the way they work is different, too.

Calling a plug/socket connection an 'interface' does cause much worry for the uninitiated but it can be justified by the fact that the cables are carrying signals. Mostly, computers' signals are coded in the American Standard Code for Information Interchange (ASCII) and communication with an outside device, like a printer or a visual display unit (VDU) can be in parallel or serial. A parallel interface, like the centronics, works with parallel wires, one for each bit of coded information, whereas a serial interface, like the RS232, uses a single wire to transmit the bits one at a time.

You will not need to worry about these technical details if you buy a complete system ready to work, but if you decide to add a new piece of equipment or buy a new software package, it is quite possible than you will run into trouble because old and new are incompatible.

The best place to start is to decide on your needs and then identify the software which will satisfy your needs. Software is a set of programs which run on a computer and direct it to perform a specific set of operations, such as calculating; comparing words to see if they are spelt correctly; searching a file for a particular name or piece of information; producing animated drawings on a screen; taking some basic accounting data, performing calculations and printing out your cash forecast in the form you require, weekly, monthly, or whatever.

When you are considering which program to buy, you will look at applications software packages. These packages are often quite specific. ACT have applications packages for accountants, building services, design, export, medical insurance, retailing, transport and many others, but some are more general and can be applied in a variety of businesses, such as costing, financial planning and graphics. If you buy a cash forecasting package, the way you put in information and the form in which the results come out may be tightly specified.

But you could buy a 'spreadsheet' package which can be just as effectively used for cash forecasting, with the big advantage that you have far more flexibility and control over the results. However, it may take you longer to learn how to use it. The usual micro packages which are often supplied with the machine are the spreadsheet; word-processing; data base; and graphics. If you buy all these programs you should check that they communicate with each other. If they do, it means you can produce your cash forecast and other financial statements with your spreadsheet, draw on files of information held in the data base, use your word processor to print a standard letter to your bank manager or your staff which incorporates some of the results and you can, if necessary, present key facts in graphical form as pie charts or histograms for emphasis. Otherwise, you have the muddle of doing each thing separately and then combining the results by hand.

Any equipment which you can touch is the computer hardware but all computers incorporate an operating system (OS) such as CP/M (control program for micros) or MS–DOS (Microsoft Disc Operating System). MS–DOS is practically identical to the IBM Personal Computer Disc Operating System (PC–DOS) because it was written for IBM by the software house, Microsoft. As the names imply, operating systems organise the work of the computer by identifying and decoding instructions, reading the applications software, letting the user know what is going on and organising the output for display on a VDU or printing out. If you do something wrong, the operating system will print 'What?' or give you an error message. The latter is usually unintelligible. You can look up what the messages mean in the manual and occasionally you may then be able to understand the problem. Manuals are notoriously bad for beginners. Once you know how your machine works you will find that the manual makes very good sense, which is not very helpful! Before you buy any package or hardware to support it, check the manual. If you cannot understand it, beware.

Another thing to check is supporting literature. Some micros are well supported by books and magazines and this may be more important in the long run than technical sophistication. A good example is the IBM personal computer. Most micro specialists regard the machine as un-exciting but it captured 40 per cent of the market within two years of its launch and, like it or not, it soon became in many ways the industry standard, supported by specialist magazines, books and a wide range of software.

Large organisations, like IBM or DEC, also provide an effective advisory and maintenance service. This means their machines may not be the cheapest on the market but in terms of total cost of implementation, remembering the cost of wasted time if you cannot get a machine to do what you want, they may still be better value. Another machine which is well supported is the Commodore, and it uses its own operating system which is very user-friendly.

At the heart of the computer is the central processing unit (CPU) where all the calculations are made. The computer works in a tedious on–off, binary arithmetic in which there are only two numbers, 0 and

1, but as it works at the speed of light, 186,000 miles per second, its cumbersome operations are still gone through far faster than the human being can react – six times round the world in a second is very fast!

A better indication of speed is that computer power is measured in millions of instructions processed per second. A super computer is one that can make at least 20 million calculations per second. Cray Computers of Minneapolis market an XMP series which can process 1,260 million calculations per second. It is used in scientific establishments like Farnborough and Harwell. Super computers are not necessary in business computing because from a computing viewpoint, our applications are relatively mundane.

The CPU uses a random access memory (RAM) to store data whilst it is working and we often use the RAM as a measure of size and power, but this is not necessarily a valid basis for comparing two machines. A micro with 64K may have far less actually available once the operating system and programs are loaded ready for use than another with 48K. The RAM is really badly named. The key thing is its flexibility, like a blackboard on which a lecturer scribbles notes, jots down words, does calculations, uses the results and finally, rubs the whole thing clean. When you use the computer, this is how the RAM works for you. In terms of the jargon, you can write to it, read from it and its memory is volatile – when you turn off the RAM is cleared of its contents.

The RAM can be contrasted to a ROM, although there are other types. Quite a few micros store programs in a read only memory (ROM) so the CPU can get (read) information out of the memory but not put information (write) into it. In effect, ROMs give you more power, but not direct flexibility.

Another factor which affects the efficiency of your machine is the size of the byte it works in. A byte equals 8 bits of data and an '8-bit' machine therefore processes information in bytes; machines which work in chunks of 16 or 32 bits are faster because they handle larger pieces of information at one time.

Coincidentally, 16- and 32-bit machines also have larger RAMs, starting at 128K and then multiplying by 2 to 256 and upwards. Overall computer speed is affected by many more factors than the size of the RAM, since the machines spend a lot of time moving data from one location to another, so if you really want to go into comparisons, the best way is to obtain benchmark reports on the machines you are interested in. You can often get these from the dealer for each machine or you can get a complete set from the magazines such as *Personal Computer World* who publish them.

Since the main memory of your machine loses its contents when you switch off, you will need some form of permanent storage for your data and programs. You can obtain sufficient permanent storage for most business purposes on floppy discs, which are like 45 rpm records, enclosed in a protective cover or on a Winchester disc which is a hard disc enclosed in a solid cover. You can store 250K or more on each floppy. A Winchester will store at least 10 million bytes (Mbytes). A hard disc system is less liable to corruption by dust and other adverse conditions and its size allows you to store all your files on it. That's a great advantage.

Networks

We have already suggested that the distinction between mainframes, minis and micros is not very significant. All modern computers use the same technology, based on chips, and are constructed to operate in similar ways. It is possible to arrange for all types to communicate with each other. The Tayside Health Authority in Scotland has a file of half a million or so records of patients in the region. Authorised users can gain access to the file through micros which can then switch through to minis and in turn to a central mainframe if the job they are doing requires it.

Peripherals

Peripherals, as the name implies, are devices surrounding the CPU including such things as the keyboards, VDUs; printer and floppy disc units. The peripherals usually operate at much slower speeds than the CPU, so they determine the overall speed of your system and, as we said earlier, there can be problems in interfacing specific peripherals to each other or to a particular computer.

It is better, if you can, to buy a complete system, starting with the software and then the hardware, including peripherals on which it will work. It is also best to make sure you get a turnkey system, ready to do your will when you are ready.

Corporate models

Computer-based corporate models were developed in the 1960s and put into use by large UK companies in the 1970s using mainframe computers. In both the USA and the UK, these corporate models are financial simulations which take basic accounting data and produce the common financial reports: income statements, balance sheets, funds statements and cash flow forecasts.

In this context, the word model simply means a representation of reality. In this book we have been concerned with cash planning. Each example that we have used has been a model of a business in cash terms. In other words, every time you predict what your cash receipts and disbursements are going to be, you are building a model. For instance, Imperial Chemicals Industries in Britain developed a long-term cash forecast model in the early 1970s. The key factors in the model were sales in tonnes, sales price per tonne, variable cost per tonne and fixed costs.

From these key factors, the company was able to calculate the cash flows generated under various conditions. The process of using a model like this under different assumptions is called simulation.

Until the late 1970s, computer models were mainly used by large companies and organisations such as government departments and nationalised industries. Smaller companies used computers for some routine jobs such as payrolls but financial models were a 'gold-plated' product that the ordinary firm could not afford.

This situation began to change when some financial models such as FCS – EPS were made available by bureaux using telephone links which enabled a user to access a large machine, perhaps in Europe or the USA to store data and to make use of a sophisticated financial model from which outputs in the desired firm could be printed locally. A number of such services are available now.

Spreadsheets

The most dramatic change occurred with the invention of the spreadsheet for use with microcomputers. The first spreadsheet program was Visicalc, available on the Apple micro and it created much of the demand for that machine, as well as generating widespread imitation. When first marketed in the UK, Visicalc cost £95 and was much more powerful than some mainframe programs costing £20,000!

As well as imitating Visicalc, the competition also introduced various improvements. The result is that you are faced with a wide choice of spreadsheets, available on all micros. Despite the choice and, of course, the continual improvements which are introduced, spreadsheets have some common features reflecting their common origins in the early mainframe corporate models. The influence of programming languages is also apparent in the symbols and signs which you have to use in order to set up and manipulate a spreadsheet.

Spreadsheet models tend to have three facets or modes in which they operate. These modes are variously labelled but they can be broadly described as:

1 Setting up the logic;
2 carrying out calculations; and
3 producing reports.

You will soon master each of these modes, especially if you have a good general idea of what you are doing and why.

Setting up the logic

One of the best ways to use microcomputers is in cash planning. Even if you are frightened of computers generally, or if you have been put off by the technicalities of trying to use a micro in the past you should now be able to use a spreadsheet for your cash forecasting because you already understand the logic of what you are trying to do.

Basically the spreadsheet is a grid of boxes, framed by a number of vertical columns and horizontal rows. You start with a rough guess as to how many columns and rows you need to accommodate your data. You need to enter a heading for each. The program will automatically assign letters to the columns and numbers to the rows. For a six-month budget you need six columns, obviously, but you may want to add one or more for six-month or quarterly summaries. Similarly, you need a row for each type of receipt or payment, plus a row for each sub-total and for the opening and closing floats.

This kind of layout is called a matrix. The intersection of the columns with the rows divides your form into a series of boxes or cells. Each cell has its own identification or identifier, given by the letter of the column and the figure of the row. Thus, a 7×12 matrix has 84 uniquely identifiable cells, as shown in Figure 12.1 where all the cells in columns A and G have been labelled, and a few from each of the other columns, to show the principle.

Columns

	A	B	C	D	E	F	G
1	A1	B1	C1	D1	E1	F1	G1
2	A2						G2
3	A3						G3
4	A4						G4
5	A5						
6	A6		C6				G6
7	A7			D7			G7
8	A8				E8		G8
9	A9					F9	G9
10	A10						G10
11	A11						G11
12	A12	B12	C12	D12	E12	F12	G12

Fig. 12.1 Spreadsheet layout

Since each available cell can now be identified, you can enter information for each cell and the computer will remember it. For instance, the titles of each month can be attached to the head of each column, as follows:

B1 – January
C1 – February
D1 – March
E1 – April
F1 – May
G1 – June

The title of each receipt, payment, total and sub-total can be attached to the successive cells in column A, thus:

A 2 – Sales volume (in tonnes)
A 3 – Sales price (per tonne)
A 4 – Receipts from sales
A 5 – Payments to suppliers
A 6 – Wages
A 7 – Rent
A 8 – Total payments
A 9 – Change in cash
A10 – Opening cash
A11 – Closing cash

The spreadsheet will now appear as in Table 12.1.

Table 12.1

Spreadsheet – budget form

	January	February	March	April	May	June
Sales volume						
Sales price						
Total receipts						
Pay to suppliers						
Wages						
Rent						
Total payments						
Change in cash						
Opening cash						
Closing cash						

You do not have to get all your headings worked out before you use the program. You can build the spreadsheet gradually and modify it at any time you wish. Similarly, you can control the width of the columns, but the size of your computer memory imposes a limit, and as you widen your columns you reduce the number you can have. The normal size of the matrix may be 255 by 255 but this would allow only very narrow columns.

Having set up the row and column titles, you now proceed to establish the logic of the spreadsheet by entering data or formulae. For instance, if your January sales are expected to be 200 tonnes at £15 per tonne, you can enter:

B2 200
B3 15

In the simplest case, receipts in January might equal the value of sales, so that you would enter in box B4 the formula to multiply B2 by B3. The precise form depends on the spreadsheet you are using but it might be: B4 = B2*B3 (* is the computer sign for multiply). Despite the = sign, this is not an ordinary algebraic equation. In Boolean algebra the expression is a logical instruction which tells your computer to calculate the value of B4 by multiplying the values B2 and B3 together. The advantage of this logical statement is that it can be used throughout the spreadsheet and for any values which may appear in B2 and B3 when you go into calculating mode. The program allows you, also, to enter a formula or some data in any other box or series of boxes by a few or even single keystrokes. Using this facility, you could instruct the program to increase the tonnage sold by 10 per cent per month by entering the appropriate formula. You can keep the price constant, or increase it every four months, as you wish.

If your payments to suppliers are 40 per cent of sales each month, you can enter in B5:B5 = 0.4*B4, and if wages are 25 per cent of sales, then in B6 you would enter B6 = 0.25*B4.

These instructions would be followed for each cell in which they appear. The computer will pick up the current value of B4 and calculate from that the value of B5 and B6. Since the value in any box is specific to that box, these values are variables. By contrast, if rent is £500 per month, that is a constant and you will enter 500 in B7. The computer will now always pick up 500 as the value in B7.

The total payments can be calculated by adding up cells B5 to B7, which can be entered in B8 as SUM (B5:B7). Remember, the exact formula depends on the program you are using. The effect of this instruction is that the computer picks up the values in boxes B5 to B7 and adds them up.

We have used the names of the boxes in the formula but in some programs you would not be able to do this. You would have to give each box value its own name. Another feature of the logic is that, as well as adding, subtracting, dividing and multiplying values, you can perform any other mathematical operation and many of them, such as working out the square root or raising to the power of ten, are available as standard operations. You can also delay or advance between columns so if receipts reflect sales in earlier months, the proportions to be received in one month can be stated in the logic. Similarly, payments to suppliers may reflect production levels for later months. Continuing with the logic of our example, if you enter in B9 B4−B8; in B10 120 and in B11 B9+B10, then B9 will find the difference between the contents of cells B4 and B8. Cell B11 would then add B9 to B10. B10 will always be 120. The process of entering figures or formulae in the boxes is now repeated for each succeeding column, but most spreadsheets have a replication formula which allows you to insert the formula into any series of cells. For instance, the instructions in B4 to add B2 + B3 can be replicated for columns C to N. All that is required is to add in B the additional instruction /R. Nothing could be simpler. On the same lines, receipts from sales in cells C2, D2, E2 etc. or C3, D3, E3 etc. can be calculated from a formula such as declining by 10 per cent per month for three months and then increasing by 5 per cent per month.

Carrying out calculations

Once you set up the logic of your spreadsheet, the real beauty of it becomes apparent. More or less at the touch of a button, the computer will work out the figures from the data and formulae which you have entered. So, in our example, the program will display the following values:

B2	200
B3	15
B4	3000
B5	1200
B6	750
B7	500
B8	2450
B9	550
B10	120
B11	670

Not only that. Provided your logic is workable, the machine will rapidly display the cash budget for the six months.

Suppose your logic is not workable? All work sheets will tell you so and many of them will also identify the line where you have made your mistake, sometimes with a useful indication of the kind of boob you have made. This can be very helpful because even the most experienced users make mistakes. If you are a beginner, obviously, you can expect to go wrong occasionally so, again, if you are having a package demonstrated, try to find out what happens if you do go wrong.

When you have got your logic working, you can change a figure and/or formula and the whole display of calculations can be changed at the touch of a button. So, if you want to know the effect on your borrowing requirement of a 10 per cent increase in sales the results can be obtained instantaneously. The changes may extend to introducing new factors, taking out factors or changing the balance. The results are seen at once. This technique is often called the 'What if' technique, because you are asking what will the result be if...? You can insert, move or delete whole rows and columns, or explore the effect of changes in factors affecting cash flow such as the balance between cash and credit terms, allowing for cash discounts at various levels; the effect of customers taking extra days of credit, or the effect of delaying payments on cash flows.

Producing reports

The third mode in which your spreadsheet operates is in producing reports. Obviously, these draw on the results calculated from the data and logic in the spreadsheet. A useful form of report would be a summary of cash flows but the reports could be extended to cover the profit and loss account (income statement), balance sheet, sources and uses of funds and so on. Often you will be using a spreadsheet to produce figures to enter into a standard report such as the income statement. The program can be set up to produce these automatically. At other times you may be using your word processing package and preparing a special report in which you wish to make use of results from the spreadsheet. Strangely enough, although you may have purchased both spreadsheet and word processing package from the same software house, you may find that their two packages do not communicate! However, a growing number are part of a set of integrated packages for word processing, database, and graphics. With the best, you can start preparing your report using your micro as a word processor. Then, when you need your cash forecasts, you can call up the spreadsheet, work on the cash forecasts or results and they include the results directly in the report. This can save a lot of time and trouble.

There are a number of factors which should be considered in choosing a spreadsheet package.

Cells. Try to decide the maximum number of boxes you are likely to use in your spreadsheet, but leave a large margin of safety. In 1984, the smallest number was about 1,300 and the largest 4 million from Powerplanner which was a middle-price package. An 8-bit machine will normally handle about 1,000 cells and a 16-bit machine about 2,500, which is ample for most people.

Memory. A limit on the spreadsheet size may be the size of the RAM. The RAM must hold both the spreadsheet program itself, the data on which it is working and provide for the display. In 1984, the minimum requirement for a spreadsheet program seemed to be about 27 Kbytes but some needed much more – 1 megabyte or even 10 megabytes in one case. A super program is not much use if it takes up most of your power.

Sorts. Another facility offered by some spreadsheets is the sorting of columns by size, or alphabetically. For cash forecasting this would mean you could highlight the months in which the bank borrowing was at its maximum. Or it could be used to highlight the periods when cash in hand was at maximum. Remember, the facility gives almost instantaneous results and could be much quicker than searching through a spreadsheet by eye.

Goal seeking. Sometimes this is called target search or reversed iteration. It is used by setting a target, for instance, of the final cash balance in hand. The program then works back through the figures and relationships and comes up with the sales needed in each period to meet the payment and produce the desired cash result. Similarly, if you state the maximum level of borrowing, the goal-seeking facility will tell you the maximum sales you can afford to achieve each month, with the needed cash required for purchases and payment of expenses.

Columns and digits. The spreadsheet may display whole numbers, two places of decimals, the formulae in use and the headings. The width of the column can be adjusted, within limits. The spreadsheet can be wider than the width of the screen and part of it can be worked on or examined through a 'window'. Windows of some packages allow different parts of the spreadsheet to be looked at simultaneously, through separate windows, sometimes co-ordinated.

Lock title. Some packages allow the titles to be locked on screen, even when you move across the spreadsheet.

Commas. Some programs allow commas for figures of 1,000 or above but many will show large figures as exponential functions. If you are a scientist or engineer, this may be quite acceptable but many people find exponentials confusing.

Logic. Programs vary in the logical functions which they offer. For instance, a statement B18>50, B19=$\emptyset$, means than if the value at B18 is greater than 50, then the value at B19 is zero. This might mean that B18 is the cash float and that B19, the bank loan, is reduced to zero whenever the cash float goes above 50.

Consolidation or overlay. The simple spreadsheets allow you to produce a succession of forecasts within the same format. Some packages allow you to transfer data between several sheets so that you can, for instance, combine a forecast with the actual results to produce a third statement showing the differences.

Statistics and finance. Some programs allow you to calculate statistics such as averages. Usually, they will also perform present value calculations, so that your cash forecasts can be used directly to see if a project is profitable or not.

Graphics. A graphics facility can turn tables of figures into bar charts, pie charts or graphs, in colour, if you wish. For instance, a graph showing the balance of cash and the sales figures can be drawn. The effect of changes in sales on cash position can be explored as you change the assumptions behind the figures. To sum up, there can be no doubt that a micro, mini or mainframe with a spreadsheet program or financial planning package is a godsend in cash budgeting. It gives flexibility, ability to make immensely detailed calculations very fast, supreme accuracy and versatility. Do remember, however, that if you do not already have a micro, you should first decide which software you will require and then buy the hardware system to support it. Do not make the mistake of buying a nice-looking micro because it was advertised on telly last night and then look for the software. That often leads to disappointment. If you already use a micro for other purposes, you should go carefully into the spreadsheets which are available for it. Do not use price as a guide. Some of the best packages are also the cheapest. If you are unsure, shop around for advice. A number of polytechnics, colleges and universities run advisory and consultancy centres. There are also many private consultancies offering advice and training. Some firms also offer rental terms so that you can try out a package for a while before deciding whether to buy. If you do buy, the cost of renting is deducted from the purchase price.

13
The impact of taxes on cash management

Since the whole purpose of tax is for the government to take cash out of your pocket, you may feel that this chapter will not have much to say. Fair comment! However, it is not what the government does, but the way that they do it that matters. For cash planning the twin problems of tax are complexity and timing.

Again, you may feel that this book cannot hope to deal with tax in any depth. This is true: the material can at best put up some warning signs on tax liabilities. There is no way we can give an authoritative guide to all aspects of the impact of tax on cash. On the other hand, there is no way a book on cash management could ignore tax! So the chapter tries to identify some of the main hazards for you and to give guidance on how to cope with them.

Liability for tax

The British government raises about £135 billion per year in taxes. Local rates account for 10 per cent, and VAT and excise duties for 20 per cent. Income tax and national insurance raise 43 per cent and, of the rest, corporation and capital gains tax raise 7 per cent of the total.

Direct taxes

Taxes on individuals and corporate bodies assessed and collected by the Inland Revenue are of greatest interest for cash planning.

Indirect taxes

Taxes on goods and services and, also, local rates do not create special problems in cash planning for most firms. Except for value added tax (VAT), indirect taxes must be paid before goods are released by Customs and Excise and, with rates, can be treated as a business expense or part of the cost of materials and supplies.

Income, corporation and capital gains taxes

Employed persons pay income tax on their earnings and are also liable for national insurance contributions which, in all but name, are another form of income tax. Both these taxes are collected together.

Self-employed persons are also liable for these two taxes. As an employer, you will be liable for income tax or corporation tax on your business profits. In addition, you pay national insurance contributions in respect of each employee, which is, in effect, a payroll tax.

Finally, other gains may be liable to capital gains tax. Each of these taxes is payable on a different basis and under separate rules, so we must look at each in turn, to see how best to include them in cash budgets.

Payroll and withholding taxes

Governments reduce the costs of collecting taxes by getting employers to do it for them, so a UK employer must withhold the income tax due on his employee's pay under the PAYE scheme and national insurance (NI) regulations. You pay the employee his or her net pay and hand over the amounts withheld to the local collector of taxes not later than 14 days after the end of each month. In addition, you must then pay the payroll tax (the employers' national insurance contribution).

Your total cash payments are the gross payroll plus the payroll tax. This is split into a net payment weekly or monthly to your employees and the tax element monthly to the collector of taxes.

There is a timing difference between these amounts but it is only important for very short-term cash budgeting purposes. For example, you may have a weekly payroll of £5,700, from which you withhold £1,700 per week in PAYE tax and NI. Your payroll tax and employer's NI is £1,500 per week. This works out at a weekly cash payment of £4,000, plus £12,800 per month (£3,200 for four weeks) or £16,000 (£3,200 for five weeks).

The sensible thing is to reckon your payroll as being £7,200 per week (£5,700 gross pay plus £1,500 employer's NI). This means you will have three or four weeks in each month when you have more cash available than you have budgeted for. If it can be used and turned back into cash before 14 days after the end of the month, fair enough, but it would be foolish to rely on this tax element for working capital. The penalties for failing to pay withholding taxes are severe because the money is certainly not yours!

Taxes on profits or gains

Income or corporation tax on profits and capital gains tax are determined annually. In preparing long-term cash forecasts, the amounts may have to be estimated but by the time these payments affect short-term budgets the amount payable should be known. The government year runs from 6 April and the tax on profits and gains is assessed retrospectively.

For income tax, the basis is the profits reported in the accounting year which ended in the previous tax year. So, if your accounting year ends on 30 September, the income tax for 1986/7 would be assessed on the profits reported in 1985/6, that is on your profits in the year to 30 September 1985. Half the income tax then becomes payable on 1 January in the year of assessment and half on 1 July in the following tax year. If your taxable profits to 30 September 1985 were £50,000 and you are liable to pay £30,000 1986/7 income tax on them, you would pay two instalments of £15,000 on 1 January and 1 July 1987.

The position for corporation tax is different. In this case, corporation tax liability is calculated on the profits made in the financial year ending on 31 March. Since company accounting years do not usually end on that date, the profits of the accounting years are apportioned on a time basis. A company having profits to 31 December 1985 of £240,000 and to 31 December 1986 of £360,000 would have profits for the financial year to 31 March 1986 of £270,000 (0.75 of £240,000 plus 0.25 of £360,000).

At the time when the inspector is assessing the profits, say in June or July, the second part of a company's profit may have to be estimated because results for the accounting year may not be available. An assessment will be issued and revised later.

Corporation tax payments

Corporation tax is payable in two ways. The first is advance corporation tax (ACT), the second is mainstream tax (MT). ACT is payable on qualifying distributions of profits, for example, when a dividend is paid. Tax at the current ACT rate is paid so as to make the dividend after tax. Suppose the current ACT rate is 30 per cent, then ACT is payable on the *dividend plus ACT*. If you pay a dividend of £7,000 you would also have to pay £3,000 ACT.

A qualifying distribution arises in some cases such as close companies, even if no cash is actually paid out as a dividend. The company is not obliged to distribute the profits, but must pay the ACT. ACT is payable within 14 days of the end of each quarter ending on 31 March, 30 June, 30 September and 31 December *and* at the end of each accounting period. So if you pay a dividend of £7,000 on 4 October, the £3,000 ACT would be payable by 14 January (14 days after the end of the quarter) unless your accounting year ends sooner. If your accounting year started on 1 November, it ends twelve months later for tax purposes, and the ACT would then be payable on 14 November.

Mainstream tax is assessed at the current corporation tax rate, which is higher than the ACT rate. If your liability for mainstream tax exceeds any ACT you have paid in the accounting period you can offset the ACT and pay the balance. Mainstream tax is due, normally, nine months after the end of an accounting period, but in any case not later than 30 days after the issue of a notice of assessment.

Even if you appeal against an assessment, the tax will be payable in full unless you apply for some or all of the amount to be postponed.

Interest on tax

Companies are allowed to make advance deposits for taxes (but not PAYE and VAT) in multiples of £500, with a minimum of £2,000 and these earn 13 per cent at the time of writing. The interest rate is reduced to 9½ per cent if the certificates are cashed. Failure to pay tax on the due date can give rise to an interest charge at 12 per cent per annum.

Capital gains tax is assessed on any gains arising in the previous tax year, so for 1985/6, you must pay on any gains in the year 6 April 1984 to 5 April 1985. Assessment may be a drawn-out process. One reason for this is that rules for deciding assessable income, or gains, and allowable expenses are detailed and complex. The net income shown in your business accounts is unlikely to be the amount agreed for tax assessment.

There may be considerable discussion between the tax inspector and your tax adviser before the liability is arrived at. Both the Revenue and the tax advisers are overworked and this slows the process down, too. The nature of the profit or gain will affect the kind of tax payable. In 1984/5 the tax on capital gains was 30 per cent. Income tax started at 30 per cent rising to 60 per cent and corporation tax was 52 per cent. However, the Chancellor had announced his intention to reduce the corporation tax rate to 50 per cent on profits earned in 1983/4, 45 per cent on 84/5, 40 per cent on 85/6 and 35 per cent on 86/7 and thereafter.

Faced with a choice of tax of 30 per cent if a profit is a capital gain, 50 per cent if it is corporate income and, possibly, 60 per cent if it is regarded as personal income, you may be excused if you develop a strong belief that the profit is best regarded as a capital gain. Equally, the tax inspector will tend to see it as personal income. Admittedly, there is often no choice after the event.

Threshold

Another factor in tax assessment is the threshold. It is common for small incomes or gains to be exempted from tax. So, for a married man, the 1984/5 threshold for income tax was £3,155, rising to £3,995 when he reaches the age of 65.

For capital gains tax, the threshold was £5,900. The importance of a threshold in cash planning depends on its size relative to cash flows and the rate of tax. At a 40 per cent tax rate, a threshold of £5,600 reduces tax by £2,240. At a 10 per cent rate, the reduction is only £560. For an individual with a small income of, say £7,000 per annum, these are significant sums. For a business with taxable profits of £200,000, they are negligible and can be ignored.

Tax shield

The value of any deduction or allowance for tax purposes can be calculated as follows:

$$\text{Amount of expenses} \times \text{tax rate} = \text{tax shield}$$

Suppose a firm has profits of £400,000 subject to tax at 35 per cent. The tax normally payable is £400,000 × .35 = £140,000. If the government allows £15,000 as a deduction from taxable profits, the tax shield is £15,000 × .35 = £5,250. The tax payable will then be:

$$£140,000 - £5,250 = £134,750$$

Taxes on profit

From a cash planning point of view, we can treat income tax, corporation tax and capital gains tax together. The important factor is that these taxes are based on assessed profits or gains. From a business point of view, you will want to know the profit which remains to you after tax.

Firms in the UK pay about 40 per cent of their income in taxes annually. That proportion seems to be fairly steady. On this basis, if you forecast you will make profits of £600,000, you can also forecast tax will be £240,000.

From a cash management viewpoint, the important thing is that receipts of £600,000 cash during one financial year will be followed by a single payment of £180,000 (corporation tax) or two payments of £90,000 (income tax). It should be possible to work out when the tax payment(s) will be due. From now on, we will refer to income tax, corporation tax, capital gains tax – and indeed any other tax assessed in this way – collectively as 'taxes on profit'.

Taxes on profit in long-term planning

Amounts and timing of taxes on profits affect long-term cash planning for projects which extend over a number of years.

Each year's cash flow will be affected by payments of tax on profits made in an earlier period. It is important to take these into account, but the big danger is that you can easily get bogged down in a mass of detailed calculations. Your tax adviser and accountant will naturally want to make a detailed assessment of the impact of each item on your tax position. The cost of the detail may be considerable and since tax rates and rules are liable to change, complete accuracy is not guaranteed. A number of studies in the UK have shown, over many years, that business people often ignore tax altogether in making long-term investment decisions. Perhaps, in view of the uncertainties, they are wise to do so. If you set an acceptable level of profit before tax, bearing in mind that tax will be payable, that may be accurate enough. However, as the purpose of cash planning is to predict the cash needs of the business you may well decide to make an estimate of when taxes on profit will be payable, and how much. A number of methods may be used.

Unadjusted tax

The simplest approach is to apply the tax rate to the net income after interest payments. This may sound naive, but it may not be so bad. It can, at least, show the effect of tax timing on cash flows, especially when tax rate or incomes are changing. On the whole you should be on the conservative side in overestimating the tax payments.

Average tax rate

Another way of handling the problem of how much tax will be payable on profits is to use an average rate. This can be expressed as a percentage of revenues. For example 20 per cent of the revenues of Princess Publications is subject to tax (because 80 per cent of the revenues are allowed as expenses) and the profits are liable to corporation tax at 45 per cent. The average rate of tax will be:

$$\text{Proportion of revenue taxable} \times \text{rate of tax} = \text{average tax rate on revenue}$$

$$0.2 \times 0.45 = 0.09$$

If the company expects to earn revenues of £1 million, then the corporation tax payable will be estimated as £90,000 (£1m × 0.09).

You do not have to use expected revenue as the basis. You may prefer to use the average rate on net income before tax. In this case, the proportion of income subject to tax will be higher than the proportion payable on revenues. Indeed, the average rate may be higher than the standard.

Suppose Princess Publications have sales revenues of £1,430,000 and commercial expenses of £1,155,000. The net income before tax is £275,000. If the Revenue disallow £11,000 expenses for tax purposes, then the taxable income will be £286,000. The proportion of income taxable is:

$$\frac{\text{Taxable income}}{\text{Net income before tax}} = \frac{£286{,}000}{£275{,}000} = 1.04$$

The current rate of corporation tax is 45 per cent of net income but the average rate for Princess Publications is:

Current tax rate × proportion of income taxable = average rate

For Princess Publications Ltd:

$$0.45 \times 1.04 = 46.8\%$$

The average rate of tax is particularly useful when tax is progressive, that is, the rate of tax rises with taxable income.

Marginal rate of tax

When tax on profits is progressive, you should also keep an eye on the marginal rate of tax. If you are considering expanding, it is the marginal rate of tax which applies, not the average rate.

In 1983/4, the rates of income tax were as shown in Table 13.1.

Table 13.1

Rates of tax, 1983/4

Income (£)	Rate of tax (%)
1 – 14,600	30
14,601 – 17,200	40
17,201 – 21,800	45
21,801 – 28,900	50
28,901 – 36,000	55
Over 36,000	60

These rates are the marginal rates within the bands shown. If you have taxable income of £14,600, then you will pay 30 per cent on it. Your average tax rate is 30 per cent (ignoring threshold allowances). Your marginal rate, if your income increases, is 40 per cent up to £17,200, when it rises to 45 per cent and so on.

Above the 30 per cent rate, your average rate of tax rises, but not as fast as your marginal rate. You can calculate your average rate by dividing the tax payable by your income. Table 13.2 gives a few examples of the average and marginal rates resulting from the 1983/84 rates.

You will see that the average rate of tax is well below the marginal rate up to the plateau level of £36,000, above which all incomes are subject to the 60 per cent rate. Above £36,000, the average rate of tax continues to rise. If your income is £200,000, your average rate of 57 per cent is very close to the marginal rate of 60 per cent. At this level and above,

Table 13.2

Average and marginal rates of tax

Income (£)	Tax payable (£)	Average rate (%)	Marginal rate (%)
10,000	3,000	30	30
14,600	4,380	30	40
15,900	4,900	31	40
17,200	5,420	31.5	45
19,500	6,455	33	45
21,800	7,490	34	50
25,350	9,265	36.5	50
28,900	11,040	38	55
32,450	12,993	40	55
36,000	14,945	41.5	60
90,000	47,345	53	60
200,000	113,345	57	60

the graduated scale will not have much effect. For cash planning, you can take both your average and marginal rates as being 60 per cent. For incomes within the graduated scale, in broad terms, the average rate of tax is useful in your long-term cash management. The marginal rate of tax is more useful in short-term cash planning and in calculating the effect of changes on your long-term plans.

Value added tax (VAT)

VAT applies to countries within the European Economic Community (EEC) and is administered in the UK by the Department of Customs and Excise. The normal rate of VAT is 15 per cent of sales value payable on most business transactions but some transactions are zero-rated, and others may be exempt. These is a big difference between being zero-rated and being exempt. Zero-rated sales are included in your taxable turnover, even though no tax is payable. Exempt sales are not.

Input and output VAT

Registered VAT traders have the big advantage that they can normally offset the VAT which they collect from customers (the output tax) against the VAT which they pay to suppliers (the input tax). Exempt businesses cannot do this.

Registration for VAT

It is the person and not the business which is registered for VAT, but the person can be a sole trader, partnership, public or private company, club or charity. Companies may have separate registration of each division. The point is that VAT extends to all the activities of the registered person. You may run separate businesses of a boarding house and a hairdressing salon. For VAT they will be taken together unless you make other arrangements.

If your taxable turnover exceeds £18,700 per annum, you must register for VAT. Again, your VAT turnover may not be the same as your sales as shown in your accounts. If clients pay your expenses whilst you are providing a service, the expenses are part of your VAT turnover, even if they are not subject to income or corporation tax. If you give away goods worth more than £10, the value must be included in your VAT turnover. Nor do you have to be making a profit on a transaction for it to be liable to VAT.

You may be trading at a loss but you are still obliged to collect VAT on your sales and to pay the amount collected, less any allowable input taxes to the local VAT officer. If in doubt, consult your accountant or the local VAT officer.

Payment of VAT

VAT is payable to the Customs and Excise quarterly on the value of taxable goods or services supplied to customers. There are strict rules for deciding the tax point at which the tax is regarded as being collected. Business persons who normally expect to receive a refund of tax may work on a monthly basis if they wish.

If you are budgeting for cash over periods of one quarter or more, the timing of VAT payments arising from operations can be ignored. The main problem in forecasting VAT in operations is to identify the proportion of costs on which input VAT will be payable and the proportion of sales on which output VAT will be collected.

Many input expenses will include VAT since it covers the supply of services such as telephone, accommodation and meals on business trips and some financial services. However, some services such as insurance are either exempt or zero-rated. From a long-term budgeting viewpoint it is probably accurate enough to calculate an average rate of VAT on turnover. This will be:

$$\text{Current VAT rate} \times \left(\frac{\text{proportion of output}}{\text{liable to output VAT}} - \frac{\text{proportion of output}}{\text{liable to input VAT}} \right)$$

For example, if the current VAT rate is 15 per cent: 20 per cent of your £200,000 output is either exempt or zero-rated; your profit margin is 10 per cent on sales turnover; and 60 per cent of your costs and expenses are liable to VAT.

Obviously, 80 per cent of your output is liable to VAT. On the input side, your costs and expenses are 90 per cent of turnover, because your profit margin is 10 per cent. Of that 90 per cent, only 60 per cent bears tax, so the proportion of output liable to input tax is $0.9 \times 0.6 = 0.54$, that is 54 per cent. Your average VAT rate is thus:

$$0.15 \times (0.8 - 0.54)$$
$$= 0.15 \times 0.26$$
$$= 0.039, \text{ that is } 3.9 \text{ per cent}$$

The VAT on £200,000 would thus be £200,000 × 0.039 = £7,800, net.

Suppose, for example, that Walton Free Ltd are building a new factory for £5 million for their own use. The company are expecting £2.4 million net receipts from sales for the next ten years. Their position will be strongly affected by VAT. If the quoted price of £5 million for the factory includes VAT, then Walton Free Ltd can claim a refund of that tax at the end of the quarter. That is the good news! The bad news is that operating receipts will be reduced by the average VAT rate. Further bad news is that the sale of the capital assets when the factory comes to the end of its life can be expected to bear VAT at the full rate.

Thus, if the full VAT rate is 15 per cent, the new factory price includes VAT and the average VAT rate will be 8 per cent on annual receipts, the projected payments and receipts will be as shown in Table 13.3.

Table 13.3

Walton Free Ltd – factory project cash flows

		Payments £	Receipts £	Amended for VAT Payments £	Amended for VAT Receipts £
January 1984	Investment	5,000,000		5,000,000	
March 1984	Refund of VAT		–		652,174
End of year (1984)	Net sales		2,400,000		2,208,000
1985	Net sales				
1986	Net sales				
1987	Net sales				
1988	Net sales				
1989	Net sales		2,400,000		2,208,000
1990	Net sales				
1991	Net sales				
1992	Net sales				
1993	Net sales		2,400,000		2,208,000
	Sale of equipment		250,000		217,400
	Sale of factory building		1,000,000		869,600
Total receipts			25,250,000		23,167,000

The percentage VAT on a price quoted as including VAT can be calculated from the following formula:

$$\frac{\% \text{ VAT rate}}{100 + \% \text{ VAT}}$$

For example, at 15 per cent VAT

$$\frac{15}{100+15} = 13.04348 \text{ per cent}$$

Thus, the refund of VAT on the £5 million factory cost is:

$$£5,000,000 \times \frac{15}{115} = £5m \times 13.0438 = £652,174$$

Similarly, at the end of the project, equipment will realise:

$$£250,000 \times \frac{100}{115} = £217,400$$

and the factory building

$$£1,000,000 \times \frac{100}{115} = £869,000$$

These calculations assume that the prices used in the example already include VAT.

If we assume that the net sales receipts include VAT, then the average VAT rate will reduce the receipts accordingly, i.e.

$$£2,400,000 - (8\% \times £2.4 \text{ million})$$

or

$$£2.4m \times .92 = £2,208,000 \text{ annually}$$

The cash payback of this project was

$$\frac{5m}{2.4m} = 2.08 \text{ years}$$

The effect of the lower annual receipts would normally have meant a longer payback period but this delay is offset by the VAT returned on the £5m in 1984. The payback in the first two years is:

	£
year 1	652,174
	2,208,000
	2,860,174
year 2	2,208,000
	£5,068,174

Thus, the payback is now less than two years and the total receipts fall from £25,250,000 to £23,167,000.

VAT on imports

Until 1984, the British government allowed VAT on imports to be paid quarterly, in line with the general VAT arrangements. Whilst the EEC accepted that this was sensible, the rest of the Community required immediate payment of VAT on importation. As a result, British businesses could save considerable sums of money by buying goods imported from the Community rather than buying them from UK suppliers. The British government, therefore, withdrew this concession. VAT, like customs duties, must be paid on importation since 1984. The concession may be reintroduced by EEC at some later date.

VAT by computer

If you are planning to use a computer for accounting purposes, it is important that the programs should handle your VAT correctly. For instance, you must be able to add VAT or not, depending on whether a group of products are subject to VAT or not and you must be able to change if the classification of the product changes. Before buying, you should ask the software vendor if the Customs and Excise have checked the program. You can also check with the local VAT office where there is usually a computer specialist.

Customs and Excise duties

Customs duties are imposed on a wide range of articles imported into the UK. In general, customs duties apply to goods imported from countries outside the European Economic Community. A wide range of countries from Abu Dhabi to Zimbabwe enjoy preference, that is, exemption from or reduction of customs duties.

In addition to the duties imposed by Parliament the EEC imposes some anti-dumping or countervailing duties and levies under the common agricultural policy.

Excise duties are the taxes imposed on a curious selection of articles, mainly alcoholic beverages and tobacco but including matches, mechanical lighters and hydrocarbon oils.

Another group of products are relieved from duty, such as educational, scientific and cultural materials, calendars to stimulate travel and documents connected with air travel. The Customs and Excise Department also maintains a long list of goods liable for duty and the relevant rates. This list enumerates thousands of items from birds' eggs to brass musical instruments, honey from various sources, nuts and spices. Customs duties are normally payable on an ad valorem or valuation basis and there are agreed GATT (General Agreement on Tariffs and Trade) rules for valuation of goods. There are five methods of valuation but they are applied in strict hierarchical order. The first rule specifies that valuation will be based on the price actually paid or payable on the goods. The second method can be used only if the first method cannot be applied, and so on. Customs value is based on the exchange rate ruling when the goods are imported. Customs duties and VAT are normally paid when goods are cleared for import. Traders may arrange a one-month deferment of duty on condition they grant a direct debit mandate to the Customs and Excise. Goods subject to customs and/or excise duties may be placed in bonded warehouses, by agreement with the Customs and Excise Department. The effect is that payment of the duties – and VAT if applicable – is deferred until the goods are taken from the warehouse. For the business person a bonded warehouse may save the tie-up of a large amount of capital and considerable savings in interest charges.

Inward processing relief is a system by which goods imported from outside the EEC for processing and subsequent export outside the EEC are relieved of customs duties and other charges. The best method to operate relief is to obtain duty suspension, which means that no duty is paid on import. This is not possible, for instance, with goods falling under the common agricultural policy; the duty must be deposited and a claim for reimbursement made when the goods are exported. This relief used to be known as drawback.

Conclusion

You have seen in this book how to apply cash budgeting to various situations. You should now have a clear idea of which of the techniques will be of use to you and which will not. Cash is essential to your business prosperity and like Aladdin's lamp it can open up powerful opportunities, but only if you put it to use. Then the trick is for you to get it back in good time for new uses. Effective budgeting and control means you will remain master of your financial situation, so that you know today what other people may start forecasting tomorrow.

The principles are clear and simple. Know the cash implications of what you propose to do. Use your cash capacity to support your business operations at least cost. Be accurate, but don't let yourself be overwhelmed by detail. Monitor what is happening to your plans and modify your actions accordingly.

Do not be overawed by cash; you may even look down on it, but never, ever, lose sight of it. The price of liquidity, and survival, is constant vigilance. The reward is peace of mind. As Joe Louis once said, 'I don't like money, actually, but it quiets my nerves'. We wish you peace of mind.

Index

accountants 84
accounting systems xiv
accrual accounting vii
accounts code 61
accrual accounting vii
accruals 2, 5
acid test 13, 164
acquisition costs 85
ACT 21
activity ix, 62 et seq., 161
actual 145-6
additional borrowing power 17
advertising 59-60, 71, 72, 186
ageing schedule 43-4, 49, 125
american standard code for information exchange (ASCII) 197
annual discounts 40
apple (computers) 188, 195, 201
application of funds *see* use of funds
applications software 197
architects 84
asset structure 15, 96
assets 1, 6, 7, 9-10, 18, 168
average costs 27
average tax rate 214 et seq
average selling price 39

Babbage, Charles 195

bad debts 8, 42, 44-5, 114, 126 et seq, 129
balance sheet 2, 5, 12, 13, 110-11, 200
bank lending xii, 2, 6, 7, 10, 15, 49, 95-6, 165, 175-7
bankruptcy xi, 188
bidding 133-4
bit 199
bonuses ix
boolean algebra 204
borrowing xi, xii, 16, 18
break-even point 161-2
British Aerospace 18
British American Tobacco (BAT) 97
British Caledonian Airways 36
British Institute of Management (BIM) 113
British Treasury 20
broad brush 73-4
budgets xiv, 142-3, 157-8
buffers 84
building Ch.10
buildings 1, 10
bureaux, computer 196
business activity 63
business expansion xii
business plans xiii, xiv

business transactions 18

Cadbury, Adrian 187
Cadbury-Schweppes PLC 10, 11, 12, 113, 187, 188-9
capital 12, 31, 109-10, 115, 168, 189-90
capital expenditure proposals 97, 99
capital gains tax 209, 210
carriage 57, 63-4, 71
carrying costs 86
cash 8
cash at start 20
cash budgets xiv, Ch.2, 61, 101 et seq, 150-4, 171-2
cash capacity 15, 16, 17
cash control xv, 13
cash cycle 3-7
cash discounts 40-2, 47-9, 124-5, 129
cash float 18, 21, 27 et seq, 82-3, 90-3
cash flows vii, 1, 18, 89-90, 97, 167, 168, 192, 200-1
cash from operations 29-33, 98-101, 166
cash from sales 126-31
cash, tax on 213 et seq
cash forecasts vii-xv, 43, 44, 73, 94, 113, 130-1, 135 et seq, 164-9, 200 et seq, 214 et seq
cash requirements 167
cash generation 31, 95, 107
cash grants 17
cells 206
certified work 137, 143-4
changes 143-4, 155
character 14
choice 6
circulating capital *see* working capital
clerical staff 70
closing cash *see* cash float
collateral 115
collection method 25
collection period 42-3
collection policy 114, 118
collections 124, 125, 129-31
collections, tax 210-12
columns 202, 207
commissioning 135
commodore (computers) 188, 195, 196
completion 135, 147-9

components 5
computers xv, 1, 10, 61, 162, 168, 188, 192, Ch.12, 220
conditions 115
consolidated cash budgeting 171-2
consolidation 207
construction 84, 134-5, Ch.8, Ch.10
  see also projects
contingencies 134, 136, 138-9
contracts 133 et seq
contributed capital 12, 109, 110
contribution 161, 164, 190
control 142 et seq, 158
corporate models 200
corporation tax xi, xii, 106, 209 et seq
corporation tax, advanced (ACT) 211
cost behaviour 159-61
cost curves 140-2, 160
cost of borrowing xii, 41-2
cost of production ix, 159 et seq
cost of purchases 49
cost of stock 84
cost over-runs 154-5
cost performance index 146-9
cost to complete 147-9
CP/M 198
CPU 198, 200
Cray computers 199
credit 10, Ch.7
credit manager 43, 119
credit period 114, 117
credit policy 114
creditors 2, 4, 10, 12, 13, 18
creditors ageing schedule 49
credit rating 119
credit standards 114-16
cumulative cost/time chart 153
current assets 9, 13, 95, 99
current cost accounting (CCA) 8
current liabilities 11, 13, 95
current ratio 13
customers 118-19
customs duties 49, 50, 70, 220-1

data base 198, 206
Data General Corpn 195
data sheet 22-4, 50-4, 99-101, 127-30, 177-9
days credit lost 48
days credit saved 41

Index

days sales outstanding (DSO) 120, 131
Debenhams PLC 9
debentures 2, 95-6, 105-7
debt ratio 16, 36, 113, 119-20, 165-6
debtors 1-6, 8, 42, 119 et seq, 129-30
decisions vii, 6
decline 188, 194
default costs 114
deferred tax 2
deficit xiii, 6, 168, 169, 191
De La Rue Co PLC 9
delinquency 118
De Lorean Cars 157
Delta Group PLC 10, 11
demand 6, 83
departments xiv, 119
  see also divisions and functions
depreciation x, xi, 10, 26-7, 31, 95-6, 98, 191
design 134, 139-40
development 133, 192
Digital Equipment Corporation (DEC) 195, 196
digits 207
direct cost of cash 19
direct taxes 210
disbursements 25, 200
discounts 8, 38-42, 47-9, 124-5, 129
discounted cash flow 94
disputed accounts 125-6, 129
distributors 12, 13, 14, 15, 16
dividends 2, 12, 18, 19, 110
divisions 60
drawback 221
drawings 12
duties 70

earnings 18, 30-1, 110
  see also retained earnings
economic environment 17, 186
  see also conditions
economic order quantity (EOQ) 86
Edwards, H 113
efficiency 142, 154, 168
electronic filing 196
employee related payments 58
employers 210
energy 82
  see also fuel
engineering 134, 170
equipment 191

see also plant
equity 115
  see also shareholders
excise 209, 220-2
  see also customs
expansion xii
expected payments 21
expected receipts 20
expected value 115 et seq
expenses 5, 18, 31, Ch. 4, 190-1
exponentials 207

factors 61
finance 207
financial budgets 162
financial environment 17
financial models 200-1
financial simulations 200
financial structure 18
finished goods 5, 83
fixed assets 2, 6, 10, 95, 96-7
fixed capital 189-90
fixed costs x, 62-3, 159-61, 190-1, 200-1
fixed overheads ix, 190-1
Fleet, Kenneth 36
float see cash float
floppy discs 199
forecast profits vii, 164-7
forecasts vii-xv, 1, 61 et seq, 158
  see also cash forecasts
formal organisation 158, 186
freight 57, 63-4, 71
fuel 58, 66, 71
  see also energy
functions 60
funds 5, 33-6, 95-6
funds statements 200

gains tax 210, 211
GATT 220
GEC Co. 18, 33-4
general administrative cost 190-1
general budget factors 61-2
global estimates 135-7
goal seeking 206
graphics 198, 206, 207
gross profit 30
growth 187, 192

Harrison, F L 132
head office 61

heating ix
heavy industry 5
Hewlett Packard 195
hire 58, 67-8, 72
historical cost accounting (HCA) 8
holiday pay ix

IBM (computers) 189, 195, 196
ICFC 37
identifiers 202
Imperial Chemical Industries (ICI) 97, 105, 113, 200-1
Imperial Metal Industries PLC (IMI) 97
imports, VAT 220
imputed cost 86
income 31
income statement viii, xiii, 30-3, 60, 110, 200
income tax 57, 209, 210
indicators 82-3
indirect cost of cash 19
indirect taxes 210
inflation 8, 18
insolvency 12
Institute of Cost and Management Accountants (ICMA) 1
Institute of Credit Management 119
insurance ix, 59, 68-70, 72, 190-1
intangibles 2
interest 2, 11, 18, 105-10, 166, 212
interest cover 107
interface 197
introduction 187, 192
inventory *see* stock
investigation costs 115
investment 12, 171, 189
investment appraisal 94
invoice 40-1, 117-18
inward processing relief 221

jobbing 170

labelling 196
labour ix
land 1, 10
large firms 1, 2, 5, 7, 16, 37, 95, 110, 113, 170-1, 202
lead time 87
lease 58, 67-8, 71
lenders xi, 16, 95
Lever Brothers 189

liabilities 10, 12, 16
liability for tax 209-11
licences 59, 70, 72
light ix
linear programming 167, 183
liquid assets 1
liquidity 222
loans 6, 7
  see also bank lending
lock title 207
logic 201-5, 207
long term assets 6
long term borrowing 105-7
long term budgeting 5, Ch. 6, 213 et seq
long term cash cycle 6-7, 21, Ch. 6
long term liabilities 11, 16, 105-7
losses 12

mainframe 196, 201
maintenance 58, 67, 71
manufacturing 5, 16, 82, 84, 134-5
margin on sales 31
marginal cost *see* variable cost
marginal tax rate 215-16
market growth 187
marketing 38, 46, 59-60, 71, 113, 186, 191
Marks and Spencer Ltd 10, 83, 106-7, 113
mass production 157
master budget 142-3, 158, 162
materials ix, 5, 83
matrix 202
maturity 187-8, 192
mergers 188
MFI 187, 189
microcomputers 196
Microsoft 198
minicomputer 196
minimum stock 89
miscellaneous 60
models 200, 201
mortgages xii, 2, 95-6, 107
MS-DOS 198
motives for holding cash 18
multiple projects 170, 172 et seq
multi-product 186

National Health Service 83, 200
national insurance 57-8, 209, 210

Index

net profit 30-1
net trade price or terms 38, 47
networks 200
net worth 115
non-cash debits 35

oil industry 5
operating systems 198
operations, cash flow from 29-36
opportunity cost 19
ordering cost 86
organisations, structure xiv
overdraft 175-7, 183-5
overdue accounts 125-6
overhead x
  see also fixed and variable
overlay 207
over-runs 154-5
overtrading 13
owners 6, 12, 95, 115

packages, computer 197-8
paper packaging and printing 97
partnership 12
Pascal, Blaise 195
payback 102-5
PAYE 57, 210 et seq
payments in advance *see* prepayments
payments to creditors 47
payout *see* payback
payroll ix, 5, 6, 70, 196, 210
Pedigree Petfoods 188
pensions 59, 70
percentage debtors to sales 42
performance 142, 145 et seq
peripherals 200
Personal Computer World 199
personnel 57-8, 65, 71
  see also salaries and wages
Phillips and Drew (P & D) 112, 166
plan, business xiii, xiv
plant and equipment x, 1
plant and machinery 10
portfolio 171, 188
positive cash management vii, x
power 58, 66, 71
precautionary cash 18
preferred asset structure 18
preliminary engineering 133
prepayments ix, 2, 8, 72
price 38-40, 46, 47, 49, 62, 137, 155, 171, 186, 190, 200

printers 197, 200
printing 97, 170
probabilities 115
procurement 134
products Ch. 11
product life cycle 187
professional firms 84
profit vii, xiv, 10, 12, 18, 30-1, 84, 134, 162, 164, 171, 211, 213 et seq
profitability 31, 83, 94, 167, 168, 169
projects Ch. 8, 170-1
  see also multiple projects
project life 98
purchasing 134

quick assets 13, 164

RAM 199, 206
rates ix, 190-1, 210
ratio analysis 13, 42, 163-4
raw materials *see* materials
realizable investments 15
receipts and payments cash budget 27-9
receipts from sales viii
recession 113
registration for VAT 216-17
reminders 118
rent ix, 58, 67-8, 72, 190
re-order level 87
reports 206
research 187, 192
reserve borrowing power 15
retailers 5, 82, 97, 187
retained earnings 12, 95-6, 110-11
retention money 137
return on assets 97, 164-5
  see also profitability
rights issue 109-10
risk 115
ROM 199
royalties 59, 70, 72

safety minimum 88
salaries 18, 57-8, 65-6, 71
  see also personnel and wages
sales viii, x, xii, xiii, 3-6, 120 et seq
sales margins 31
saturation 187, 192-4
scheduled performance index 149-54
S-curve 139-40
security 59, 68, 72, 139-42

self-employed 210
selling 59-60, 71, 72
services 58, 66-7, 71, 84
shareholders 2, 7, 12, 13, 18, 95-6, 115
share issues 95, 110
shield, tax 213
short term budgeting 24-5
short term cash cycle 3-6, 21
site managers 136
small firms xiv, 37
software 197
sole proprietor 12
sorts 206
sources and uses of funds 33-6
speculative transactions 18
spreadsheet 196, 201-8
standard cost Ch. 9, 163
statements 118
statistical analysis 196
statistics 207
stockout time 87
stocks ix, 1-6, 9, 10, 18, Ch. 5, 196
structure of assets 15
sub assemblies 83
 see also work in progress
sub contracting 170 et seq
sundries see miscellaneous
superannuation see pensions
supplies 57, 63, 71
supply of cash 6
surplus 6
synthesis 136, 137

tangibles 2, 8
target profit 162, 164
target search 206
tax xi, xii, 2, 17, 57, 59, 70, 72, 105, 110, Ch. 13
tax shield 213
Taylor Woodrow PLC 10, 11
Tayside Health Authority 200
tenders 134
terms of trade 40, 42, 114, 117
Thomson, Sir Adam 36
Thorn Electrical 18
threshold, tax 213
time overruns 154-5
times interest covered 107
timing 19, 56, 71-2, 142
total borrowing power 16
trade credit Ch. 3, Ch. 7, 191

trade discounts 38
Trafalgar House 84
training 157
transactions 18
transport 63-4
travel 58, 68, 72
types of contract 155
types of expenses 56-60
types of market 46
types of product 189
types of project 98-9

unadjusted tax 214
uniform accounting 61
unit costs 159-61
usage rate 88
use of funds 33-6

valuation of assets 7
variable costs 159-61, 190, 200-1
variable overheads x, 62-3
VAT xi, 49-50, 52, 70, 209-11, 216-21
Visicalc 201
visual display unit (VDU) 197, 200
volume 190
volume discounts 40

wages 18, 57-8, 65-6, 71
 see also personnel and salaries
weighted average price 39-40
wholesalers 12, 13, 14, 15, 82
Wimpey, George PLC 9, 11
winchester disc 199
withholdings 57
withholdings tax 210
word processing 196, 206
working capital 3-6, 7, 8, 13, 37, 95, 96, 99, 116, 120, 145, 163, 191
working papers 24, 52-3, 180
work in progress 2, 9, 83-4